S0-ADL-251

STALIN, HITLER, AND EUROPE

STALIN, HITLER, AND EUROPE

VOLUME ONE

The Origins of World War II

1933–1939

by JAMES E. McSHERRY

THE WORLD PUBLISHING COMPANY

Cleveland and New York

The Wollman Library
BARNARD COLLEGE
Columbia University

WITHDRAWN Barnard
FROM
THE WOLLMAN LIBRARY
BARNARD COLLEGE

741
.M24

V.1
Cop. 2

Copyright © 1968 by JAMES E. McSHERRY

Published by The World Publishing Company
2231 West 110th Street, Cleveland, Ohio 44102

Published simultaneously in Canada by
Nelson, Foster & Scott Ltd.

All rights reserved. No part of this book may be reproduced
in any form without written permission from the publisher,
except for brief passages included in a review appearing in a
newspaper or magazine.

Library of Congress Catalog Card Number: 67–31018

PRINTED IN THE UNITED STATES OF AMERICA

Preface

Close students of Soviet diplomacy eventually come to resemble the psychiatrist who, greeted by a colleague with a cheerful "good morning," pondered after the other had passed: "Now just what did he mean by that?" But in the case of the U.S.S.R.'s European policy from 1933 to 1941, and especially in 1938 and 1939, we can form a reasonably accurate idea of just what Stalin meant by each of his moves.

No significant Soviet publications covering the period have ever appeared and probably never will as long as a Communist government controls the archives in Moscow.[1] Most of the pertinent German documents are available, however, and the British documents from 1938 to the outbreak of the war in September 1939 are now in print. French-British relations were so close during 1938 and 1939 that one can trace French policy in some detail through the British minutes and correspondence. A number of diplomats in responsible positions at the time have also published their memoirs, and the U.S. and Italian documents provide valuable supplements. Thus, with two elements of the equation known, Britain-France and Germany, it is not too difficult to determine the value of Russia. One other factor makes the study of Soviet foreign policy during this period especially rewarding: The diplomatic "pot" was boiling more furiously than at any other time in recent European history; whether fearful, cautious, confident, or overconfident, Stalin reacted—and most of the reactions may be traced.

152899

Like the rifleman in combat, the scholar must rely on a multitude of largely unsung supporting troops—the professional librarians. In the case of this volume, special thanks are due the staffs of the Libraries of the University of Illinois and Southern Illinois University, the Library of Congress, the Army Library in the Pentagon, the Library of the Department of State, the National Archives, and the Library of the Hoover Institution on War, Revolution, and Peace.

J. E. McS.

The Hoover Institution
Stanford University

Contents

	Preface	v
1	*Japan—Delicate Dynamite* September 1931—August 1938	3
2	*Retreat from Rapallo* February 1933—April 1934	23
3	*Litvinov and the League* December 1933—February 1938	35
4	*Mainstream to Munich* March–September 1938	58
5	*Munich: The Tributaries*	75
6	*Stalin's Desperate Diplomacy* October 1938—March 31, 1939	99
7	*The Last of Litvinov* March 15—May 3, 1939	129
8	*Stalin Coaxes Hitler . . .* May 4—July 22, 1939	146
9	*. . . and Beats the Anglo-French Team*	164
10	*Hitler Plays the Russian Card* July 19—August 25, 1939	196
11	*Stalin Fans the Flames* August 22—September 17, 1939	231
	Appendices	255
	Notes	271
	Bibliography	305

STALIN, HITLER, AND EUROPE

Volume One
1933–1939

Since the time of the formation of the Soviet Republics, the States of the world have divided into two camps: the camp of Capitalism and the camp of Socialism.

SOVIET CONSTITUTION OF 1923

The more powerful enemy can be conquered only by exerting the utmost effort, and by necessarily, thoroughly, carefully, attentively and skillfully taking advantage of every, even the smallest, "rift" among the enemies, of every antagonism of interest . . .

LENIN, "LEFT WING COMMUNISM . . . ," 1920

. . . the basic rule for us until the final victory of Socialism in the whole world, namely that one must exploit the antitheses and contradictions between two capitalist powers, between two systems of capitalist states, and incite them against one another. As long as we have not conquered the whole world, as long as, from the economic and military standpoint, we are weaker than the capitalist world, we must adhere to the rule that we must know how to take advantage of the antagonisms and contradictions existing among the imperialists. . . . We are at present between two foes. If we are unable to defeat them both, we must know how to dispose our forces in such a way that they fall out among themselves; because as is always the case when thieves fall out, honest men come into their own. But as soon as we are strong enough to defeat capitalism as a whole, we shall immediately take it by the scruff of the neck.

LENIN, NOVEMBER 26, 1920

1

Japan—Delicate Dynamite

September 1931—August 1938

By the end of 1929 Stalin had defeated Trotsky and his other opponents and was the unchallenged master of the Soviet Union. In the same year the First Five-Year Plan was approved, and the merciless drive to industrialize a great but backward nation began. The necessity of selling raw materials and agricultural products abroad in order to buy machinery and other capital goods demanded good relations with foreign countries. At the same time deprivations caused by the export of many necessities and peasant opposition produced by collectivization meant that any serious foreign conflict would be extremely dangerous to the regime.

While not ideal, the attitude of the "capitalist world" toward the U.S.S.R. was reasonably satisfactory. A number of the smaller European powers still refused the Soviet Union *de jure* recognition as did all of the American republics except Mexico and Uruguay. Relations with China had ended when Chiang Kai-shek turned on the Communists in 1927. But none of these were powerful states; only the United States among the great powers had not yet recognized the Soviet Government.

As the two outcasts of post-Versailles Europe, Russia and Germany found themselves natural allies. The April 1922 Treaty of Rapallo between the two countries was followed by a treaty of friendship in April 1926, the Treaty of Berlin (Appendix A), and a conciliation agreement of January 1929. German businessmen found Russia one of their best foreign markets, especially during

3

the first years of Soviet industrialization, and the Red Army furnished the Reichswehr with secret training and experimental facilities in the U.S.S.R.

Despite the ideological difference between Fascism and communism, relations with Italy were quite "correct" if not especially cordial. Commercial agreements were concluded in August 1930 and April 1931 and comparatively few conflicts existed between Rome and Moscow.

As an avowed opponent of the Versailles system, the Soviet Union was automatically an opponent of French policy. Memories of the *cordon sanitaire* still rankled and Moscow viewed with suspicion France's strong ties with Poland. Communist propaganda in turn provoked French suspicion and resentment, but thousands of French owners of unpaid tsarist bonds held the greatest grudge against Russia.

During most of the nineteenth century Britain and Russia had been rivals in Asia, and Japan's decision to attack Russia in 1904 had followed the Japanese-British alliance of 1902. With Germany, the cause of the 1907 entente, temporarily impotent, this historic enmity assumed a new shape. Communist efforts to proselytize the masses of the colonial and semicolonial countries of Asia had failed in China in 1927 but still disturbed British imperial interests elsewhere, e.g., on the frontiers of India and in the Middle East. London severed diplomatic relations with the Soviet Union in 1927, charging that Soviet commercial organizations in the United Kingdom served as a mask for espionage and other illegal activities. Although ambassadors were again exchanged in the fall of 1929, in Soviet eyes Britain and France remained the inveterate enemies of the U.S.S.R.

Japanese troops had evacuated Siberia in 1922, and a convention of 1925 secured Japanese withdrawal from Northern Sakhalin. In the following years little occurred to disturb relations between the two countries, and Japan observed strict neutrality in 1929 when the Red Army temporarily occupied part of Manchuria to protect the Soviet interest in the Chinese Eastern Railway.

The U.S.S.R. had participated in the World Economic Conference in May 1927 and subsequently in the meetings of the Preparatory Commission on Disarmament. Nevertheless Moscow still regarded the League of Nations with dislike as an instrument of the captialist powers which could be used to organize an anti-Soviet bloc of capitalist states.

This, in very brief summary, was the international situation of the Soviet Union on September 18, 1931, when the Japanese Army began the complete occupation of Manchuria and opened the chapter of modern history that ended aboard the U.S.S. *Missouri* in 1945. In the midst of the First Five-Year Plan, with the collectivized peasants thoroughly hostile to his regime, and with only negligible military forces in the Far East, Stalin adopted a policy of appeasement far more abject than that for which he later castigated the British and French.

At the end of the year Soviet Foreign Commissar Litvinov proposed a Soviet-Japanese nonaggression agreement. During the first months of 1932 his ambassador in Tokyo pressed the suggestion in several conversations only to be told that the matter was receiving careful consideration. On March 10, 1932, the U.S. Ambassador to Japan reported that "the Soviets have taken every precaution against being involved in the conflict . . . have avoided taking steps to oppose or check Japan's military actions in North Manchuria, and have maintained, in the face of some provocation, a strictly neutral attitude." [1] Before the end of the month the Soviet-controlled Chinese Eastern Railway was carrying Japanese troops with the tacit approval of Moscow.

In a note of April 20, the Secretary General of the League of Nations suggested to Litvinov that Soviet officials in Manchuria might be authorized to furnish information or evidence to the League-appointed Lytton Commission which was then in the Far East investigating the Sino-Japanese conflict. Litvinov immediately refused on the ground that his government was not a member of the League, had no part in the appointment of the commission and no representation on it, and thus could not "assume any responsibility" for the commission's conclusions. The following month Moscow even refused members of the commission permission to cross Soviet territory.[2]

By the fall of the year the policy of appeasement seemed to promise rewards. On October 28 U.S. Ambassador Grew reported from Tokyo that he had learned "on good authority" (presumably Soviet) that the Japanese seemed to be seriously considering the offer of a nonaggression pact. Indeed, the Soviet Embassy expected one would be signed before the end of the year.[3] This optimism, if real, was premature. Early in December Japanese forces advanced to the western terminus of the Chinese Eastern Railway at Manchuli and Soviet and Japanese troops faced each other across the Manchurian (now "Manchukuoan") border for the first time. On December 12 the Soviet and Chinese Governments announced the resumption of diplomatic relations. Tokyo could not criticize this step, "but nevertheless," reported Grew, "in all official and press communications on the subject, there is an undertone of feeling that the resumption of relations means that the Soviets have definitely taken a stand inimical to Japan."[4] And on December 31 the Japanese at Harbin moved eastward along the Chinese Eastern with the aim of occupying all of the line to its eastern terminus on the Soviet border.

In February 1933 the Japanese Cabinet decided to withdraw from the League of Nations, and on the 24th, in an unmistakable gesture, the Japanese delegation walked out of a League meeting. Japan "has prepared to burn her most important bridge with the outside world," Grew reported on the 23rd. "This step indicates the complete supremacy of the military and a fundamental defeat for the moderate elements in the country." He warned that the "military themselves and the public through military propaganda" were ready to fight rather than surrender to Western pressure, and any attempt to compromise on the part of the Japanese Government "would almost certainly result in further assassinations if not in internal revolution." Much of the public and army considered war with Russia or the United States or both inevitable. "The military and naval machines are in a state of high efficiency," continued the ambassador. "They possess complete self-confidence and arrogance. The Navy is becoming more bellicose. In the present temper of the Army and Navy and the public there is always the risk that any serious incident tending to inflame public opinion might lead Japan to radical steps without counting the cost thereof."[5] Presumably the Soviet Embassy reported to Moscow in similar terms.

Although seriously concerned about the threatening developments in the Far East, Stalin apparently feared to take any step which might provoke the hotheads among the Japanese military. Thus in a note of March 7, 1933 to the Secretary General of the League, Litvinov refused to have anything to do with a League Advisory Committee on the Chinese-Japanese conflict. As an organ of the League, wrote the Foreign Commissar, the committee would have to submit its recommendations to the League Assembly, and the U.S.S.R. would have no influence over the Assembly's decisions since it was not a League member. The majority of the countries represented on the committee, he continued, had no diplomatic ties with the Soviet Union and were thus more or less hostile toward it. "It would clearly be difficult for a Committee thus constituted to cope with this task of coordination as regards the Soviet Union, which is deprived of the possibility of having any contact with the majority of its members and individually with those whose interests are most likely to coincide with its own." [6]

At about the same time (reported by Grew on March 9) a Soviet representative approached the U.S. Embassy in Tokyo. Although the Japanese Foreign Office and many businessmen favored a nonaggression pact with the U.S.S.R., said the Russian, the Japanese Army opposed a move which would tie its hands. Japan was frantically preparing for war with her armaments factories working overtime. Since China could offer little resistance, these preparations were obviously for a war with the United States and the Soviet Union. The Japanese were especially afraid of a *rapprochement* between the two countries, continued the Soviet official, and he observed in conclusion that his government was in great need of diplomatic relations with the United States. Moscow could not repay the old Russian debts owed in the United States, for it would then have to pay all of the tsarist bonds. To obtain recognition, however, the Soviet Government was willing to grant economic favors and concessions.[7]

At the Washington Conference in 1921 the British and Japanese had agreed to terminate their 1902 alliance, but apparently Stalin still considered Britain a tacit ally of Japan. Hence the arrest of several British subjects in Moscow on March 11 and 12, 1933 may have been intended as an indirect warning to Tokyo—a move which, without provoking the Japanese military, would demonstrate Soviet willingness to take vigorous action. Six British engineers employed by the Metropolitan-Vickers Company in installing electrical generating equipment in the U.S.S.R. were falsely accused of sabotage and espionage. Despite a warning from London that Russian imports would be barred from the United Kingdom, the Soviet Government proceeded to "feature" the defendants in one of the propaganda trials characteristic of Soviet "justice." On April 19 two of the men were sentenced to terms of imprisonment, three to expulsion from the U.S.S.R., and one was acquitted. The same day a British proclamation suspended the importation of a wide range of Russian products. Although the Soviet Union was no longer as vulnerable as at the beginning of the First Five-Year Plan, Britain furnished one of the best markets for Soviet exports and the embargo must have been a severe economic blow.

At the end of June 1933 Litvinov, who was attending the World Economic Conference in London, had several conversations with Sir John Simon, the British Foreign Secretary. After the latter had rejected Litvinov's proposal that the embargo be lifted before the two engineers were freed, it was agreed that the two actions should take place simultaneously. The Foreign Commissar, however, avoided committing the agreement to paper.

On July 1, presumably at noon as arranged, Litvinov was informed that the embargo had been rescinded. At 7:25 that evening the Narkomindel (People's Commissariat of Foreign Affairs) informed William Strang, the British chargé in Moscow, that the two prisoners would be released at 9:00 the same evening. Together with another member of the embassy staff, Strang proceeded to the prison. Although the prisoners were brought into the prison courtyard and the necessary formalities completed, at the last moment one of the Soviet officials, a certain Sheinin representing the Procurator, declared that a necessary document was missing and the release could not take place until the next day. Strang thereupon objected strenuously and made ostentatious preparations to "camp" in the courtyard until the two men were freed:

I [Strang] then telephoned to Mr. Vyvyan at the Embassy, again in M. Sheinin's presence, and instructed him to telephone London to warn the Foreign Office of the delay and the reason for it . . . Mr. Vyvyan telephoned a little later to say that he had been unable to telephone to London as the line was out of action . . . The time was then about 10:20. Mr. Vyvyan, on my instructions, drafted and despatched my telegram No. 444 in order to acquaint you with the position.

I then settled myself in a corner of the garden, with Mr. Thornton [one of the prisoners], to wait. About 11.5 Mr. Sheinin rushed out, called us together round the table again, and announced that everything was now in order and that the prisoners were free. He did not, so far as I could see, produce any document, and I doubt whether there was any.

Strang was left with the impression "that no necessary documents were in reality missing, and that the officials at the prison were indulging in play-acting." [8]

Apparently the Soviet authorities were attempting to allow a whole day to elapse between the cancellation of the embargo and the release of the prisoners and thus give the impression that the British Government had been the first to weaken. Alarmed by Strang's vigorous reaction, they abandoned the attempt, but a TASS communiqué released at 11:00 that evening was worded to convey the same idea: "On July 1 the British Government raised the embargo on the import of Soviet goods," it stated. "On the same day, at its evening session," the Presidium of the Central Executive Committee (since 1936 the Presidium of the Supreme Soviet) commuted the sentences to expulsion from the U.S.S.R., and the prisoners "were released on the evening of 1 July." [9]

Toward the end of 1933 the Soviet position in the Far East seemed to improve somewhat. Grew reported on September 29 that most foreign observers in Tokyo considered a Soviet-Japanese conflict inevitable, probably in 1935 or 1936, but that the situation did not appear critical at the moment. Red Army forces in eastern Siberia had been strengthened significantly since 1932, and Soviet spokesmen now adopted a firmer tone when speaking of Japan. At the same time there had been no Japanese attempt to mobilize public opinion against the U.S.S.R.[10]

Litvinov visited the United States from November 7 to 25, 1933 and negotiated recognition. William Bullitt was appointed the first U.S. Ambassador to the Soviet Union, and Moscow appointed Alexander Troyanovsky, the former ambassador to Japan, to the Washington post. On December 24 Bullitt reported that all the government and Party leaders with whom he had spoken expected a war with Japan. The U.S.S.R. was so desirous of peace, he continued, that "even our moral influence is valued very highly . . . It is difficult to exaggerate the cordiality with which I was received . . . Stalin, who until my arrival had never received any ambassador, said to me 'at any moment, day or night, if you wish to see me you have only to ask and I will see you at once.' "

The following spring, on April 16, 1934, Bullitt reported from Moscow that many Soviet leaders, including Litvinov and Voroshilov, the Defense Commissar, had "expressed the opinion to me that the largest single deterrent to an attack by Japan this spring was recognition of the Soviet Government by the United States. They believe that the Japanese Government was uncertain as to the extent to which our relations had become intimate and feared an eventual attack by the United States in case of war." During the winter of 1933/34 work on the double tracking of the Trans-Siberian railroad had continued, and other preparations had been made for a war in the Far East. In the same dispatch Bullitt observed that all the Soviet leaders considered a Japanese attack inevitable. Voroshilov and other military leaders feared a conflict in the near future, but Litvinov and his colleagues in the Narkomindel felt that Japan would not attack in the spring or summer of 1934.[11]

On June 21, 1934 Litvinov and Lord Chilston, the British Ambassador to Moscow, discussed a proposed general security pact for Eastern Europe, an "Eastern Locarno." Judging from the British press, the Foreign Commissar observed, London seemed opposed to the idea. "He complained with considerable animation that it seemed impossible to know the attitude of the British Government." He had learned nothing at Geneva nor had any word been forthcoming from London. In concluding the conversation "M. Litvinov said he wished Soviet Union could have more understanding and better *political* [italics Chilston's] relations with Great Britain because in his mind there was no doubt that Great Britain and Russia were the most important factors for peace of the world." [12]

In London on July 3, Soviet Ambassador Maisky called on Sir Robert Vansittart, the Permanent Undersecretary of State for Foreign Affairs. His government earnestly desired better relations with Britain, declared the ambassador, and frankly admitted that this desire was motivated largely by fear of Germany. "There were, he said, two points at which his countrymen were suspicious of British policy, to wit, Japan and Germany." Vansittart replied that an objection had already been lodged in Moscow regarding statements that Britain was trying to involve Japan with the U.S.S.R. in the Far East. Nevertheless, said Maisky, Moscow entertained "a genuine apprehension, or misapprehension" regarding Britain's Far Eastern policy:

. . . to which Sir R. Vansittart replied that the Soviet Government themselves must have produced that impression, for no well-informed person—and M. Maisky himself was, of course, among the best informed—could for a moment credit so fantastic a tale as that of a British desire for warfare in the Far East. The theory ran against every element of commonsense. . . . His Majesty's Government wished, of course, to be on as good terms with Japan as their commercial differences with her permitted; and they also wished, of course, that Russia, too, should be on as good terms as possible with Japan. Their interests, financial and commercial, in the Far East were far too great for any other attitude to be possible.

With regard to Europe, Vansittart assured the ambassador that Britain was prepared to welcome the Soviet Union into the League and also favored the idea of an East European security pact.[13]

On July 13 Foreign Secretary Sir John Simon himself declared in the House of Commons that Britain would warmly welcome Soviet membership in the League. It was presumably a few days later that, according to Litvinov, Simon personally assured Maisky that Britain opposed any Soviet-Japanese war, would do everything possible to prevent it, and would give Japan absolutely no support. "For the first time since recognition by Great Britain," Litvinov remarked to Bullitt on July 29, "we now have actual diplomatic relations." Neither he nor Chicherin, his predecessor as Foreign Commissar, had ever discussed serious matters with the British Embassy in Moscow, and the Soviet Ambassador to London had been little more than a consul. "Both in London and in Moscow we are now discussing all the problems of the world freely and in the most friendly manner." Bullitt reported that the "delight of the Soviet Government" over the "reversal" of British policy was "universal and profound." [14]

The published British documents reveal no deliberate reversal of policy, i.e. no one in the Foreign Office seemed to feel they were adopting a radically new attitude toward the Soviet Union. With Russia's previous isolation from world developments, however, the diplomats of the two countries had little to discuss other than matters of trade and, in the case of the British, complaints regarding Communist propaganda statements in the Soviet press. Closer ties between France and the U.S.S.R., efforts to establish an Eastern pact system, and the Soviet decision to enter the League naturally led to more meaningful discussions with London. To Litvinov this development may actually have seemed like a major change in British policy. In any event he must have considered it advantageous for the U.S.S.R. if the rest of the world, Tokyo especially, believed that close ties existed with Britain.

The *"rapprochement"* with London appeared to have eased the Narkomindel's fears of a Japanese attack. On July 29, 1934 Litvinov told Bullitt that Britain's changed attitude had eliminated all danger of an attack. In the fall he remarked to the ambassador "that he had no fear whatsoever of a Japanese attack in the foreseeable future." The Japanese were having much more trouble than they had expected in Manchuria. During the winter, Maisky urged, apparently with some energy, an official British visit to Russia. (An entry of February 28 in Anthony Eden's diary referred to "poor old Maisky with his invitation burning a hole in his pocket no doubt." The Soviet Ambassador also promised an interview with Stalin.) Eden, a Parliamentary Undersecretary but not yet in charge at the Foreign Office, made the visit to Moscow from March 27 to 31, 1935, and on April 2 Litvinov assured the U.S. chargé that Britain and the U.S.S.R. would in the future collaborate closely in their foreign policies and mentioned

Japan specifically. A few weeks later Lord Chilston informed Bullitt that he and Eden had finally "been able to disabuse the Soviet Government of any idea that Great Britain was urging Japan to attack the Soviet Union." [15]

In the summer of 1935 Japanese forces penetrated farther into Inner Mongolia, and during the winter of 1935/36 a number of clashes occurred on the border of Soviet-controlled Outer Mongolia. Litvinov told Bullitt on February 21, 1936 that he feared no early attack by Japan. The Japanese Army was having too much trouble in Manchuria and North China and Japan's finances were in poor shape. Stalin, however, apparently considered a word of warning in order and on March 4 he granted a personal interview to Roy Howard, an American newspaperman. "If Japan ventures to attack the Mongolian People's Republic," warned Stalin, "we will have to assist the Mongolian People's Republic." Eight days later, on March 12, a Soviet-Outer Mongolian mutual assistance pact was signed at Ulan Bator.[16]

During a conversation at a diplomatic reception in Moscow on April 2, at which Bullitt was present, Defense Commissar Voroshilov warned the Japanese Ambassador that Moscow desired peace, but an attack on Outer Mongolia would be answered by a counterattack twice as strong. The ambassador mentioned unmarked frontiers and attempted to depreciate the seriousness of the clashes. The commissar replied that the border was very well marked and Soviet forces would repel any attempts to cross it. The ambassador then stated that the Japanese commander in Manchuria was a thoroughly responsible person and no further difficulties were likely. "Voroshilov answered that he did anticipate further difficulties and that if war should break out soon Japan unquestionably would be defeated." Two days later, however, the Narkomindel official in charge of Far Eastern affairs told Bullitt that the latest information indicated Japan had no intention of attacking Outer Mongolia or the U.S.S.R. in the immediate future; junior Japanese officers seemed to have instigated the recent border incidents against the will of both the government in Tokyo and the Commander-in-Chief in Manchuria.[17]

In Nanking on May 20 the Soviet Ambassador to China informed an American journalist that "Soviet policy vis-a-vis Japan was now one of defiance based on the theory that a strong attitude would be more likely to prevent Japanese aggression and resultant war than a weak." During the course of a dinner he gave the following evening, the ambassador made similar remarks to the Chinese Foreign Minister and a member of the U.S. Embassy: [18]

> He said that his Government had discovered that the Japanese misunderstood conciliation as weakness and that boldness was probably the best preventive of war. . . . Referring to Manchurian border incidents, he said that his Government had denied to the Japanese Government the contention of the latter that boundaries were vague and had said that if any military parties crossed them into Soviet territory military action would result; that the Soviet Union would be glad if Japan did not regard such border incidents as *casus belli* but if Japan made them pretext for war then the Soviet Government "could not help it."

The new policy of "toughness" in the Far East reflected primarily the increased strength of the Red Army in eastern Siberia and possibly, to a lesser degree, the better relations with Britain and France.

At the end of 1936 Litvinov was able to demonstrate the new policy in action. The convention governing Japanese fishing in Siberian coastal waters since 1928 was due to expire at the end of 1936. After protracted negotiations, the protocol of a new treaty had been agreed upon and was to be signed on November 20. At the same time negotiations in Berlin had led to the Anti-Comintern Pact, an agreement with Tokyo ostensibly providing for cooperation in suppressing Communist activities in Japan and Germany. This was signed on November 25, 1936, and on November 16 the Japanese Foreign Minister had admitted to the Soviet Ambassador that an agreement with a third state was being concluded but denied that it was directed against the U.S.S.R. or would affect Japanese-Soviet relations. To the dismay of the Japanese, the Soviet Government thereupon refused to conclude the fisheries convention. At the last moment, however, Moscow relented and on December 28 extended the existing convention for another year.[19]

Press reports from Manchukuo, relayed from Tokyo on May 16, 1937, foreshadowed the next significant incident: Citing the alleged failure of Manchukuoan authorities to appoint representatives to a joint dredging committee, the Soviet Government had announced its intention of abrogating a 1934 agreement regulating navigation on the Amur. During June Soviet troops occupied several islands in the Amur some 120 kilometers below Blagoveshchensk. The islands were on the Manchurian side of the channel, and the Japanese claimed that the action meant the end of free navigation of the river. On June 29 the Japanese Ambassador in Moscow protested to Litvinov, and the next day Japanese artillery sank a Soviet gunboat in the vicinity. On July 2 Litvinov agreed to the withdrawal of Soviet forces with the understanding, according to the Narkomindel account, that neither side would occupy the disputed territory. A few days later, however, a Japanese-Manchukuoan company occupied the islands and provoked nothing more than an official protest from Moscow.[20]

One can only speculate about the true meaning of this incident. Marshal Tukhachevsky, the Deputy Commissar of Defense and actual military head of the Red Army, had been demoted to a minor post on May 11. Early in June he and several other senior officers were executed, allegedly for conspiring with Germany. These executions marked the spread of the Great Purge to the Soviet armed forces and to the higher and middle ranks of Soviet society generally. By occupying the Amur islands, Stalin may have intended to demonstrate to the Japanese that troubles at home had not weakened the Soviet Union abroad. Alternatively, the occupation of the islands may have been merely part of the new policy of "toughness" toward Japan. In any event Stalin decided against a major frontier incident; purely Mongolian forces had been involved in the earlier incidents on the Outer Mongolian border, but only Soviet troops could be used on the Amur.

Japanese aggression against China finally flared into open warfare with the Chinese central government on July 7, 1937, and in Moscow on December 20, 1937, U.S. chargé Henderson had a very confidential conversation with the Chinese Ambassador. The latter explained that he had arrived in Moscow as ambassador in November 1936. Before his appointment he had been considered a firm believer in Soviet-Chinese friendship and had been on friendly terms with Bogomolov, the Russian Ambassador, and other Soviet officials in China: [21]

. . . in China Bogomolov had been free in making oral assurances of Soviet readiness to assist China in case of war with Japan . . . in Moscow at the time of my arrival, I was unable to get in touch with him. He did call upon me to say good-bye prior to his return to China some time after my arrival but avoided discussing political problems. I found that Litvinov was also evasive. In response to my overtures he usually replied that he preferred to have important matters involving Soviet-Chinese relations discussed at Nanking.

Bogomolov and influential groups in China friendly to the Soviet Union continued during the spring and summer of 1937 to endeavor to make the Chinese Government believe that if it would undertake to offer armed resistance to Japan it could confidently expect the armed support of the Soviet Union. . . .

I must state out of fairness that neither Litvinov nor any other high Government official in Moscow has ever given me any promises of Soviet armed support to China against Japan. Nevertheless, they have not taken recommended measures to end the campaign of belligerency carried on by their representatives and friends in China.

Bullitt, now the U.S. Ambassador to Paris, dined alone with Leon Blum, the French Socialist leader and Vice Premier, on October 22, 1937. Blum expressed extreme skepticism regarding the Soviet position: [22]

He had had many discussions with Litvinov in Geneva recently. Litvinov had talked to him frankly as an old friend. Litvinov had said that he and the Soviet Union were perfectly delighted that Japan had attacked China. He believed that Japan would be so weakened financially and economically and would have such enormous difficulty in digesting a conquered China that the Soviet Union was now completely assured of peace in the Far East for many years to come. Litvinov had added that the Soviet Union hoped that war between China and Japan would continue just as long as possible and would result in an attempt by the Japanese to swallow just as much of China as possible. . . . Litvinov had said that whereas before the Japanese attack on China, Japan had been most hostile and aggravating, today the Japanese were all politeness and butter in their relations with the Soviet Government.

In June 1937, while relations between China and Japan still remained fairly peaceful, Moscow had provoked the Amur-islands incident but quickly decided not to press the matter to the point of a serious conflict. By the summer of 1938, however, the situation had changed radically: Although strong forces remained in Manchuria, Japan was deeply involved in China and no longer possessed the same freedom of action as a year earlier.

On July 6, 1938 a small Soviet cavalry patrol appeared on top of Changkufeng, a hill on the Soviet-Manchurian border southwest of Vladivostok in the area where Korea, Manchuria, and the Soviet Maritime Provinces come together. On the 11th Soviet infantry or engineers occupied the crest of the hill and began digging in and putting up barbed wire. Four days later the Japanese chargé in Moscow protested that the hill was on the Manchurian side of the frontier, and on the 20th the Japanese Ambassador made a similar protest. As early as July 17, however, a Tokyo correspondent of the *New York Times* was "confidentially informed that the situation had not reached the point where war was necessary." Another dispatch to the same paper on the 22nd reported the Japanese public as "almost unanimously opposed to taking steps that might lead to war with Russia if there is any possible honorable way to avoid a conflict." The same day the Associated Press reported a Japanese Foreign Ministry denial "that Japan had threatened to use force to eject Soviet soldiers" at Changkufeng. From Tokyo on July 25 a *New York Times* correspondent wrote that "the most recent developments make an amicable solution in the near future almost certain." The same day in Moscow Litvinov told the U.S. chargé that "he did not believe that this incident would result in hostilities" since "he was informed that the Japanese military authorities were opposed to precipitating a conflict with the Soviets."

And four days later (July 29) Soviet troops began digging in at Shachofeng, a hill just north of Changkufeng. This was too much for the senior Japanese officer on the spot, Lieutenant General Kamezo Suetaka. If his forces had ignored this new action, he wrote some six weeks later, "the same sort of unlawful irruption would occur more often along the frontiers," and the danger of an all-out war with the Soviet Union would have grown. Thus during the early morning of July 31 the Japanese attacked and took both Changkufeng and Shachofeng.

In the next ten days Red Army infantry and tanks made repeated counter-attacks, and artillery pounded the Japanese positions with increasing accuracy and effect; the Soviet artillery tactics resembled those used on the Western Front in 1916. Soviet air attacks began on August 1; planes bombed not only the front-line positions but also the nearby Japanese railway and targets in Korea proper. As early as August 2 a *New York Times* correspondent in Tokyo had "authoritatively learned that the Japanese military authorities have no intention of sending war planes over Soviet territory in retaliation . . . and that they insist that Japanese troops on the spot absolutely obey orders from Tokyo." Since no Japanese planes opposed these attacks at any time during the incident, Tokyo was clearly trying to avoid enlarging the scope of the hostilities. Litvinov had reached this conclusion by August 5 when he assured the U.S. chargé that he "knew" Japan desired no war with the U.S.S.R. Red Army circles also shared this opinion, the chargé reported, and were determined to force the Japanese to withdraw.

In Moscow on August 4, the Japanese Ambassador had suggested to Litvinov a restoration of the situation before July 11, i.e., before the Soviet occupation of Changkufeng, while the Foreign Commissar demanded a restoration of the situation before July 29. The ambassador saw Litvinov again on the 7th and suggested a mutual limited withdrawal which was also rejected. The two conferred once more during the evening of August 10, and the Foreign Commissar finally agreed to a cease-fire with both sides retaining the positions they held as of midnight of the 10th (local time). The cease-fire became effective at 12:00 noon on August 11, and by the 15th Japanese forces had voluntarily withdrawn from all of the contested ground. During the fighting Tokyo had committed most of one peace-strength infantry division, while the Red Army had used three somewhat understrength rifle divisions plus hundreds of tanks and planes. The Japanese lost over 500 killed and 900 wounded and estimated Soviet casualties at 4,500 to 7,000.[23]

At the time and later, many journalists were convinced that the Russians had staged the Changkufeng incident to reduce Japanese pressure on the Chinese. On the other hand it may have been merely a probe to determine just how deeply Tokyo was committed to the China venture. But in retrospect a third explanation seems even more likely.

Although prominent old-Bolshevik leaders of the anti-Stalin opposition had been tried and sentenced as early as 1936, the wholesale phase of the Great Purge began, as previously mentioned, in June 1937 with the execution of Marshal Tukhachevsky and several of his colleagues.[24] By drastically reducing the number of foreigners in the U.S.S.R. and isolating those who could not be expelled, Stalin attempted, with some success, to conceal the extent of the dreadful affair from the outside world. As early as the spring of 1937, the N.K.G.B. had arrested or exiled many Soviet citizens who had had business or personal dealings with foreign diplomatic missions or foreign residents. The remaining persons in this category appeared to be in constant fear of arrest, even those authorized to maintain contacts with foreigners. Loy Henderson, the U.S. chargé, reported that members of the embassy staff "hesitate to continue or to develop such contacts as they already have since they do not wish to be instrumental in causing misfortune to innocent persons."

Tourists with valid Soviet visas arriving at Leningrad during the summer were not permitted to land, and the U.S. Embassy even had to make "strenuous representations" to the Narkomindel to secure a visa for a newly-assigned staff member. Road and rail traffic across the Polish frontier was also severely restricted. By September 20, 1937, Henderson reported that he and his colleagues could still see Soviet officials whose duties forced them to receive foreigners, could talk with a few Soviet citizens who were still permitted to associate with foreigners, could speak to Soviet employees of the mission and their own household servants, and could "chat occasionally with those few persons who still are not alarmed to find a foreigner sitting by them at the theater, in a tramcar, on a park bench, and so forth."

In the same dispatch Henderson observed that practically all the other diplomatic missions were trying to determine the fate of their arrested nationals. German citizens seem to have been the main targets of this drive, a number having been arrested as early as November 1936. It "is quite possible," wrote Henderson on December 31 of that year, "that the Soviet authorities feel that the German Government, through its representation and German citizens in the Soviet Union, has been able to keep itself too well informed." By October 8, 1937, some 382 German nationals were in Soviet prisons; by November 1 the figure had grown to 508. With the deportation of almost a hundred prisoners in the intervening months, 408 German citizens were known to be in custody as of February 7, 1938, but the German Embassy estimated that it had never been informed of the arrest of an additional 200.

During the summer and fall of 1937, the Soviet Government requested those states with which it was not on good terms to reduce the number of their consulates in the U.S.S.R. to match the number of Soviet consulates in the countries concerned. Thus, in the Soviet Union, five Italian, five German, two Japanese, and two Polish consulates were closed. Early in January 1938 the Narkomindel made a similar request to Britain, Turkey, Iran, Afghanistan, Czechoslovakia, Norway, Sweden, Estonia, and Latvia. In 1937 the Auswärtiges Amt (the German Foreign Office) had considered abandoning a twelve-day courier service between Berlin and Tokyo via Siberia. But on February 22, 1938, General Köstring, the German military attaché in Moscow, told the State Secretary in Berlin that one of his last sources of information had disappeared with the closing of the German consulates. "Under those circumstances he would have to urge especially that nothing be changed in the present arrangement of our courier trips, for what the couriers saw on the way and could then report to him was in the present situation actually the last remaining source of information outside of Moscow." [25]

During the spring of 1938, Stalin may have thought he had succeeded in concealing the full effects of the purge from the outside world. But then on June 13 General Genrikh S. Lyushkov, the senior N.K.G.B. officer in the Far East, defected to Manchukuo, and his presence in Tokyo was revealed on July 3—three days before the Soviet patrol appeared on Changkufeng. By this time the Great Purge was reaching its climax, and even the purgers were being purged (hence Lyushkov's flight). As Walter Duranty, the Moscow correspondent of the *New York Times,* wrote on July 21, "It is possible the Japanese are convinced the Soviet regime is so weakened by the effects of purges that Japan can take risks." And the third secretary of the Japanese Embassy in Moscow made a similar statement to reporters when he arrived in Japan on August 4: "The Soviet purges and the recent flight of General G. S. Lushkoff from Siberia to Japan seem to have created the impression in some quarters that the Soviet Union is disintegrating, but this is a great mistake." [26]

It seems very probable that the Changkufeng incident was staged simply to offset the impression Lyushkov's flight, and presumably his testimony, had made on the Japanese high command. When expecting an attack, even an animal snarls and bristles up and tries to appear fearless.

CONFRONTED by a powerful and dangerous Japan, whose government could not always be depended upon to act rationally, Moscow adopted what must now be recognized as some of the standard tactics of Communist diplomacy (State Department and Central Intelligence Agency please note):

1) At the beginning, while the Red Army was still very weak in the Far East, a painfully correct attitude accompanied by efforts to secure a *détente*, if possible even a nonaggression agreement; at other times and vis-a-vis other powers, the standard term has been "peaceful coexistence."

2) A vigorous, belligerent action against a third power—the arrest and trial of the Metropolitan-Vickers engineers. This could not provoke any really dangerous British reaction, and would demonstrate to Tokyo that the Soviet Union was a genuine rather than a teddy bear (or, to use a later term, "paper tiger"). The closest recent parallel to this gambit was probably the Chinese Communist raid over the Himalayas into India in 1962.

3) Efforts to demonstrate that the Soviet Union was on good terms with France and Britain and even with Germany and Poland (more of this in the next chapter). In other words, the Japanese should not expect any of the European powers to attack Russia merely because she was embroiled in the Far East.

4) Once the Japanese were safely involved in China, a series of

increasingly serious border incidents to convince them that China—not Russia—offered indeed the most profitable field for aggression. Stalin apparently provoked the Amur islands and Changkufeng incidents to counter any belief in Tokyo that the Soviet Union was paralyzed by the Great Purge. This is undoubtedly one of the standard ploys of Soviet diplomacy: When weakened at home or contemplating a retreat that may give an impression of weakness, then make an offensive move abroad. (But not one likely to provoke a serious reaction; Stalin made his moves at Changkufeng with a great deal of caution—first the occupation of Changkufeng proper, then the occupation of Shachofeng. These are now called salami tactics.) Later examples are the shooting down of a British transport over Germany soon after Stalin's death in 1953, and the resumption of nuclear testing in 1961 as a prelude to abandoning a deadline for a German peace treaty.

But Stalin seems to have deliberately provoked a much more serious conflict on the Outer Mongolian border, May–September 1939 (see Chapter 7); no reason can be found in specific developments within the Soviet Union or in Soviet-Japanese relations. Apparently the idea was at a convenient moment to convince the Japanese Army once and for all that an all-out war with Russia would be disastrous.

From Stalin's point of view, Litvinov's efforts at collective security were a failure. His own pact with the Germans was an almost fatal blunder as Hitler demonstrated on June 22, 1941. But in the Far East, Stalin scored an unqualified success: Instead of occupying all of eastern Siberia, as they might have done after the German attack on European Russia, the Japanese refused to be tempted and instead carried out their plans for an attack on Singapore, the Philippines, and the Dutch East Indies.

2

Retreat from Rapallo

February 1933—April 1934

While the position of the Soviet Union in the Far East had improved markedly by the time of the Changkufeng fighting, a potentially far greater danger had been developing in the west since Hitler's assumption of power in 1933. At first, although concerned about the growing strength of the avowedly anti-Communist and anti-Soviet National Socialist Party in Germany, Soviet officials hoped responsibility would have a sobering effect on the Nazis. In July of 1932 the rather worried manager of the Soviet news agency TASS expressed to Gustav Hilger, the economic expert of the German Embassy in Moscow, his conviction that even a National Socialist government would maintain the good relations with Russia which were to Germany's ultimate advantage. The press official assured Hilger confidentially that the Soviet press had been ordered to avoid any appearance of interfering in German politics and any criticism of German policy. "All he feared was that the accession of Hitler might be followed by a rather disturbing period of transition before normal relations could again be achieved." In a report to the Central Executive Committee on January 23, 1933, Molotov declared that Germany occupied "a special place in our foreign relations. Of all the countries maintaining diplomatic relations with us, we have had and now have the strongest economic connexions with Germany. That is no accident. It arises from the interests of the two countries." [1]

Hitler became Reich Chancellor on January 30, 1933, and the

next day Dirksen, the German Ambassador in Moscow, reported that the event had "caused great uneasiness here." On February 6 State Secretary Bülow of the Auswärtiges Amt (the German Foreign Office) wrote Dirksen that he should discount alarming rumors, even those from Berlin. "Here as elsewhere," he concluded, "one still boils with water." On the 15th, during a detailed discussion of policy toward Russia, Hitler agreed with Foreign Minister von Neurath that it was necessary to maintain the existing political, economic and military relations with the U.S.S.R. and said he would allow no changes in existing German policies.

Although the burning of the Reichstag building on February 27 afforded an excuse for the legal suppression of the German Communist Party and the installation of a National Socialist dictatorship, there was some truth in Bülow's statement. Germany was still disarmed and even Poland posed a formidable threat to the 100,000-man Reichswehr. Thus peaceful assurances characterized the first years of Hitler's regime. In a speech to the Reichstag on March 23, 1933, he declared that [2]

The Government of the Reich are ready to cultivate with the Soviet Union friendly relations profitable to both parties. It is above all the Government of the National Revolution who feel themselves in a position to adopt such a positive policy with regard to Soviet Russia. The fight against Communism in Germany is our internal affair in which we will never permit interference from outside. Our political relations with other Powers to whom we are bound by common interests will not be affected thereby.

Nevertheless, partly as a result of the still unsettled situation in Germany, a number of Soviet trade offices were raided and searched and several Soviet commercial officials arrested or manhandled, both by police and Nazi Party toughs. Litvinov protested to Dirksen as early as April 3. The next day Hitler approved an extension of the German-Soviet Berlin Treaty of 1926 and the conciliation convention of 1929. The extensions had been signed in 1931 but parliamentary difficulties in Germany had prevented ratification. The formal exchange of the instruments of ratification took place on May 5, 1933, but nine days later, in a report to Berlin, Dirksen complained that the Soviet press had not "responded to the positive position of the entire German press toward the Soviet Union on the occasion of the extension of the

Berlin Treaty" but instead had "continued to expatiate on every single, meaningless incident that has occurred in connection with a Soviet citizen in Germany." [3]

Concluding a conversation with Dirksen on May 16, Litvinov observed that his government's basic attitude toward Germany remained unchanged. It was convinced that friendly relations with National Socialist Germany were as feasible as friendly relations with Fascist Italy. The Soviet Government was uncertain only regarding future German policy. In the issue of the Comintern journal dated the preceding day, a writer had warned of the aggressive plans of Nazi Germany: [4]

The plan of foreign policy of the National-Socialists is as follows: Germany, Great Britain and Italy must make an alliance for a joint struggle against the U.S.S.R. Poland must be cut off by handing over the Corridor to Germany and separating West Ukraine from it. The Soviet Union must be dismembered. Soviet Ukraine together with West Ukraine must be converted into an "independent" bourgeois state under the aegis of Germany. The remaining bourgeois Russia must open up Siberia for German colonisation and enterprise.

While attending the World Economic Conference in London, Hugenberg, the German Minister of Economics, Food and Agriculture, released a memorandum to the press on June 16. One way in which Germany could again be made internationally solvent, he declared, would be to "open up to the 'nation without space' areas in which it could provide space for the settlement of its vigorous race and construct great works of peace." The world economic depression, he continued, was really caused by a decline in consumption. "War, revolution, and internal decay made a beginning in Russia and large parts of the east." This development had been intensified by the artificial impoverishment of the "civilized countries of the world having the greatest power of consumption. This destructive process is in the meantime still going on. It is necessary that it be stopped."

Litvinov made light of the release the next day in a statement printed in *Izvestia* three days later, but indicated that he considered it an attempt to "defame" the Soviet Union. On June 19 Deputy Foreign Commissar Krestinsky remonstrated with Dirksen regarding Hugenberg's memorandum, claiming it was a direct attack upon the U.S.S.R. Although the text made no reference to settlement in the east, Krestinsky stated this was the case and that any settlement in Eastern Europe would have to be at the expense of Russia. Three days later in Berlin the Soviet Ambassador handed State Secretary Bülow an official protest: Hugenberg had made an "appeal for war against the USSR," and Germany was "asking for Soviet territory to colonize." This note appeared in *Izvestia* on June 24.[5]

As early as April 27, 1933 Soviet authorities had indicated their wish to discontinue one of the three joint experimental stations in Russia (air, armour, and chemical warfare). General von Bockelberg, chief of the German Army Weapons Office, was received with marked friendliness, however, when he visited Moscow from May 8 to 28 at the invitation of Deputy Defense Commissar Tukhachevsky, and plans for discontinuing the station seemed to have been dropped. At a dinner given by Dirksen in honor of the visitor on May 13, Voroshilov requested the ambassador, when in Berlin, "to inform the authoritative German offices that the Soviet Government wanted to continue its good relations with Germany as in the past; a sign of this attitude of the War Commissariat in particular might be the friendly reception accorded General von Bockelberg."

Nevertheless, on the heels of the general's departure and even before he had arrived back in Berlin, Soviet authorities demanded the immediate liquidation of the stations. In a conversation with Dirksen on June 3, Krestinsky mentioned French accounts of disclosures of the secret Soviet-German military cooperation, allegedly made by von Papen while Chancellor. The Deputy Foreign Commissar observed that the accounts deserved little credence, but "it was perhaps more advantageous and safe for both sides—the German and the Soviet—to undertake to reduce cooperation and forestall possible attacks." The deactivation of the stations continued and, despite some initial Soviet hostility, was completed in a friendly fashion on September 15.[6]

The next conflict arose over the Reichstag-fire trial. On or before September 19 Hitler had indicated that Soviet correspondents should not be admitted to the proceedings, not even the TASS representative. But the TASS and *Izvestia* correspondents proceeded to Leipzig, where the trial was to be held, and were arrested there on September 22. The two correspondents were soon released and the responsible German official apologized. But the bar on attendance at the trial remained in force, and on September 26 the Soviet Government announced the expulsion of German journalists in the U.S.S.R. In a conversation with the German chargé the same day, Litvinov hinted that the conflict could be ended by admission of the Soviet journalists to the trial and if it were made clear in Germany that illegal molestation of a Soviet citizen would result in prosecution.

Also on the same day, at a conference of department heads, Hitler stated that restoration of good relations with Russia was impossible as the Soviet leaders would never forgive the National Socialists for having smashed communism in Germany. At the same time he was opposed to breaking off relations or furnishing the pretext for a break and agreed that Bülow should make some reassuring statements to the Soviet Ambassador. Illegal acts, e.g., unjustified arrests, against Soviet citizens in Germany were also discussed, and as Bülow noted the consensus of opinion appeared to be that while all Russian complaints could not be satisfied "substantial efforts ought to be made to remove at least some of the grievances."

In October, during negotiations between the Soviet Ambassador and an official of the Prussian State Police, the latter agreed that the Soviet journalists should be admitted to the trial; in return the ambassador promised that their reporting would be wholly objective, the Russian radio would refrain from anti-German agitation, and the German journalists would be readmitted to the U.S.S.R. The matter was finally settled on these terms during a discussion on October 28, 1933 between Neurath and Litvinov who had stopped in Berlin en route to the United States. This, however, was the only matter discussed in any detail during the conversation.[7]

A WRITER in the June 22, 1933 issue of the *Communist International*, the Comintern journal, declared that the National Socialists intended to form an anti-Soviet capitalist bloc based on a German-Polish agreement "according to which Germany will receive the corridor from Poland, and Poland, in turn, will be compensated at the expense of Soviet Ukraine." On December 21 Litvinov informed Bullitt that his government expected an attack by Japan in the spring and felt it must secure its western frontier in every way; he did not fear an immediate attack in the west, but "if the probable war with Japan should drag on for two years he anticipated a joint attack by Poland and Germany, acting in concert with Japan." A few days later, on January 1, 1934, Karl Radek, the editor of *Izvestia*, spoke "with the utmost frankness" to a member of the German Embassy. It was clear, said Radek, that Germany had no intention of attacking the U.S.S.R. in the near future. But should the Soviet Union become engaged in a desperate war with Japan, Germany might well seize the Corridor and then soothe Polish national pride with an offer of compensation in the Ukraine. Three and a half months later, however, Bullitt reported Litvinov's admission that he did not believe rumors of an actual Polish-German agreement for an attack on the U.S.S.R.[8]

Neither Litvinov, Radek, nor any other Communist propagandist mentioned still another danger: that the extremists among the Japanese military might convince themselves that Germany and Poland would indeed attack the Soviet Union should it become involved in a war with Japan. Thus a major aim of Soviet policy until the spring of 1934 seems to have been not to prevent such an attack but rather to make it clear that a German attack was either not contemplated or not possible.[9]

As early as February 20, 1933 Dirksen reported from Moscow that private assurances had relieved the worst Soviet fears regarding Germany's future policy, but could not take the place of a public govenmental statement. "There is also disappointment here over the fact that even the substitutes for such official Government statements, such as friendly telegrams on special occasions or interviews of a positive nature on the part of Germany, have been omitted." Two days later in a letter to the Moscow embassy, Neurath mentioned Soviet "wishes repeatedly expressed to us at certain intervals since the fall of the Brüning Cabinet, to receive from the Reich Government assurances of an official or semi-official nature that there was no change in our policy toward the

USSR." On February 28 Krestinsky complained to Dirksen that statements regarding the unchanged nature of Germany's policy toward Russia had all been made privately. "The public at home and abroad was not informed about the intentions of our Russian policy." [10]

In an interview with Hitler on April 28, the Soviet Ambassador read a prepared statement objecting to actions against Soviet nationals and commercial interests in Germany and the tone of the German press. In order to "pass over the excesses that have already occurred," it would be necessary to "bring about a decisive change in the method of action" and also [11]

to make known to the general public the friendly foreign policy attitude of the German Government toward the USSR . . . For otherwise it would soon be hardly possible to find people inside and outside both countries who, in the face of the systematic repetition and continuation of the above-mentioned actions, would be able to believe that the previous relationship had actually been maintained between the Union of the Soviet Socialist Republics and the German Reich. . . .

The German press should be provided with information designed to inform the people who support the German Government in a way corresponding to the actual intentions of the Reich Cabinet toward the USSR.

At the beginning of October and again on October 23, a semiofficial representative of the Narkomindel suggested to Twardowski, the German chargé in Moscow, that any settlement of the journalists controversy be accompanied by a short, general, and presumably public statement which would mention "recent misunderstandings and incidents" that the two governments regarded as "no longer in existence." An agreed communiqué of October 31 was released, but it dealt only with the dispute regarding the journalists which had been settled according to the principle that "mutual relations must remain unaffected by the difference between the governmental systems in the two countries." Strang, the British chargé in Moscow, seems to have accurately summed up this particular phase of Soviet diplomacy in a dispatch of August 9, 1933: [12]

Their major fear is from Japan . . . As, however, the threat from Germany, unlike the threat from Japan, is not imminent as Germany is isolated in Europe, the Soviet Government are not likely to adopt with Germany the subservient tone they are wont to use with Japan, but will employ the aggressive diplomatic tactics which they find have paid them in the past with other countries, and will not leave the Germans at rest until they publicly abjure, if they can, both interference in Soviet internal affairs and the promulgation of a policy of colonisation or territorial readjustment at the expense of the Soviet Union.

For the first few months after Hitler assumed power, the Polish Government displayed an unmistakably hostile attitude toward Germany. Toward the end of 1933, however, Marshal Pilsudski decided to accept an understanding with the Third Reich. The Führer received the new Polish Ambassador, Lipski, on November 15, and an agreed release stated that the interview "resulted in the full agreement of both Governments in the intention to take up the questions affecting the two countries through direct negotiations and also to renounce any use of force." After some further negotiations, a nonaggression "declaration" was signed in Berlin on January 26, 1934, and the ensuing *rapprochement* lasted until the beginning of 1939.

Early in December 1933 the Soviet Government had invited Polish Foreign Minister Beck to visit Moscow and at about the same time also suggested a joint declaration to the effect that Poland and the U.S.S.R. considered the political and economic independence of Finland and the Baltic states essential and would consult together should that independence be threatened. Moscow sounded the Latvian Government on the subject on December 21 and the Finnish Government on the 23rd. Helsinki replied that it considered the declaration unnecessary, and the governments of the Baltic states adopted a negative or at best lukewarm attitude which ended the matter. According to a later Polish explanation in London, Warsaw had felt obliged to go along with the proposal in order to quiet Litvinov's unfounded suspicions regarding Polish-German conversations. At the same time, to avoid offending Germany, the Poles had proposed that the states concerned be consulted, believing that the Finns, at least, would reject the declaration.[13]

Moscow certainly had nothing to lose from this maneuver. Had it succeeded it would have demonstrated to the world in general and Japan in particular that Russia enjoyed good, indeed close relations with Poland. Even though nothing came of the proposal, the fact that the Polish Government was willing to cooperate indicated that it was planning no combination with Germany against the U.S.S.R.

After abandonment of the joint Polish-Soviet declaration, the Red Army leaders sought a reassuring public gesture from Germany. On January 10, 1934, Defense Commissar Voroshilov spoke for an hour with Nadolny who had replaced Dirksen as German Ambassador to Moscow:

Voroshilov immediately turned the conversation to the sympathies and good relations that existed between Japan and Germany and naturally caused great concern in the Soviet Union owing to the situation in the Far East. . . . He dwelt a particularly long time on Hitler's *Mein Kampf*, in which connection he finally said that two words of the Chancellor's in public would be enough to [destroy?] the impression that the anti-Soviet tendency of the book still had validity today. . . . he came back to this time and again.

Three days later, Yegorov, the Chief of Staff of the Red Army, remarked to Colonel Hartmann, the German military attaché, that he would like to meet and have a frank conversation with the new commander of the German Army, General von Fritsch, and the new Chief of Staff (Chief of the Truppenamt), General Ludwig Beck. Hartmann replied that an invitation to Berlin could easily be obtained. "Yegorov, however, indicated that he was thinking of a visit of Germans in Moscow. . . . The wish which he expressed and which he dwelt on for some time in his conversations was not a figure of speech, and it is also more than a feeler; it seems to me actually to be an unofficial invitation." [14]

With Colonel Jozef Beck's official visit to Moscow in mid-February 1934, Litvinov finally secured one of the friendly gestures he sought. As the Foreign Commissar pointed out in the welcoming speech, Beck was the first member of a Polish cabinet to pay the U.S.S.R. an official visit. Although the political discussions were quite general, the Polish Foreign Minister was received with a great deal of pomp. "The Bolsheviks imitated the splendour of the old Tsarist receptions," he later wrote. Military leaders, including Voroshilov and Yegorov, were especially friendly. Before Beck's departure it was agreed to renew a 1932 nonaggression treaty and raise the respective legations in Moscow and Warsaw to embassies.[15]

The next move took place on March 20 when Moscow suggested a ten-year extension of its nonaggression agreements with the Baltic states, dating from 1932 in the case of Estonia and Latvia and 1926 (prolonged in 1931) with Lithuania. Signature of the instruments took place in Moscow on April 4. A 1932 nonaggression treaty with Finland was also extended three days later, but similar action on the agreement with Poland was delayed until May 5. Other favorable developments followed: Hungary had established diplomatic relations with the U.S.S.R. on February 6, and Rumania and Czechoslovakia granted *de jure* recognition on June 9. Bulgaria took a similar step on July 23, and even Albania followed suit on September 17, leaving Yugoslavia as the only country in Eastern Europe without diplomatic ties with the Soviet Union.

Litvinov made his last attempt to secure a friendly public gesture from Germany on March 28, 1934 during a conversation with Ambassador Nadolny. "He felt that it was unsatisfactory for the desire for good relations to be expressed only in speeches" and handed the ambassador the draft of a joint statement on the Baltic states: Both countries would "obligate themselves in their foreign policy to adhere undeviatingly to the necessity of maintaining the independence and inviolability of the Baltic countries mentioned and to avoid any sort of action that would indirectly or directly damage this independence." Nadolny cited the fate of the projected Polish-Russian declaration on the same subject and asked if the Foreign Commissar contemplated a secret exchange of statements: "Litvinov replied that of course it was to be a public agreement. . . . Finally, Litvinov confirmed to me briefly that the actual purpose of the protocol was to foster an improvement of the relations between the Soviet Union and Germany and [italics supplied] to *give evidence of the relaxation of tension.*" The same evening Krestinsky and Voroshilov also urged the declaration, and the latter indicated that it was not merely Litvinov's private idea.

Berlin rejected the proposal on April 9, and Nadolny informed the Foreign Commissar on the 14th. On the 21st Litvinov summoned the ambassador and read a lengthy reply which appeared in *Pravda* on April 27. The aim was evidently to put Germany in a bad light before world public opinion: [16]

The Soviet Government does not find in the German Government's statement a single convincing reason or argument against the signing of a protocol for the non-violation of the independence and integrity of the Baltic States. . . . In this connexion I would like to challenge another suggestion by the German Government, to the effect that the regrettable estrangement in Soviet-German relations pointed out by the German Government is due to the Soviet Government's attitude to the National-Socialist regime in Germany. The Soviet Government, during the sixteen years of its existence, has demonstrated its ability to maintain the best of relations with other States regardless of their internal regime. The real causes of this estrangement are sufficiently well known to the German Government.

Apparently Litvinov had abandoned all hope of a friendly word from Germany. Too, by this time an ostensible *détente* with Berlin had lost much of its potential value. If we may believe the statements by the Foreign Commissar and his associates as reported by Bullitt on April 16, 1934, the Narkomindel no longer feared an imminent Japanese attack.

IN HIS DISPATCH from Moscow on August 9, 1933, Strang described quite accurately the problem of the Soviet leaders in 1933 and 1934: "Their major fear is from Japan," and "the threat from Germany, unlike the threat from Japan, is not imminent." Indeed, they may not have even expected the Nazi regime to survive for very long. According to General W. G. Krivitsky, Stalin began to take Hitler seriously only after the Nazi Blood Purge of Röhm and his followers in 1934—certainly the French Communist Party began to show interest in cooperating with the Socialists only after this event.

But it would be too much to say that Germany was more the pawn than the object of Soviet foreign policy in 1933–34. Stalin was probably trying to keep the options open (to use an expression of the 1960's). Nevertheless some of the moves with respect to Berlin were made with third powers in mind, e.g., the attempt to secure a friendly gesture and thereby prevent any inflation of Japanese hopes, and the decision to discontinue the military experimental stations in the U.S.S.R. and thus remove a possible booby trap in the path of a growing Franco-Soviet *rapprochement.*

3

Litvinov and the League

December 1933—February 1938

According to later French accounts to the British, Herriot had assumed the premiership of France in June 1932 determined to seek a reconciliation with Germany. When this proved impossible, he had embraced the idea of close ties with Russia as insurance against future German aggression. France and the Soviet Union signed a nonaggression pact on November 29, 1932, and Herriot visited the U.S.S.R. in August of the following year. Accompanied by a number of air force officers, French Air Minister Cot made a similar visit in September. The Franco-Soviet entente developed slowly, however, since Herriot's influence declined and the Quai d'Orsay opposed any hasty moves.

According to the French account, the Soviet Government had at first urged an outright alliance. Fearing this might be interpreted as an attempt to encircle Germany, Paris proposed instead a collective security agreement embracing Russia, Poland, Czechoslovakia, and Germany and guaranteed by France, a sort of "Eastern Locarno." Moscow reluctantly agreed but insisted on the inclusion of the Baltic states. Under the terms of this initial version, the remaining signatories were to come to the aid of one of their number attacked without provocation by another signatory. Should Russia be attacked by a member of the system, France would come to her aid, and if an attack on France violated the Locarno Treaty the U.S.S.R. would come to her assistance. But Locarno forbade French aid to a Russia attacked by Germany, and thus it would be necessary for the Soviet Union to join

35

the League of Nations; France could then come to her aid under the provisions of the Covenant.[1]

Litvinov informed Bullitt of the negotiations on December 21, 1933. Because of the threat from Japan, said the Foreign Commissar, the Soviet Union would take every possible step to secure its western frontiers; although reluctant to join the League and preferring to keep its hands free, it was willing to pay this price for an agreement with France. Four days later Stalin told Walter Duranty of the *New York Times* that "if the League were to turn out an obstacle, even a small one, that made war more difficult, . . . then it is not impossible that we shall support the League, notwithstanding its colossal defects." In a speech to the Central Executive Committee on the 28th, Molotov cited the withdrawal of Japan and Germany from the League, claimed that the two countries had withdrawn in order to gain a free hand, and observed that "even the League of Nations stands to some extent in the way of 'freedom' of action for the interventionists." "Not being doctrinaires," said Litvinov in a speech to the same body the next day, "we do not refuse to use international associations or organizations, whether those already in existence or those which may be founded in the future, if we have or shall have reason to believe that they serve the cause of peace." [2]

A new French Government was formed under Doumergue in February 1934, and in order to avoid any impression of eagerness, the new Foreign Minister, Barthou, left the project in abeyance for two months. Barthou eventually exchanged ideas with the Soviet Ambassador in Paris and finally discussed the matter with Litvinov at Geneva on May 18. The French Ambassador in Berlin informed State Secretary Bülow of the general nature of the projected alliance on June 7, and returning from Geneva Litvinov himself stopped in Berlin on June 13 and urged the pact on Neurath. Barthou expounded French views on the subject during a conference with Simon in London on July 9, and the Foreign Secretary agreed that the British Government would support the proposal in Berlin and Warsaw.[3]

But it was with the greatest reluctance that Stalin accepted close ties with France and membership in the League; apparently only the continued hostility of Germany persuaded him to do so.

As early as August 4, 1933, Molotov had assured Dirksen that the Soviet attitude toward Germany remained unchanged, no matter what the country's internal political structure might be. Nor would Moscow's policies toward Germany change as long as the latter did not change her policy toward the U.S.S.R. Discussing the visits of Herriot and Cot, Helfand, a Narkomindel official, told the German chargé on September 22 that the Soviet Union had no interest in a coalition with France or Poland unless Germany should try to form an anti-Soviet coalition. And Tukhachevsky had a long talk with the chargé on October 31, 1933: "Don't forget, my friend," he concluded, "it is politics, your politics alone, which separate us, not our feelings, our most friendly feelings for the Reichswehr." 4

Commenting on rumors of a Franco-Soviet pact in a memo of December 26, the German chargé in Moscow pointed out that such a tie would solve Russia's problems in Europe and many in Asia. "It would become a full-fledged member of the most powerful European combine, an inviting idea for Soviet diplomacy, which has had to endure the bitter lot of a pariah for 14 years." But such a tie would also curtail Moscow's carefully guarded freedom of action and might produce unwanted consequences. Hence the French proposals would be accepted "only if no other way out with similar security guarantees presents itself." Future German policy would largely determine the final choice. "If we decide to make the Russians an offer that takes account of their need for security and peace and reestablishes the old relationship of confidence between the Rapallo Powers, it seems to me probable that they will drop the French offer." 5

The speeches by Molotov and Litvinov on December 28 and 29 contained, in addition to references to the League, several friendly remarks regarding Germany. "Our relations with Germany have always occupied a special place in our foreign relations," said Molotov, and added that "the USSR has for its part no reason to change its policy towards Germany." Litvinov emphasized the advantages to both countries of good relations:

We were the only big country which wished to have nothing to do with the Versailles treaty and its consequences. . . . Enormous advantages, both for Germany and for us, followed from the political and economic relations established between us. With these to rely on, Germany could speak more boldly and confidently with the victors. . . . Of course, we have our own opinion about the German regime, and of course we sympathize with the sufferings of our German comrades, but we as Marxists are the last who can be reproached with allowing sentiment to prevail over policy. The entire world knows that we can and do maintain good relations with Capitalist States whatever their regime, even if it is fascist. . . . We want to have the best relations with Germany, as with other countries. Nothing but good can come from such relations, for the Soviet Union and for Germany.

Five days later Litvinov admitted in effect that the remarks were meant as a warning when he told the German Ambassador that "in the interest of German-Russian relations" (Nadolny's paraphrase) he had wished "to open the eyes of the German people to where they were drifting." [6]

In a conversation with a German journalist early in January 1934 (reported by Nadolny on the 10th), Radek emphasized that the door was still open for a reconciliation. "Do not believe that something has already been decided," he said in reference to French-Soviet relations. "We shall do nothing that could commit us for a long time. Nothing will happen that would permanently block our way to a common policy with Germany. The dangers in the Far East are very great. But as soon as it is evident that war can be avoided there, which I myself believe, then new possibilities will develop for us with Germany in Europe." Radek "gave repeated assurance that nothing had been decided and nothing final would be decided." On the 13th Nadolny reported that Twardowski, the second ranking member of the embassy, had had a friendly two-hour conversation with Red Army Chief of Staff Yegorov. The latter "did not conceal his sympathies for the Reichswehr" and "repeated once more: Change your policy and everything will be all right again." [7]

In his report to the seventeenth Party congress on January 26, Stalin himself declared that Soviet policy was based upon national interests rather than ideology: [8]

Some German politicians say that the USSR has now taken an orientation towards France and Poland; that from an opponent of the Versailles treaty it has become a supporter of that treaty, and that this change is to be explained by the establishment of the fascist regime in Germany. This is not true. . . . Our orientation in the past and our orientation at the present time is towards the USSR, and towards the USSR alone. And if the interests of the USSR demand rapprochment with one country or another which is not interested in disturbing peace, we take this step without hesitation. . . . The point is that Germany's policy has changed.

Following the formal unveiling of the "Eastern Locarno" in Berlin during the first part of June 1934, Litvinov did what he could to secure German acceptance. But Nadolny, who had eagerly worked for a *rapprochement* with the Soviet Union, received no support from Neurath and in consequence resigned. Twardowski, who remained on as chargé, apparently concluded that an attitude of cool reserve toward the Narkomindel was advisable. Nevertheless Litvinov could still convey hints through third parties, and on June 18 Italian Ambassador Attolico informed Twardowski of a conversation regarding the Eastern pact the previous day. The ambassador had remarked that Germany was unlikely to accept the pact, and Litvinov had replied that the pact would then be concluded without her. Should Poland also refuse to sign, he was ready to conclude a bilateral assistance agreement with France. Late in June or early in July (reported by Twardowski on July 2) the Foreign Commissar remarked to the Italian Ambassador that a regular alliance was not yet being considered and would only come about should the Eastern pact fail; Attolico had received the impression that a general Franco-Soviet treaty covering all possibilities was quite likely.[9]

In a memo communicated to most of the interested governments on September 10, 1934, the Auswärtiges Amt explained in detail its objections to the Eastern Locarno but did not conclusively reject the idea. Although favoring bilateral pacts, the German Government did not wish "altogether to reject the idea of multilateral pacts" or to exclude other possibilities. And in a note of September 27 to French Foreign Minister Barthou, Beck summarized Polish objections, the main one being that Poland simply could not take part in the alliance unless Germany were also a member.

These quite predictable reactions should have opened the way for a straight French-Soviet alliance. But at Marseilles on October 9, together with King Alexander of Yugoslavia, Barthou was assassinated, and his successor, Pierre Laval, preferred to seek an understanding with Germany. The negotiations with Russia had gone too far for Laval to drop them, however, and at Geneva on December 5 he and Litvinov signed a protocol in which they promised to refrain from any negotiations with third powers which might preclude an Eastern pact. Both governments also undertook "not to abandon these negotiations without having first agreed on the uselessness of pursuing them further. In such an event they will consult with each other as to the new assurances which it would seem opportune to them to give to each other in the same spirit and with a similar objective in view." At this time the Czechoslovak Government stated that it too accepted the idea of an Eastern pact and considered itself also bound by the protocol. And in a statement to the press on the 9th, Litvinov pointed out that the protocol "imposes no restrictions on bilateral agreements between the USSR and France.[10]

New French and Anglo-French efforts during January and February 1935 to secure German participation in the Eastern pact proved fruitless, and on March 16 Hitler announced the reintroduction of conscription—thereby openly violating the Treaty of Versailles. In April at Geneva Litvinov and Laval worked out the draft of a bilateral French-Soviet agreement; Laval and Soviet Ambassador Potemkin continued the negotiations in Paris and signed the treaty (Appendix B) on May 2, 1935. A similar Soviet-Czechoslovak mutual-assistance agreement (Appendix C) was signed at Prague on May 16 but was made dependent upon prior action by France under the terms of the French-Soviet treaty.

During the next few months Britain and France did not completely abandon efforts to secure an Eastern pact, and Laval refrained from presenting the bilateral agreement to the President of France for ratification by decree but rather submitted it to parliament. The treaty finally came before the Chamber of Deputies on February 11, 1936 and was approved 353 to 164 on the 27th. On March 7, claiming that the French-Soviet pact was incompatible with the Treaty of Locarno, Hitler occupied the Rhineland and for the first time violated a treaty which had not been imposed by force but had been signed by Germany of its own free will. Five days later, on the 12th, the French Senate approved the agreement with Russia 231 to 52.

Nevertheless, Stalin still preferred an understanding with Germany. Local Soviet officials had made numerous pro-German statements to Hilger, the economic expert of the German Embassy, when he visited the Ukraine during the late spring of 1935. In a "very friendly conversation" of May 8 with Count Schulenburg, who had succeeded Nadolny as German Ambassador to Moscow, Litvinov had expressed hope for a more general nonaggression treaty which would "lessen the significance of the Franco-Soviet Pact" and lead to better Soviet-German relations. On July 15, 1935, David Kandelaki, chief of the Soviet trade delegation in Berlin and rumored to be close to Stalin, took advantage of a purely commercial discussion with Reichsbank President Schacht to ask if political relations could not be improved. And at a German Embassy reception in Moscow on October 26, Tukhachevsky expressed deep regret over the break. Should the two countries march together, he said, they could dictate peace to the rest of the world, but if they clashed Germany would discover that the Red Army had learned a great deal in the meantime.

Kandelaki, who had left for consultations in Moscow at the end of October, returned to Berlin during the first part of December, probably on or about the 9th. On the 9th or 10th, Twardowski, who had been recalled from Moscow to be Deputy Director of the Cultural Policy Department of the Auswärtiges Amt, made an appointment for a courtesy call on Soviet Ambassador Suritz. Bessonov, the Counselor of the Soviet Embassy, visited Twardowski immediately after this and asked how German-Soviet relations might be improved. Although Twardowski pointed out that he no longer had any responsibility for political affairs, Bessonov insisted on discussing the matter.

The conversation with the Soviet Ambassador, presumably on December 10, began the same way. Suritz asked Twardowski,

as an old acquaintance and an expert in German-Russian relations, to give him my advice as to what should be done to improve German-Soviet relations and above all what he personally could do to achieve this end. . . . M. Suritz went into all manner of details and wanted to know whether I considered a development of the Berlin Treaty to be feasible; what effect the strengthening of economic relations would have on the political situation; whether a development of cultural relations was possible; whether he should intensify his social activities in Berlin, etc. I declined to go into any of these details. It emerged very clearly from this whole conversation that M. Suritz has strict instructions to do everything in his power to bring about, at least outwardly, an improvement in mutual relations.

Bessonov called on the official at the Auswärtiges Amt responsible for Eastern Europe on December 21; after discussing trade negotiations, he enquired regarding the German attitude toward the Soviet-French treaty and the proposed Eastern pact. Told that Germany could not accept such a pact and regarded the Soviet-French agreement as directed against her, the Soviet diplomat then advanced the idea of a bilateral nonaggression pact to supplement the Berlin Treaty. In conclusion, Bessonov explained that he regarded the conversation as unofficial and purely private on his part.

Even Molotov finally had something to say on the subject in a report to the Central Executive Committee on January 10, 1936:

The Soviet Government would have desired the establishment of better relations with Germany than exist at present. . . . But the realization of such a policy depends not only on us, but also on the German Government. . . .

Side by side with the reckless anti-Soviet foreign policy of certain ruling circles in Germany, on the initiative of the German Government an agreement between Germany and the USSR was proposed and concluded on 9 April 1935, for a five-year credit of 200 million marks. . . .

The development of commercial and economic relations with other States, irrespective of the political forces that are temporarily ruling those countries, is in conformity with the policy of the Soviet Government. We think that it is also in keeping with the interests of the German people, and it is the business of the Government of Germany, of course, to draw practical conclusions from this.

In the face of all these cautious advances, however, German officials maintained an attitude of polite but cool reserve.[11]

For their part the French seem to have placed no great reliance on the tie with Russia. Alexis Léger, the Secretary General of the French Foreign Ministry, told the British chargé in Paris on June 20, 1934 that France would have to accept a bilateral alliance with the U.S.S.R. if Germany would not agree to the Eastern pact. Although Soviet military assistance might be of little value, France could draw on Russia's vast resources. Conversely, should France rebuff the Russians, the latter might seek an arrangement with Germany and offer her these resources. Barthou also mentioned this possibility during his talks with Simon in London on July 9, 1934, a few days after the liquidation of Röhm when Hitler had apparently decided in favor of the Reichswehr and traditional policies. The same fear troubled Léger on July 25 when he told a member of the British Embassy that Moscow did not really desire a peaceful Europe and an understanding with Germany would suit its purpose better than one with France. The Soviet Government, he said, had turned to France only because no agreement with Hitler's Germany was possible, but this might no longer be true.[12]

As LATE AS APRIL 1934 French Communists, like their German comrades less than two years earlier, seemed to reject all cooperation with Social Democrats. Apparently the only form of united front they considered acceptable was the "united front from below," i.e., the capture of the Socialist rank and file. On July 27, however, the two parties agreed to work together in opposing Nazism and preparations for war and in defending democratic liberties. The French-Soviet pact was signed on May 2, 1935, and during the same month the Radical, Communist, and Socialist parties cooperated in Paris municipal elections. Leaders of the three parties spoke from the same platform on June 28, and on Bastille Day their followers marched in a single demonstration. Finally the seventh congress of the Comintern, which met in Moscow during July and August 1935, formally proclaimed a new policy of the "united front from above," i.e. cooperation with Socialist leaders.

Although Dimitrov, the Secretary General of the Comintern, stressed cooperation by "local organizations through local agreements" (essentially the "united front from below"), he stated that Communists would even support a popular front government should it become necessary "in the interests of the proletariat." In his report to the congress, as printed in the Comintern journal, the term "united front" monopolized most of the subheads: "United Front of the Working Class Against Fascism," "The United Front in the Countries where the Social Democrats are in Office," "The United Front and Youth," "Women and the United Front," "The Anti-Imperialist United Front," "The Government of the United Front," "Content and Forms of the United Front," etc. In his concluding address, Dimitrov stated that the Communists were prepared "to undertake joint action with other parties fighting against fascism." They were "ready to fight jointly for any immediate tasks which, when realized, will weaken the position of fascism and strengthen the position of the proletariat." The Communists were willing to do this, he added, "to prevent the abrogation of bourgeois democratic liberties, forestall fascism's terrorist vengeance upon the proletariat" in "the countries of bourgeois democracy." [13] The example of Germany seemed to have finally made an impression; there the Communists had refused to the very end to cooperate with the Social Democrats against the Nazis.

In France on January 11, 1936, the Communist, Socialist, Radical, and several smaller parties and organizations announced the formation of a "popular front." Although the leftist coalition gained a large majority in the April elections and the Communists did especially well, they declined to enter the Blum government formed in May but promised to support it. The popular-front period in French politics lasted until January 1938, and the Blum government of March and April of that year was also based on the original coalition; but the Daladier government of April 1938 was definitely of another complexion.

It was in Spain during the Civil War, however, that the popular-front policy reached its most perfect development. The Spanish garrison in Morocco had revolted in July 1936, and throughout the ensuing conflict the Spanish Communist Party advocated moderate and nonrevolutionary domestic policies and did its best to mobilize against Franco the members of as many classes and parties as possible.

Although stemming from purely domestic issues, the Civil War soon developed into a limited international conflict. Hitler furnished aid to the rebels almost immediately, and Louis Fischer later wrote that by "October 12, 1936, the Spanish Republic was lost. If the Russians had not brought in their first airplanes, tanks, and military advisers that month the war in Spain would have ended in 1936 with a Fascist triumph." Soviet equipment and personnel may have been in Spain as early as September 8; they were in action by October 24 when Fischer spoke to a Ukrainian tank driver at the front. [14]

A combination of three motives probably induced Stalin to intervene in Spain. The first was a desire to tie down German forces in an area as remote from the Soviet frontier as possible. As one of the keenest and most objective students of the Spanish conflict has pointed out, "Spain was a long way from Russia and, by using Spanish workers the Soviet Union did not have to commit herself to an open war with Germany." The Loyalists unwittingly served as mercenaries and were reinforced by liberals from the West and unwanted foreign Communists from the U.S.S.R. "Thus all the Soviet Union needed to supply was a minimum of equipment and technical assistance, just enough to keep Loyalist resistance from collapsing." [15]

Second, Stalin apparently wished to retain the supposed loyalty of the "international proletariat." As a "responsible Soviet official" remarked to U.S. chargé Henderson in Moscow on August 3, 1936, "Soviet leaders" felt "that if the Soviet Union is to continue to maintain hegemony over the international revolutionary movement it must not hesitate in periods of crisis to assume the leadership of that movement." Moscow considered leftist and liberal support abroad quite valuable during the 1919–20 period of Allied intervention and Soviet-Polish conflict. Writing in 1929 as a Soviet partisan and reflecting the opinions of the highest Narkomindel officials, Louis Fischer claimed that "Moscow appealed to Left Opposition elements to obstruct the interventionist policies of their governments, and at least in England the results were appreciable. . . . Labour sentiment—especially in England—was able to mobilize a strong body of public opinion which hastened the day when the policy of intervention was scrapped." During the summer of 1920, at the height of the Polish-Soviet War, the "proletariat" was aroused everywhere in Europe, according to Fischer. " 'Hands off Russia' became a universal slogan." [16]

. . . fiery appeals from Moscow to "The Workers of the World" supplied Labour opposition with material for protest.

Campaigns to prevent the forwarding of war materials to Poland developed in all transit countries. Working men in Czecho-Slovakia stopped and searched trains moving in the direction of the Polish frontier and refused to pass them when munitions were discovered. Danzig, the most important port for Polish traffic, witnessed stirring scenes. Longshoremen and sailors went on strike. Ships stood in the harbour for days upon days waiting for navvies who sometimes did not come; and British troops had to be employed in the unloading of supplies. . . .

Opposition to Allied intervention against Russia grew strongest in England. . . . The British trade unions, then very Radical and pro-Russian, objected strenuously to such measures. They wanted no war on the Soviet Republic. Not only did they obstruct the shipment of munitions to Poland: they organized a serious movement to paralyse any effort the Government might undertake on behalf of the Warsaw regime.

As late as February 1938, in his "letter to Ivanov" published in *Izvestia*, Stalin warned that "without considerable help from the working class of capitalist countries," Soviet workers and peasants could not "vanquish the bourgeoisie of other countries." Without "considerable help from the international proletariat," the "final victory of socialism" in the U.S.S.R. could not be achieved. Therefore "we must organize political help of the working class of bourgeois countries for the working class of our country in the event of military attack on our country," continued Stalin. [17]

In this respect, Soviet aid to the Spanish Loyalists paid dividends and was responsible for much of the pre-1939 and post-1941 sympathy for the U.S.S.R. in leftist and liberal circles in France, Britain, and the United States. "If the egotistical patriotism which I saw emerging from Bolshevik headquarters in 1935 and 1936," wrote Louis Fischer in 1941, "had barred the way to Soviet participation in the Spanish struggle in 1936, I would have despaired of Russia, and I think I would have turned away from Russia then." [18]

Why, instead of holding my tongue, did I not come out in 1937 or 1938 as a critic of the Soviet regime? . . . in 1938, the Soviet government's foreign policy was still effectively anti-appeasement and anti-Fascist, much more so than England's or France's or America's. It helped China with arms to fight Japanese aggression. It helped Spain with arms to fight the Nazis and Mussolini. . . . I did not know how long it would last. But while it lasted I hesitated to throw stones in public.

Still a third possibility should be considered: that by preventing an early Nationalist victory and conducting an all-out propaganda campaign in the West for aid to the Spanish Republic, Stalin hoped to embroil France and perhaps Britain in a conflict with Germany and Italy. Orlov, the chief of the N.K.G.B. in Spain, relates how a certain "General N." returned from Moscow in the summer of 1937 with the information that the Politburo had adopted a new line. Instead of furnishing all the materiel and personnel (pilots and tank crews) needed for a Republican victory, the policy was now to let the conflict drag on as long as possible. Soviet assistance to Spain seems indeed to have declined sharply in 1937 but apparently did not end entirely until mid-1938.[19] At the same time the Politburo "decision" may not have been entirely voluntary but rather dictated by the sinking of Soviet merchant ships by Italian and Nationalist submarines, the fear of becoming directly involved in a war with Germany and Italy, and the necessity after July 1937 of sending munitions to China. In any event, by the summer of 1938 Stalin can hardly have entertained any further hopes of British or French embroilment.

THE SOVIET UNION had been admitted to the League of Nations on September 18, 1934, and in the following years Litvinov made a number of speeches at Geneva, speeches which still have a sincere ring and certainly contained sound advice. "Peace is indivisible," he warned, and collective security imperative. During the Italian conquest of Ethiopia in 1935 he demonstrated that his government was willing to sacrifice good relations with Italy for such a cause. In a statement at a meeting of the League Council on September 5, 1935, Litvinov declared that "one of the parties to the conflict [i.e. Italy] is a State with which the Soviet Union has been maintaining invariably friendly relations for over ten years, with which it sincerely desires to continue these relations, which it would least of all wish to cause any harm, collaboration with which both in the League of Nations and outside it, for the maintenance of peace in Europe, we highly appreciate, and, finally, a nation which enjoys in my country deepest respect and sympathy."

The Foreign Commissar admitted that once before—during the Japanese occupation of Manchuria in 1931—the Council had not done everything possible to prevent a conflict. "But this is exactly a thing to be remembered now, for we all still feel in what measure that case weakened the League of Nations, diminished its authority and contributed to the creation of the politically unstable, menacing situation in which the world finds itself and even, may be, to the arising of the present conflict. The repetition of that precedent would certainly have a cumulative effect, and in its turn would stimulate new conflicts more directly affecting the whole of Europe." [20]

Nine days later, in an address to the League Assembly, Litvinov denied that his delegation had any intention of "siding with one or the other party to the conflict, or of defending anyone's interests. . . . For the Soviet delegation there is only a question of defending the Covenant of the League as an instrument of peace. This instrument has already been somewhat damaged by previous attempts and we cannot allow a new attempt which would put it completely out of work. We may need it more than once and probably on still more serious occasions." [21]

In a note to the Italian Ambassador in Moscow, the Foreign Commissar stated on November 22, 1935 that "the Soviet representatives at Geneva voted for, and the Soviet Government adhered to, the measures collectively and practically unanimously drawn up by the League of Nations. Any other conduct would have meant a rejection of the principles of the League of Nations, a rejection of the collective organisation of security, the encouragement of aggression in the future, and a denial of the possibility of displaying international solidarity in the cause of maintaining and consolidating peace which is the foundation of the Soviet Government's policy and for the sake of which it entered the League of Nations." [22]

Hitler reoccupied the Rhineland on March 7, 1936, and ten days later Litvinov warned the League Council that "one cannot struggle for peace without at the same time defending the integrity of international obligations, particularly such as have direct bearing on the maintenance of existing frontiers, on armaments and on political or military aggression. One cannot struggle for the collective organisation of security without adopting collective measures against breaches of international obligations.

"We do not, however, class among such measures collective capitulation in face of the aggressor, in face of an infringement of treaties, or collective encouragement of such infringements, and still less collective agreement to a bonus for the aggressor by adopting a basis of agreement, or other plans, acceptable or profitable to the aggressor.

"We cannot preserve the League of Nations, founded on the sanctity of international treaties (including the Covenant of the League itself), if we turn a blind eye to breaches of those treaties or confine ourselves to verbal protests, and take no more effective measures in defence of international undertakings.

"We cannot preserve the League of Nations if it does not carry out its own decisions and pledges, but, on the contrary, accustoms the aggressor to ignore its recommendations, its admonitions or its warnings.

"Such a League of Nations will never be taken seriously by anyone. The resolutions of such a League will only become a laughing-stock." [23]

Speaking to the Assembly on September 21, 1937, after the outbreak of the Spanish and Chinese-Japanese conflicts, Litvinov stated that it "may now be considered an axiom that the League's passivity during the Manchurian conflict had as its consequence, some years later, the attack on Ethiopia. The insufficient activity of the League in the case of Ethiopia encouraged the Spanish experiment. The failure of the League to take any steps to help Spain encouraged the new attack on China. Thus we have had four aggressions in the course of five years. We see how aggression, when it meets with no check, passes from one continent to another, assuming larger and larger dimensions every time.

"Yet I am firmly convinced that a resolute policy pursued by the League of Nations in one case of aggression would rid us of all the other cases. Then—and only then—would all States become convinced that aggression does not pay, that aggression should not be undertaken." [24]

As early as January 14, 1936, the Narkomindel organ *Journal de Moscou* had stated that the "friends of peace" could "no longer count on the policy of certain great powers who have always during the years since the war been the supporters of collective security and the League." The next day an unofficial Kremlin agent told U.S. chargé Henderson that the Soviet Government placed no reliance on French military assistance; the French shopkeeper would fight only if France were attacked. But these remarks may have merely reflected dissatisfaction with the delay in ratifying the French-Soviet pact—which came before the French Chamber of Deputies on February 11. On the 16th Litvinov expressed some concern regarding the action of the French Senate but told Bullitt that he felt the Deputies would approve the agreement. "I believe the British will adhere to the policy they pursued before 1914," said the Foreign Commissar. "They may even make fewer commitments than they then made to the French. But at the last minute faced by the fact of German aggression they will make war." [25]

But Hitler reoccupied the Rhineland in March without provoking any meaningful British or French reaction, and in a speech to the Central Executive Committee on November 10, 1936, the Foreign Commissar spoke of the "bankruptcy of the policy of those States which have agreed to the Soviet proposals in words, have made declaration after declaration about collective security, the indivisibility of peace, the firmness of League of Nations principles, and about regional pacts, but which in fact sabotage all these ideas . . . governments which ignored the violation of international treaties and indisputable acts of aggression, which courted those guilty of these acts and curried favour with them in the hope that they would be satisfied with their successes and say 'we will sin no more.' " [26]

The Soviet trade delegation in Berlin had been negotiating a new commercial agreement, and by March 6 only a few minor points remained to be settled. But on the 7th, a few hours after

Hitler announced the reoccupation of the Rhineland, Moscow ordered the negotiations suspended. When it became apparent that Britain and France contemplated no effective action, however, talks were resumed and the agreement was signed on April 29, 1936. Yet as Bessonov and one of his colleagues from the Soviet Embassy pointed out to an Auswärtiges Amt official on May 4, any expansion of trade between the two countries

was bound to be severely handicapped by the bad relations between Germany and the Soviet Union. It was absurd that two States which were interested in mutual economic relations should be campaigning against each other in the political sphere in an almost unprecedented manner. . . . the Soviet Government—despite increasing scepticism in Moscow—still saw a possibility of achieving a political *détente*.

Nine days later Göring received Kandelaki and his assistant and expressed satisfaction over the signing of the trade agreement. "All his efforts," said Göring, "were directed towards making closer contacts with Russia again, politically too, and he thought that the best way would be through intensifying and expanding mutual trade relations." Schacht spoke to Kandelaki in more restrained terms the next day; nevertheless, when talks on prolonging the agreement began in October, both sides seemed inclined to make concessions.

And at the end of December 1936, when Kandelaki again approached Schacht and asked about the possibilities of increasing German-Soviet trade, the latter suggested an end to Communist agitation as a prerequisite. After reporting in Moscow, Kandelaki appeared once more on January 29, 1937 with a definite proposal for German-Soviet negotiations. The proposal, he declared, was made in the name of Stalin and Molotov and with their approval. (Since Kandelaki's assistant was present during the conversation, this was undoubtedly true.) The Soviet Government, he continued, had no desire to establish policies opposed to German interests, was prepared to open negotiations—through regular diplomatic channels if desired—on improving relations between the two countries, and was also prepared to keep the exchanges secret. Schacht suggested a direct approach to the Auswärtiges Amt, but Kandelaki asked him to find out how the suggestion would be received.

Schacht informed Neurath on February 6, and the Foreign Minister discussed the matter with Hitler four days later. "The Führer and I are agreed," he informed Schacht on the 11th, that talks "could lead to no result at the moment, at most would be used by the Russians to achieve the closer military alliance they are seeking with France, and also if possible to attain still closer relations with England." And as the experiences of the French and British had demonstrated, promises to discontinue Comintern propaganda were worthless. [27]

In a dispatch from Paris on January 14, 1937, the correspondent of *The Times* (London) had mentioned "persistent reports in the Press here crediting M. Blum, the Prime Minister, with the intention of offering to Germany economic negotiations on a large scale without preliminary political conditions in the near future." The correspondent went on to discount these rumors, however, and ten days later cited Blum's rejection of bilateral deals in a speech at Lyons: "it is in view of a general settlement, or within a general settlement," said the French Premier, "that we seek a solution of the Franco-German problem." Nevertheless, after a conversation on February 4, 1937, Davies, the new U.S. Ambassador to Moscow, reported "the impression that Litvinov was somewhat apprehensive lest there should be some composition of differences between France, Great Britain and Germany." And five days later, Walter Duranty, the *New York Times* correspondent in Moscow, claimed that the Soviet Government expected no help from the West. If France and Britain, the argument went, "can be tricked into allowing Fascist control of Spain, which gravely threatens their own interests, there is little chance of their aiding the Soviet Union save by mild protests and pseudo-sanctions." [28]

Potemkin, the Soviet Ambassador to Paris, was recalled to Moscow on April 4 to serve as Deputy Foreign Commissar. Kandelaki was transferred to Moscow at the same time, and Suritz took over the mission in France. Also at the beginning of April, rumors of the Kandelaki-Schacht conversations began to circulate in Paris and London and were repeatedly denied by the German and Soviet press in the next few weeks. Finally, on May 18,

Litvinov called on Foreign Minister Delbos and Premier Blum in Paris. According to the official communiqué, the two had

an extensive and friendly exchange of views with M. Litvinoff, during which they were glad to be able to take note of the friendly relations existing between the two countries, as also of their common aim to maintain the organization of indivisible peace by means of collective security. They reaffirmed their fidelity to the pact uniting the two nations and their determination to pursue, within the framework of the League and in accordance with its principles, a loyal policy of international collaboration.[29]

The Foreign Commissar referred to Spain and the "cowardly conduct" of France and Britain when he talked to Davies on July 10. The British Ambassador in Berlin was violently pro-German, he continued, and Foreign Secretary Eden apparently no longer had the same free hand under the new Prime Minister, Chamberlain. Nevertheless Litvinov still professed to believe assurances, which he stated Eden had given, that Britain would never allow Germany a free hand in Eastern Europe. [30]

But Lord Halifax, a member of the British Cabinet, arrived in Berlin for a visit on November 17, 1937 and was received by Hitler at Berchtesgaden two days later. On the 22nd French Foreign Minister Delbos told Bullitt that French public opinion would not allow abrogation of the pact with Russia. Moreover "he still feared greatly that Germany and the Soviet Union would come to an immediate agreement if France should abandon Russia altogether." The following month, December, the Foreign Minister visited Warsaw, Bucharest, Belgrade, and Prague—but not Moscow. Neurath himself spoke to Delbos at the station during a short layover in Berlin. Although highly gratified and encouraged by this gesture, French Premier Chautemps told Bullitt on December 4 that he could not "formally abandon" the alliance with the U.S.S.R. [31]

In an "election" speech of November 27, Litvinov had declared that some of the great powers accepted the idea of collective security in principle but went "no further than words and declarations, and words and declarations cut no ice with the aggressor." "You think," he remarked to the audience, that "they are groping for a deal with the aggressor. You can think so if you like, but my position does not allow me to express such doubts, and I must leave them to your responsibility." In another "election" speech on December 8, Dimitrov warned that the fascist powers were feverishly preparing for large-scale war "with the toleration of the bourgeois-democratic powers" which "even sacrifice the interests of their own people."

In a conversation with the Moscow correspondent of *Le Temps* around the middle of January 1938, Litvinov expressed dissatisfaction with Delbos and with France's current policy. The Soviet Union, he declared, could reach an understanding with Germany and would do so if Soviet-French relations did not improve. And shortly after the middle of the month, the Soviet Ambassador in Paris complained to Delbos that the French Government seemed to be seeking a *rapprochement* with Germany and hinted that his government would counter any moves of this sort by itself immediately coming to terms with Germany. (Were Kandelaki's feelers a year earlier designed to give plausibility to such threats?) Given a choice, the Foreign Minister replied, Germany would certainly prefer better relations with France, and Paris would anticipate any move Moscow might make. Returning from a January session of the League Council, Delbos admitted to Bullitt on February 1 that he had suggested to Litvinov at Geneva that better Franco-German relations would be to the ultimate advantage of the Soviet Union. A very acrimonious discussion had followed, and the Foreign Commissar seemed quite hostile to such a reconciliation. Schulenburg, the German Ambassador in Moscow, had been confidentially informed of Litvinov's threat to the French journalist and considered it deliberate. The Narkomindel, he reported to Berlin, feared the pact with France had lost its importance and Paris was only maintaining it to prevent a Soviet-German understanding. The Soviet press had adopted a mild tone toward Germany in the last few weeks, and no attacks had been made during a recent meeting of the Supreme Soviet. "The Soviets wish to create the impression that they too can change their course, and in this way Litvinov hopes to force concessions from France." [32]

Early in February Berlin announced the dismissal of War Minister General von Blomberg and the replacement of Foreign Minister von Neurath by von Ribbentrop. Both Blomberg and Neurath had generally been regarded as responsible conservatives and moderating influences on German policy. Bad news from Britain followed hard on the heels of the ominous developments in Germany: Foreign Secretary Eden resigned on February 20 and in the House of Commons the next day spoke of a fundamental difference of opinion with Chamberlain regarding a "most important decision of foreign policy which did not concern Italy at all." [33] Finally on March 11, 1938 Austrian Chancellor Schuschnigg accepted an ultimatum from Berlin, and the next morning troops of the Third Reich were marching into Austria.

"OUR ORIENTATION in the past and our orientation at the present time is towards the USSR, and towards the USSR alone," Stalin told the seventeenth Party congress at the beginning of 1934. "And if the interests of the USSR demand rapprochement with one country or another which is not interested in disturbing peace, we take this step without hesitation." As Stalin later demonstrated, the "interests" of the Soviet Union might even demand a *rapprochement* with a country which *was* interested in disturbing the peace. Nevertheless, his remarks in 1934 were a reasonably frank statement of Soviet policy. (One of the problems of students of Soviet diplomacy is that its spokesmen quite frequently speak the plain, unvarnished truth!)

In other words, Stalin saw advantages and no major disadvantages in his various maneuvers of 1933–37. At the beginning of the period he sought to keep a foot in each camp; at the same time he was still seeking a friendly German gesture to discourage Tokyo from any rash moves. Later Hitler's adamant hostility left little choice other than the Anglo-French camp. But this choice was not necessarily dictated by German intransigence. From the orthodox Communist point of view, a conflict between France and Britain on the one hand and Germany or Italy or both on the other could only redound to the ultimate benefit of the Soviet Union and communism in general. As late as the spring of 1924, Stalin mentioned certain possible "reserves of the revolution": "contradictions, conflicts and wars (the imperialist war, for instance) among the bourgeois states hostile to the proletarian state." [34] It was therefore logical for the Soviet Government and Western Communists to encourage British and French resistance to German and Italian aggression. In the event of war, the Soviet Union would be safely insulated since it had no common border with Germany or Italy. And as we shall see, after 1936 Moscow was no longer seriously concerned about a possible Polish-German combination.

The one thing Stalin feared above all was a genuine *rapprochement* between the aggressive and peaceful powers; a real and lasting "spirit of Locarno" meant the end of any Soviet hopes for unearned gains in Europe. Even worse, if not fighting or on the verge of fighting among themselves, the other great powers of Europe might easily turn against the U.S.S.R.—the old Soviet nightmare.

Unlike Molotov, his successor as Foreign Commissar, who hardly dared sneeze on his own initiative, Litvinov had a fairly free hand in the day-to-day conduct of foreign affairs. And most of the foreigners who dealt with him seem to have retained a certain respect for Litvinov personally; even the spiteful remarks in the dispatches of some of the German diplomats, Nadolny especially, were obviously written to appease National Socialist prejudices and did not necessarily reflect the writers' true feelings.

This was the era of Litvinov and the League, of his "indivisible peace" and futile struggle for collective security. But Stalin clearly believed in divisible peace and collective insecurity for other countries, and Litvinov must have been aware of his master's real aims and desires. Yet he could still advocate collective security and resistance to aggression with a clear conscience—even if the Soviet Union had remained on the sidelines, Britain and France would have been much better off if they had gone to war at any time before 1938.

In 1946 Litvinov was serving obscurely in the Foreign Commissariat as one of Molotov's assistants. In June, a few months before he retired, he granted a private interview to Mr. Richard Hottelet, an American journalist. Relations between Russia and the United States were already beginning to deteriorate, and Hottelet

asked what would happen if Washington granted all the current
Soviet demands. We would immediately come back with a new
set of demands, replied Litvinov. At about this time Litvinov also
had a conversation with Walter Bedell Smith, the new American
Ambassador to Moscow, and warned that he saw "nothing better
before us but a prolonged period of armed truce." The ambassador's account of this conversation went to Washington as a
classified telegram, and Hottelet informed the embassy but refrained from publishing his story while Litvinov was still
alive—to have done so would have meant the latter's immediate
arrest and probably execution. For several days after the interview, Hottelet later recalled, he had expected to hear at any
moment that Litvinov had been arrested. [35]

Why were these two statements made? Why did Litvinov risk
his life and the security of his family to convey these warnings
against any attempt to appease Moscow? Simply because he had
seen at first hand the result of one attempt at appeasement and
feared Stalin would become infected with the fatal *hubris* that
had afflicted Hitler in August 1939. Maxim Maximovich was at
the height of his fame as Foreign Commissar in 1930–39, but he
may have rendered the greatest service to his country when he
was old and almost forgotten—in two private conversations in
1946.

4

Mainstream to Munich

March–September 1938

In Moscow on March 14, Litvinov told U.S. Ambassador Davies that the British Government's acquiescent attitude was responsible for the *Anschluss*. Although not immediately threatened, Czechoslovakia was now in danger. Should Germany attack the Czechs, France would have to come to their aid, "otherwise it would also be the end of France." Great Britain would in turn be forced to come to the aid of France, "willy nilly." He ended by predicting new German aggression before the end of the year and warned that war was a definite possibility in the summer. The next day the Foreign Commissar expressed to British Ambassador Lord Chilston the opinion that Hitler would soon deal with Czechoslovakia. Because of the weak attitude of France and Britain he feared no active opposition. And in connection with the French obligation to Czechoslovakia, Litvinov mentioned that the Soviet-Czech pact was dependent upon the one between France and Czechoslovakia.[1]

At a diplomatic reception shortly after the conversation with Chilston, the Foreign Commissar told several foreign correspondents that the U.S.S.R. would come to the aid of Czechoslovakia if France did. When asked how this could be done (the Soviet Union had no common frontier with either Germany or Czechoslovakia), he merely replied that "means would be found."[2]

Two days later, on March 17, Litvinov made a formal statement for the press. After citing Soviet adherence to the League of Nations, other efforts to guarantee peace, and warnings against "international inaction," he pointed out that, unlike earlier instances of aggression, the German action against Austria had occurred in the center of Europe. Although the new development menaced the small nations especially, their "inevitable enslavement" would dangerously weaken the position of the great powers. After mentioning the danger to Czechoslovakia, the Foreign Commissar announced that his government, "as heretofore," was ready to "participate in collective actions the scope of which should be decided in conjunction with the Soviet Government" in order to halt further aggression and eliminate the growing danger of a "new world massacre." Moscow was prepared "to commence immediately with other States in the League of Nations or outside of it the discussion of practical measures called for by the present circumstances." [3]

"The issue of either war or a virtually complete Fascist domination of Europe" would be decided during the coming summer, Litvinov predicted to Davies on the 23rd. He feared Czechoslovakia might succumb to very strong pressure because of lack of confidence in France and lack of mutual French-Soviet confidence. The "extreme probability" of a Fascist dominated continent existed, with only the U.S.S.R. and Britain retaining their independence; "nothing but an immediate reversal of policy by Great Britain would prevent this because the smaller states are slipping surely into the Fascist orbit." [4]

A month later on April 24, *Izvestia*, the official voice of the Soviet Government, declared that a consistent and honest French policy based on the pact with the U.S.S.R. [5]

would have meant such unequivocal defeat for the fascist aggressors that it would certainly have . . . changed the whole international situation. . . . France is being dragged in the wake of English foreign policy, yet England needs the support of France at least as much a France needs that of England . . . A more resolute French foreign policy would undoubtedly exert a great influence on that of England, and would bring with it a change of attitude on the part of a number of small states. . . . even 'moderate capitulation,' further concessions to the fascist states, mean under the present conditions . . . a great risk for France.

The purely Party press expressed itself in much stronger language. The general line was that the British and French *bour-*

geoisie, fearing their own working classes, were willing to sacrifice the national interests of their countries rather than oppose the Japanese militarists and especially Hitler and Mussolini whom they regarded as insurance against social revolution. Certain elements in Britain and France were in fact attempting to direct fascist aggression against the Soviet Union. The various articles almost invariably contained an appeal for working-class unity and pressure upon the British and French Governments to force the abandonment of these policies. [6]

Stalin himself followed this line in a few passing remarks he devoted to the subject during a rather long conversation with U.S. Ambassador Davies on June 5. When Davies requested his views upon European developments, Stalin declared that "reactionary elements in England, represented by the Chamberlain Government," were strengthening Germany in order to make France dependent upon England and, ultimately, to make Germany strong against the U.S.S.R. In "his opinion Chamberlain did not represent the English people and . . . would probably fail because the fascist dictators would drive too hard a bargain. . . . the Soviet Union had every confidence that it could defend itself." [7]

Although Soviet propaganda neglected no opportunity for urging British and French resistance to aggression, a minor incident during the first part of May illustrated Stalin's aversion to categorical declarations of his own determination to oppose Hitler. On April 30 and May 1 the two leading Communist papers in Czechoslovakia, *Rude Pravo* (Czech language) and *Rote Fahne* (German), reported an announcement by the Comintern radio station in Moscow, that "30,000 Soviet bombers will appear over Berlin the day the first German soldier crosses the Czechoslovakian frontier." On May 9 TASS denounced the articles as an invention broadcast by a Fascist station in Rome. The report was not only denied by the Soviet press but by several articles in the Communist press abroad.[8]

More circumspectly worded articles on Soviet declarations and intentions aroused no reaction, however. On May 8 Kalinin, the titular head of the Soviet state (Chairman of the Presidium of the Supreme Soviet), received several delegations of foreign workers who had come to Moscow for the May Day celebrations. According to the *Prager Presse* of May 11, a Czech trade-union official asked Kalinin "whether the Soviet Union would come to the aid of Czechoslovakia if the Republic were attacked without provocation and France rendered assistance." [9]

The Soviet Union [Kalinin replied] has always and without reserve honored the treaties concluded with other nations . . . and if necessary would fulfill all her obligations toward Czechoslovakia and France to the last letter. . . . If the Treaty of Friendship between the Soviet Union, France, and Czechoslovakia were as strong as we wish it to be, then it would influence Britain also to choose other directions for her policy than those so far followed.

Soviet spokesmen went even further privately. In Berlin on May 6 the Soviet chargé d'affaires told the U.S. Ambassador that under no circumstances would Russia furnish military assistance to Czechoslovakia independently of France. The attitude of Rumania and, especially, Poland would make the provision of Soviet aid difficult, but he hoped this attitude "could be overcome provided a general common action were joined against Germany." [10]

At the end of March, Konrad Henlein, the leader of the Sudetendeutsche Partei, received his orders from Hitler in Berlin; it was agreed that the SdP should demand what Prague could not grant. In a speech at Karlsbad on April 24, Henlein announced his demands. The most important were full autonomy for the Sudeten German area, guarantees for Germans living outside the area, and complete liberty to profess and follow Nazi political principles. If Czech statesmen desired good relations with Germany, they must revise Czech foreign policy which had placed the state among the enemies of the German people—in other words abandon the French and Soviet alliances and trust in the mercy of Hitler. Following the speech tension grew steadily on both sides of the border. On May 19 troop movements were reported in Germany, and the next day the SdP broke off negotiations with the Czechoslovak Government. On the afternoon of May 20 Prague ordered a partial mobilization, and on the 21st, upon instructions from London, British Ambassador Henderson warned German Foreign Minister Ribbentrop that Britain might well become involved in the event of a German attack on Czechoslovakia. On the following day Henderson delivered to the Auswärtiges Amt a personal message from Lord Halifax who had succeeded Eden as Foreign Secretary. "If a resort is had to forcible measures," wrote Halifax, Ribbentrop should not "count on this country's being able to stand aside." In Paris on the evening of the 21st, Foreign Minister Bonnet announced that France would aid her ally if German troops crossed the Czech border, and the next day French Premier Daladier warned the German Ambassador that France would have to fight whether she wanted to or not. [11]

The crisis was without foundation. No unusual German troop movements had taken place, and Hitler had no intention of attacking Czechoslovakia at that time. The Communist press, however, was quite jubilant over the apparently strong Western reaction: [12]

In face of the firm demeanor of the Czechoslovaks, the French government stepped in and made it clear . . . that France intended to abide by its obligations . . . The world knows that the Soviet Union steadfastly abides by its international obligations. The Czechoslovak-Soviet Pact states:
"Both governments simultaneously recognize that the obligation between these two for mutual aid shall take effect only if . . . France shall come to the aid of the victim of the aggression."
The fulfillment of the pact, therefore, signified that Hitler would see himself confronting the Soviet Union as well. . . . It turned out that the moment France ceased to yield, England could become a serious force of peace. . . .
For twenty-four hours, there was a united peace front—and the fascist beast drew back growling. . . .
From this it follows that for all the friends of peace and above all for the international labor movement it is necessary to close their ranks more tightly . . . and to compel the governments of France and England to defend world peace together with the Soviet Union against the fascist aggressors.

In a long speech at an "election" meeting in Leningrad on June 23, Litvinov surveyed the international scene in detail and elaborated somewhat on this theme. Repeating the claim that the Western democracies feared war because of the probable social consequences, the inevitable demands of the working class, Litvinov asked why the fascist powers displayed no such fears. "Threats, blackmail, and bluff" were their principal weapons, he explained; they had invariably attacked weak, unarmed countries. He hinted that hopes of turning fascist aggression against the Soviet Union were vain: "aggressors will always seek new prey in those territories whose masters have shown their flabbiness and their inability to defend their positions." The fascist leaders dared only attack "weakly-defended" countries where "short distances" were involved; "neither the one nor the other will they find in our country." The speech was published in the Leningrad press on the following day but appeared in none of the Moscow Russian-language papers. It was, however, printed in the July 5 *Journal de Moscou*, the Narkomindel paper intended mainly for foreign diplomats. [13]

Izvestia expounded the same idea on July 17. After claiming that Chamberlain was prepared to sacrifice not only the interests of the smaller powers but even those of France, in order to convert her "into a devoted 'junior partner,'" the article declared that the fascist powers were not so dangerous in themselves. Their strength lay rather in the "pusillanimity, the vacillations, the cowardice, the shortsightedness of the countries of 'Western Democracy'." The article charged Britain and Chamberlain with "the greatest responsibility . . . the responsibility whether or not a new world war breaks out." [14]

Soviet Ambassador Maisky, who had just returned to London from leave in the U.S.S.R., told Foreign Secretary Lord Halifax on August 17 that German policy was at least "50 percent bluff." The weak attitude of Britain and France exaggerated the impression of German strength, both in Germany and abroad, and "constituted a real danger for peace." That evening Maisky expressed the same views to the U.S. chargé; fifty per cent of Hitler's threat was bluff but the temptation might be too strong for him to resist "if he thinks there is a gambling chance that Great Britain will not fight." In Moscow on September 8, Deputy Foreign Commissar Potemkin talked to Lord Chilston: There would be no war, he predicted, mainly because the German Army was not yet prepared and the German people were opposed. Potemkin also remarked that the U.S.S.R. was only obligated to intervene if France were actually engaged against Germany.[15]

While claiming that a strong Anglo-French stand would halt Hitler, Soviet spokesmen attempted to discount the likelihood of a German attack on Russia. In his speech of June 23, Litvinov pointed out that it was really the treaties imposed by France and Britain that had been violated and the position of the Western powers that was threatened. Yet from "the reactionary foreign press, one might gain the impression that the successes of the aggressor countries are a defeat, mainly, for the Soviet Union." One might believe, he continued, that the treaties of Versailles, Saint-Germain, etc. "had been worked out and written by the Comintern or, at least, by the Soviet Government." The fascist powers were dreaming of unlimited aggression, Litvinov continued, and for this reason no country, "however strong and remote," could be certain that "the waves of frenzied aggression will not roll to its own borders, even though in the distant future." If, contrary to Soviet expectations, the U.S.S.R. were attacked, he concluded, "we know that the defence of our country is in strong and capable hands." [16]

In the conversation with the U.S. chargé in London on August 17, Maisky predicted German hegemony over southeastern Europe would inevitably follow the fall of Czechoslovakia. Supported by the resources of that area, Hitler would then be able to attack either the U.S.S.R. or Britain and France. In view of the natural difficulties of a Russian campaign and growing Soviet strength, he was unlikely to choose the former. The chargé reported the Soviet Ambassador "gave the most curious impression of self confidence, that he feels that Great Britain and France are the ones in real danger; and that Russia can take care of herself." [17]

During these conversations Maisky repeated that Moscow was prepared to aid Czechoslovakia—after France. With Stalin's "full authority" he assured Jan Masaryk, the Czech Minister to London, that the U.S.S.R. would fulfill her obligations the instant France acted. Russia would move at once if France met her commitments, he assured the U.S. chargé—who pointed out to Washington that "by inference, if France would not fight, Russia will do nothing." [18]

Hitler was scheduled to speak at Nuremberg on September 12,

and it was widely feared his speech might be the signal for war. On the 9th Foreign Secretary Lord Halifax instructed British Ambassador Sir Nevile Henderson in Germany to deliver a personal warning for the Führer, a warning in which Halifax envisaged as "inevitable" a "general conflict from which Great Britain could not stand aside." But Henderson strongly advised against such a personal warning on the grounds that it would infuriate Hitler (!), and instead Prime Minister Chamberlain made an unofficial statement to a group of journalists on the 11th. The German Government, he said, should not believe "that a brief and successful campaign against Czechoslovakia could be safely embarked upon without the danger of the subsequent intervention first of France and later of this country." "But after all," continued the Prime Minister in his concluding remarks, "Herr Hitler has repeatedly expressed his own desire for peace and it would be a mistake to assume that those declarations were insincere." [19]

The Führer's speech the next day did not signal war, but disorders in the Sudetenland cost a number of lives. On the 13th Prague declared martial law in the border districts and peace was soon restored. The Czechoslovak Cabinet had agreed on September 5 to grant practically all of the demands Henlein had made at Karlsbad; in view of Berlin's actual aims, *Sudetendeutsche* acceptance was of course impossible, and the security measures of the 13th afforded the SdP leaders a convenient excuse for presenting an ultimatum and breaking off negotiations with the government in Prague.[20]

In the face of these developments, Daladier and Bonnet apparently lost their nerve. In a message to Chamberlain on the 13th, the French Premier declared that a German invasion of Czechoslovakia must be avoided at any cost, otherwise France would be forced to fulfill her obligations. He recommended that a three-power conference be proposed to Hitler immediately (Britain, France, and Germany). Chamberlain had for some time been considering a personal talk with Hitler. The latter's speech and Daladier's message decided the matter; a request for a meeting was telephoned to Berlin late in the evening of September 13, and Hitler's agreement was received the next day.[21]

Upon Chamberlain's arrival at Berchtesgaden on the 15th,

Hitler informed him that the Sudeten problem must be solved—
either peacefully or by war. Chamberlain agreed that the only
solution was the cession of the Sudetenland. He must, however,
consult with the cabinet before making any decision. Hitler in
turn promised to order no attack in the meantime. Chamberlain
flew back to London the next day (the 16th) and met with the
inner cabinet that evening; a full cabinet meeting took place the
next day. Premier Daladier and Foreign Minister Bonnet arrived
in London on the 18th, and during discussions lasting from 11:00
A.M. until after midnight it was agreed that Britain and France
should urge the Czechoslovak Government to cede those territories with a German majority. In return Prague would receive an
Anglo-French guarantee of the new frontier. The French cabinet
also agreed the following morning and the proposal was presented
to President Beneš that afternoon.[22]

The Czechoslovak Government's first reaction was negative.
Beneš posed two questions to Soviet Minister Aleksandrovskii the
same day (the 19th): (1) If France fulfilled her treaty obligations
would the U.S.S.R. do likewise? (2) In the event of an attack,
Prague intended to appeal to the League of Nations; would the
Soviet Union come to the aid of Czechoslovakia as a member of
the League, i.e. regardless of treaty provisions and even though
France refused her support? Aleksandrovskii requested instructions from Moscow, and at 7:00 P.M. on the 20th answered the
first question in the affirmative. Soviet aid would also be forth-
coming, he said, should Czechoslovakia appeal to the League.
Apart from the questionable extent and effectiveness of eventual
Russian support, any German military campaign against Czecho-
slovakia would probably have been in its final stages by the time
the League action envisaged by Moscow had been carried out.[23]
Hence almost irresistible British and French pressure was decisive.
Prague was warned that a rejection of the proposal would cause
London and Paris to wash their hands of the whole affair, and the
Czechoslovak Government officially agreed on the afternoon of
September 21.[24]

Chamberlain's second meeting with Hitler took place at Godesberg on September 22. Upon being informed that France, Britain,
and Czechoslovakia agreed in principle to the transfer of the

Sudetenland, Hitler simply remarked that the proposal was no longer adequate. Germany could not guarantee the new Czechoslovak frontier before Polish and Hungarian claims had been satisfied, and the transfer of German areas would have to take place within a few days. In his own words Chamberlain was "profoundly shocked" at Hitler's reaction, and a fruitless discussion followed.[25]

The situation appeared hopeless. Chamberlain remained overnight at Godesberg and consulted with London via telephone. The next afternoon the British and French Governments informed Prague that they could no longer advise against a mobilization. The Czech mobilization order was broadcast at 10:30 P.M. on the 23rd, and half an hour later at Godesberg Hitler and Chamberlain came together for a second conversation. The Führer handed over a memorandum demanding Czech evacuation, beginning on the 26th, of territories indicated on an attached map. During the conversation Hitler was informed of the Czech mobilization and declared that this development settled the whole affair. Chamberlain asked if the memorandum was his last word and was answered in the affirmative. Hitler added that the Czech mobilization would in fact force him to take certain military measures. The British Prime Minister thereupon remarked resignedly that there was no point in continuing the conversation. He had done everything possible to avoid war but in vain. The Führer in turn declared that military measures did not mean an invasion of Czechoslovakia. Chamberlain then stated that he would transmit the memorandum to Prague, and Hitler agreed to extend the time limit to October 1.[26]

In the meantime Litvinov was making what were essentially propaganda speeches even though they contained a great deal of truth. Evidently he and Stalin had abandoned all hope of British and French resistance to Hitler and had decided to establish the purity of the Soviet position beyond question. On September 21 at Geneva the Soviet Foreign Commissar declared that[27]

the Soviet Government bears no responsibility whatsoever for the events now taking place, and for the fatal consequences which may inexorably ensue. . . . the Soviet Union abstained from any intervention in the negotiations of the Czechoslovak Government with the

Sudeten Germans . . . from all advice to the Czechoslovak Government . . . When, a few days before I left for Geneva, the French Government for the first time enquired as to our attitude in the event of an attack on Czechoslovakia, I gave in the name of my Government the following perfectly clear and unambiguous reply.

We intend . . . *together with France,* to afford assistance to Czechoslovakia *by the ways open to us.* . . . Independently of this, we should consider desirable that the question be raised at the League of Nations . . . with the object, first, of mobilising public opinion and, secondly, of ascertaining the position of certain other States, whose passive aid might be extremely valuable. It was necessary, however, to exhaust all means of averting an armed conflict, and we considered one such method to be an immediate consultation between the Great Powers of Europe and other interested States, in order if possible to decide on the terms of a collective *démarche.*

This is how our reply was framed. It was only two days ago that the Czechoslovak Government addressed a formal enquiry to my Government as to whether the Soviet Union is prepared in accordance with the Soviet-Czech pact, to render Czechoslovakia immediate and effective aid *if France, loyal to her obligations, will render similar assistance,* to which my Government gave a clear answer in the affirmative.

On the same day in Berlin the Soviet chargé told the counsellor of the U.S. Embassay that "under no circumstances would Russia lend military assistance to Czechoslovakia except in common action with France." [28]

A singular feature of Soviet pronouncements between the *Anschluss* and Munich was the almost invariable reminder that the U.S.S.R. was obliged to come to the aid of Czechoslovakia only if France were already engaged. It seems safe to assume that Stalin's own aims and convictions were the basis of this particular line—that he desired and to the extent of his power encouraged a conflict between the "capitalist" powers in which the U.S.S.R. could remain on the sidelines. It was only natural for him to assign his own motives to others: Stalin quite probably believed the claims of his own propagandists, that "reactionary circles" in France and Britain were seeking to turn Nazi Germany toward the east. If these "reactionary circles" believed a German attack on Czechoslovakia would automatically involve the Soviet Union, they would, of course, do everything in their power to provoke such an attack and then prevent any action by their own governments. The repeated disavowal of any unilateral obligation to

Czechoslovakia was closely related to Soviet efforts to discount the likelihood of a German attack on the U.S.S.R.

German military preparations had continued after Prague's acceptance of the British-French plan became known on September 21. Even Bonnet became alarmed. By the evening of the 22nd Halifax and the French Government had agreed that they could no longer advise against a Czech mobilization. The French Ambassador in Berlin expected a German attack on the 24th. On the 23rd Daladier decided that the Godesberg talks had failed and that Britain and France were assuming a terrible responsibility in restraining a Czechoslovak mobilization. The British and French notes reversing an earlier recommendation against such a measure were handed over in Prague late that afternoon.[29]

Litvinov seems to have been aware of these developments. According to his own account, the Czechoslovak Government had in fact inquired sometime after the 21st if Moscow would still consider itself bound by the Czechoslovak-Soviet pact in the event of a breakdown in the Chamberlain-Hitler negotiations and a Czech decision to fight.[30] The Foreign Commissar evidently considered an unmistakable word of warning necessary—not to Hitler but to the "reactionary circles" in France and Britain. From Moscow's point of view, rumors then circulating regarding unconditional Soviet support of Czechoslovakia made such a warning particularly desirable. In addition, on the morning of the 23rd, the Soviet Government had been obliged to inform Warsaw, quietly and without press releases, that a Polish attack on Czechoslovakia would result in the abrogation of the 1932 Polish-Soviet nonaggression treaty.

Therefore during the afternoon of the 23rd Litvinov made yet another statement in which he defended and re-emphasized the provision of the Czech-Soviet pact that required the U.S.S.R. to provide aid only after France had acted. In the negotiations leading to the treaty, declared the Foreign Commissar, the Czechoslovak Government itself had "insisted that Soviet-Czechoslovak mutual assistance should be conditional upon assistance by France . . . Thus the Soviet Government had no obligations to Czechoslovakia in the event of French indifference to an attack on her." Referring to Prague's query regarding the Soviet attitude should

Czechoslovakia decide to fight, Litvinov pointed out that since Prague had accepted the eventual abandonment of the pact with the U.S.S.R.,[31]

the Soviet Government had undoubtedly also had the moral right to renounce that Pact. Nevertheless, the Soviet Government, which, for its part, did not seek pretexts for evading the fulfilment of its obligations, had replied to Prague that, *in the event of France granting assistance* [italics supplied] . . . the Soviet-Czechoslovak Pact would again enter into force . . . only the representative of a Government with a clear conscience and clean hands in the sphere of the fulfilment of international obligations could speak as he [Litvinov] did.

Earlier in the day Halifax had authorized R. A. Butler, the Parliamentary Undersecretary of State for Foreign Affairs who was then at Geneva for a meeting of the League, to inform Litvinov that Chamberlain was "making a supreme effort at Godesberg" to reach an agreement on a fair and orderly transfer of the Sudetenland to Germany. Should Germany reject this effort and resort to military action, it would produce a "deep and immediate effect" upon British and French public opinion. Butler was therefore requested to sound Litvinov on exactly what action the Soviet Government would take in the event of a German attack on Czechoslovakia and when they would take it.[32]

Butler and Lord De La Warr, another member of the British delegation, spoke with Litvinov shortly after he had made his statement. Although promising Soviet support, the Foreign Commissar managed to evade any discussion of the type of support and how it would be made effective: [33]

We asked him whether he could develop further the [statement made in the speech] . . . and in particular at what point Soviet Government would be prepared to take action. He said he could say no more than that if French came to the assistance of the Czechs Russians would take action. . . . they might desire to raise the matter in the League; this would not alter the proposition that he had stated, namely, that Czechoslovak-Soviet Pact would come into force. . . . He had for long been hoping for conversations between Great Britain, France and Russia, and he would like to suggest . . . a meeting . . . together with Roumania and any other small Power who could be regarded as reliable . . . and preferably in Paris, and so show Germans that we mean business. . . . Geneva meetings never impressed the Germans. He would be ready then to discuss military and air questions, upon which he was not posted, since he had been away from Russia for such a time. He could not therefore tell us to what extent Russian army was mobilised or air force ready to assist Czechoslovakia. He referred to rumours in German press that Russia had already provided Czechoslovakia with a certain amount of military assistance and said he could not confirm them personally.

Chamberlain flew back to London with Hitler's memorandum on the 24th, and the cabinet met several times on the 24th and 25th. Daladier had already ordered a partial mobilization on the 24th, and on the 25th the Czechoslovak Government rejected the Godesberg memorandum. Daladier and Bonnet consulted with the British leaders in London on the 25th and the morning of the 26th, and the French Premier declared that France would support her ally should the Germans attack. Chamberlain agreed with this position and stated that Britain would support France. He had decided, however, to make a final appeal to Hitler and at the same time warn him that France would have British support if she came to the aid of Czechoslovakia. That afternoon (the 26th) Lord Halifax authorized a communiqué which was released to the press later in the evening: If "a German attack is made upon Czechoslovakia, the immediate result must be that France will be bound to come to her assistance and Great Britain and Russia will certainly stand by France." [34]

Sir Horace Wilson carried the appeal to Berlin in a letter the same day and presented it to Hitler at 5:00 that afternoon. Chamberlain proposed that the details of the transfer of the Sudetenland be settled at a conference of German and Czech representatives; if desired by both parties, Britain would also take part. The communication provoked an angry outbreak; in the end, although willing to receive Czech negotiators, the Führer declared that the Sudetenland must be delivered up by October 1. During the course of a speech at the *Sportspalast* in Berlin that evening (the 26th), he announced that if Beneš had not yielded the Sudetenland by October 1, Germany would occupy the territory by force. At the same time he stated that this was his last territorial claim in Europe, praised Chamberlain's efforts to maintain peace, and expressed disinterest in Czechoslovakia after other minority claims had been satisfied: "Wir wollen gar keine Tschechen!" (We want absolutely no Czechs!) [35]

Soon after midnight (morning of September 27) Chamberlain announced that since the Führer had no faith in Czech promises, Britain would assume the responsibility for seeing that they were carried out if only Germany would settle the details of the transfer by negotiation. Hitler received Sir Horace and the British Ambassador again shortly after noon on the 27th. The Czechs had only two choices, he said, accept or reject the demand to turn over the Sudetenland by October 1. If they rejected it, the result would be the total destruction of Czechoslovakia. Sir Horace then delivered Chamberlain's warning: If France in pursuit of her treaty obligations "became actively engaged in hostilities against Germany, the British Government would feel obliged to support her." That afternoon the British inner cabinet decided to mobilize the fleet and auxiliary air force. In a radio address at 8:30 in the evening, Chamberlain saw "nothing further that I can usefully do in the way of mediation."

However much we may sympathize with a small nation confronted by a big and powerful neighbour, we cannot in all circumstances undertake to involve the whole British Empire in a war simply on her account. . . . but, if I were convinced that any nation had made up its mind to dominate the world by fear of force, I should feel that it must be resisted. . . . war is a fearful thing, and we must be very clear, before we embark on it, that it is really the great issues that are at stake.

But at 8:40 the Foreign Office received via telephone from the embassy in Berlin the text of a personal letter from Hitler to the British Prime Minister. In it the Führer assured Chamberlain that his desires regarding Czechoslovakia were limited to the German areas. Nor would the Czechs in those areas suffer under German occupation. The Czechoslovak Government was conducting a delaying maneuver in order to mobilize support in Britain and France, "and thus to achieve the possibility of a general war-like conflagration." Hitler therefore urged Chamberlain to continue his efforts toward peace and "bring the Government in Prague to reason at the very last hour." [36]

On the morning of the 28th Chamberlain wired Hitler that he was prepared to discuss the transfer of the Sudetenland in Berlin together with a representative of the Prague government; France and Italy could also be represented if desired. We "could reach agreement in a week," wrote the Prime Minister. "I cannot believe that you will take responsibility of starting a world war which may end civilisation for the sake of a few days' delay in settling this long standing problem." The French also urged the idea, and in a personal message Chamberlain requested Italian support. Upon receiving Mussolini's endorsement of the proposal early in the afternoon of the 28th, Hilter agreed.[37]

The last Soviet propaganda gesture prior to Munich was made the same evening. That morning Kirk, the U.S. chargé in Moscow, had delivered to the Narkomindel a suggestion from Washington that the chief of state or government of the U.S.S.R. make a formal appeal to Germany and Czechoslovakia to preserve the peace—an appeal similar to one made by President Roosevelt on September 26. In the evening Deputy Foreign Commissar Potemkin (Litvinov was still in Geneva) handed Kirk an official written answer which mentioned previous Soviet efforts to maintain the peace and stated that an international conference would be the best means of averting war. "Faithful to its aspiration for peace the Government of the U.S.S.R. is prepared at the present moment as well to support the proposal put forward by the Government of the United States . . . for the calling of an international conference and to take an active part therein." (Roosevelt had suggested such a conference on the evening of the 27th but the U.S. Embassy in Moscow had not yet been officially informed.) Kirk pointed out that neither his communication that morning nor Roosevelt's appeal of the 26th had mentioned a conference and expressed regret that the Soviet Government had not seen fit to make the appeal suggested. Potemkin disclosed the true purpose of the Soviet reply at the end of the conversation when he mentioned that both the U.S. suggestion and the Soviet reply would be published in the press the next morning.[38]

According to Marxist-Leninist dogma, the still terribly vulnerable "land of Socialism" (the U.S.S.R.) was surrounded by powerful and unalterably hostile capitalist states. The greatest danger in Stalin's eyes was that these might unite to crush the power which would otherwise be their eventual nemesis. At the time Moscow did not desire an international conference as much as it feared one from which it was excluded. As Potemkin told German Ambassador Schulenburg on September 29,[39]

What was happening now was the rebirth of the "notorious" Four Power Pact, which wanted to force its will on Europe, and whose first appearance he had witnessed—several years ago in Rome. The Soviet Government firmly maintained that the Czech dispute should be solved by a *general* conference. The Soviet Union had already made a proposal to that effect in March last (after the Austrian *Anschluss!*). The view of the Soviet Government was now fortunately supplemented by President Roosevelt's suggestion.

In London the same morning, Soviet Ambassador Maisky called on Lord Halifax at the latter's request. He was "particularly anxious," the Foreign Secretary explained, that the Soviet Government should understand why it had not been invited to send a representative to Munich. The Soviet interest in the matters at stake was as great as Britain's, but Hitler and Mussolini would simply refuse to sit down with a Soviet representative. Although no invitation had been sent to Moscow, Britain and France wished to maintain their "understandings and relations" with the U.S.S.R. They were, in fact, well aware of how important it was to work as closely as possible with the Soviet Government, and for this reason he had asked Butler and Lord De La Warr to approach Litvinov at Geneva. At the conclusion of the conversation, Maisky thanked the Foreign Secretary for the information and expressed the hope that his government would be kept informed of the developments at Munich. Halifax promised to do this and in summarizing the conversation in a dispatch to the embassy in Moscow observed that Maisky's general attitude was "one of some suspicion, but not one of resentment in face of facts, which he was perforce obliged to admit. And, as our conversation proceeded, he seemed to discard some of the suspicion." [40]

The Munich conference itself was little more than a formality. The discussion began shortly after noon on September 29 and general agreement was reached early that evening. The details were settled during the night and the actual agreement signed early in the morning of September 30, 1938.

5

Munich: The Tributaries

As early as 1936, in discussing the course of any future campaign against Germany, Marshal Smigly-Rydz, the head of the Polish Army, warned General Gamelin, vice president of the French Conseil supérieur de la Guerre, that Poland could not allow any Soviet attack against East Prussia over Lithuanian or Polish territory. If the Bolsheviks ever entered Poland or Lithuania they would never leave. Of our former masters, continued the marshal, we could get along fairly well only with the Austrians. We dislike but respect the Prussians and consider the Russians the worst of all. He was willing to consider Polish-Soviet cooperation only in the air, and even in this case Poland would provide nothing more than temporary landing fields.[1]

On May 16, 1938 French Foreign Minister Bonnet, who had just returned from a League meeting, told William Bullitt, the U.S. Ambassador to Paris, of important discussions he had had with Polish, Rumanian, and Russian representatives at Geneva. The Poles would not support France if the latter declared war on Germany as the result of an attack on Czechoslovakia; and should the Red Army attempt to cross Polish territory in order to aid Czechoslovakia, Poland would declare war on the U.S.S.R. immediately. Comnen, the Rumanian Foreign Minister, had declared "equally categorically" that a Soviet attempt to cross Rumanian territory would provoke an immediate Rumanian declaration of war. Five days later the Polish Ambassador, who had just returned to Paris from Warsaw, gave Bullitt the same information. The Polish air force would even attack Soviet planes en route to Czechoslovakia. Polish air units had been concentrated

75

near the Polish-Rumanian border for this specific purpose and might even attempt to interdict any flights over Rumanian territory if the Rumanian air force were unable to halt such transit.[2] Although the Rumanians subsequently modified their stand somewhat, the Polish Government remained adamant—even a year later when Poland herself was threatened.

Significant Russian help could only reach Czechoslovakia via the railway system of southern Poland, the British Ambassador reported from Warsaw on June 14, "but any such attempt, implying military occupation, would inevitably be resisted by Poland."[3] With regard to aerial assistance, the Polish Chief of Air Staff had recently informed the British military attaché that Polish fighters had attempted to intercept some Soviet bombers en route to Czechoslovakia. The attempts had failed, however, because "various routes" had been followed and the flights were made at night.[4]

"His chief nightmare at the moment" Bonnet told Bullitt on August 30, "was the prospect that if the Soviet Union should attempt to send an army to the support of Czechoslovakia, Rumania and Poland would both declare war on the Soviet Union." The French Foreign Minister was convinced that Poland and Rumania would attempt to remain neutral as long as possible; the only aid which Czechoslovakia could expect from the U.S.S.R. would have to come by air. Eleven days later the British Ambassador in Warsaw again warned that even this would be opposed:

The one eventuality which might throw Poland into the German camp would be any attempt by the U.S.S.R. to send help to Czechoslovakia across Poland . . . It is argued that once Soviet armies were on Polish soil another war would be necessary to turn them out . . . Should Russian help be confined to sending aeroplanes across Poland the effect on public opinion would be equally bad, and active measures would probably be taken to prevent any such passage.

The ambassador felt, however, that if France and Britain declared war on Germany and the Soviet Union took no action, public opinion would eventually lead to Polish participation on the side of the Allies. On September 13 the Polish Ambassador to Britain told Halifax that although his government would try to remain neutral, Poland would probably eventually be drawn into any general war; in line with Pilsudski's policy, Foreign Minister Beck wished "to orientate the policy of Poland as closely as possible with that of London." [5]

On September 20 the French Ambassador to Warsaw informed Beck that Moscow had promised to make no attempt to send troops or planes across Polish territory. But on September 23 Moscow threatened to denounce the 1932 nonaggression treaty should Polish troops attack Czechoslovakia, and in a conversation with British military chiefs in London on the 26th General Gamelin mentioned the possibility of Soviet action against Poland. "Although I did not stress the point," he later wrote, "it was evident that the prospect of Russia invading Poland did not please our allies very much." Finally, in Paris on the 28th, Gamelin instructed the Soviet military attaché, who was leaving for Moscow, to inform Defense Commissar Voroshilov that the French were making every effort to keep Warsaw on their side and hoped the U.S.S.R. would not attack Poland without previously informing Paris.[6]

Poland's position was complicated by still another factor aside from her determination to allow no transit of Soviet troops or aircraft. While engaged in a life and death struggle with Soviet Russia in 1920, she had been forced to cede the predominantly Polish Teschen district to Czechoslovakia. This action had embittered relations between the two states throughout the interwar period.

As early as May 1938 Foreign Minister Beck expressed the official Polish "line" when he warned the Quai d'Orsay that any concession by Prague on the subject of minorities which did not include the Polish minority would immediately provoke tension between Poland and Czechoslovakia. And on June 10, 1938, General Stachiewicz, the Polish Chief of Staff, assured the British military attaché that Poland would not make the first move against Czechoslovakia, but the Polish minority in Teschen must share in any concessions Prague might make to other nationalities. The Polish chargé called at the British Foreign Office on August 9 and explained that the Polish Government wanted London to tell Prague "that there must be no discrimination as between the treatment eventually accorded in any settlement to the Sudeten

Germans and that accorded to the Polish minority." On August 30 the British chargé in Warsaw reported on a conversation with Foreign Minister Beck: The Polish Government expected that the Polish minority in Teschen "should receive treatment equal to that of Sudeten Germans in any settlement." Although "determined to maintain this formula," Poland "would not seek to enlarge it." [7] Warsaw supported this position with diplomatic notes and even with troop movements.

Litvinov was ostensibly considering the problem at the end of May when he asked Coulondre, the French Ambassador, what France would do if Poland, "having attacked Czechoslovakia, should be in turn attacked by the USSR?" Coulondre replied that the French alliances with Poland and Czechoslovakia were defensive pacts, i.e. applied only in cases of unprovoked aggression, which seemed to satisfy Litvinov. But on June 5 the Foreign Commissar instructed the Soviet Ambassador in Paris to pose the question officially. Bonnet referred the matter to the legal experts of the Quai d'Orsay who pointed out that the U.S.S.R. was not required to take any action before France had intervened. Upon receiving this reply from Coulondre, Litvinov mentioned still another hypothesis: "that, for one reason or another, the Soviet Union should intervene without France having moved." [8] In his instructions of the 5th, the Foreign Commissar had mentioned that he was not at all worried about rumors of the *démarche* leaking out; they might in themselves help to restrain Poland. But Litvinov may also have been "fishing" for some reliable indication of French determination to resist Germany. (For a clear example of this tactic, see the last part of Chapter 7.)

In a note handed over in Prague on September 21, the Polish Government demanded a decision on the Teschen region, "a decision immediate and analogous to that which the Czechoslovak Government has taken with regard to the German problem." The next day the Czechoslovak Foreign Minister asked the Soviet Minister to inform Moscow that Poland was concentrating troops all along the frontier with Czechoslovakia; it would be advisable, he continued, for the Soviet Government to warn the Poles that the Soviet-Polish nonaggression pact would lose its validity in the case of a Polish attack. Moscow could hardly refuse, and on the morning of the 23rd Deputy Foreign Commissar Potemkin asked the Polish chargé to call and handed him a note: [9]

The Government of the USSR has learned from various quarters that Polish Government troops are being concentrated . . . in readiness . . . to occupy by force part of the territory of the Czechoslovak Republic. In spite of the widespread and alarming character of these reports, the Polish Government has so far not denied them. . . . if there should be no such denial, and if . . . Polish troops should in fact cross the frontier of Czechoslovakia . . . the Soviet Government . . . in virtue of Article 2 of the non-aggression pact concluded between the USSR and Poland . . . would be compelled to denounce the said pact without further notice.

At 7:00 that evening the Polish chargé delivered the written answer: Polish defense measures were exclusively the business of the Polish Government which was not obliged to give any explanations and was well aware of the terms of the treaties to which it was a party. He also declared that his government was particularly surprised at the Soviet *démarche* since it had taken no measures on the Polish-Soviet frontier. Contrary to the usual development of affairs of this nature, the Polish Foreign Ministry announced the exchange of notes on the evening of the 23rd, and the communiqué appeared in the press the next day. But the matter was not mentioned in the Soviet press until September 26 when *Izvestia* published an official statement.[10]

At about the same time Moscow made what Beck later called a "somewhat theatrical military demonstration." Parts of two Soviet army corps, together with motorized and armoured units, were moved up to the Polish frontier. The Poles were convinced, however, that no mobilization had been ordered and took no special steps aside from air patrols along the border.[11]

A somewhat transparent campaign designed to demonstrate the depth of Polish feeling and determination with regard to the Teschen area culminated on September 30 in a Polish ultimatum demanding an immediate and unconditional evacuation of the territory. The Czechoslovak Government agreed, and in Paris on October 3 Bonnet told the U.S. Ambassador that [12]

Litvinov had been in Paris in hiding during the critical days . . . On the morning of the expiration of the Polish ultimatum . . . he (Bonnet) had had a private and secret conversation with Litvinov and had asked . . . whether or not if Poland should attack Czechoslovakia the Soviet Union would attack Poland in accordance with the promises made to Praha . . . and the public announcements to this effect . . . Litvinov had replied that the Soviet Government would do nothing in support of Czechoslovakia.

Bonnet's veracity has frequently been questioned, but in view of the general feeling of relief immediately after Munich he can hardly have felt it necessary at that time to justify his actions. At any rate the statement attributed to Litvinov did not contradict apparent Soviet policy. Once the Western powers had sacrificed Czechoslovakia to Germany, there was no point in encouraging Prague to resist other demands which could not conceivably involve Germany and the West in World War II. Worse, any effective support for Czechoslovakia could only drive Poland closer to Berlin.

THE CZECHOSLOVAK-SOVIET PACT was signed in 1935 and the next year Prague financed repairs of certain Rumanian rail lines in Transylvania and Bessarabia to improve connections with the new ally. In 1937 King Carol assured General Gamelin that Soviet forces would be allowed to pass through northern Rumania in order to reach Czechoslovakia. But the King demanded that the assurances be kept secret since he did not want the matter discussed in Rumania; he would act when it was necessary. By 1938, however, Bucharest apparently had no intention of allowing the passage of Soviet troops. The new Rumanian constitution of February 1938 contained the same article as the old one: No foreign troops could "enter or pass through Rumanian territory except by virtue of a law." On May 1, 1938 King Carol told a senior official of the Czechoslovak Foreign Ministry that the Rumanian Government could not formally approve flights of Soviet aircraft over its territory but would ignore any flights that actually took place. It was impossible, however, to allow transit of Soviet ground forces. Only one division per week could be moved via the one-track railroad. In addition Moscow could be expected to use the occasion as an excuse for occupying large areas of Rumania. Finally, the Soviet Government was neither willing nor able to provide aid. Eight days later Rumanian Foreign Minister Comnen warned Bonnet that his government could not agree to the passage of troops.[13]

At Geneva on May 12, replying to a question from Bonnet, Litvinov stated that aid for Czechoslovakia was only feasible if Poland and Rumania would allow Soviet troops to march through. Since France was allied to these two states, she should secure their permission. The Foreign Commissar also recommended French-Soviet military staff talks.[14]

At a meeting of the foreign ministers of the Little Entente powers in Bled on August 21 and 22, Foreign Minister Comnen informed his Czech opposite number that passage of Soviet ground forces through Rumania was impossible. Should Soviet planes fly over Rumania to aid Czechoslovakia, however, Bucharest would close its eyes and make only a formal protest for the record. The French Ambassador to Rumania mentioned this possibility to Comnen on September 6, and the latter remarked that at an altitude of three thousand meters it hardly required an act of will. He was quick to point out, however, that under the terms of the Rumanian-Polish alliance, Bucharest could only act (positively?) in agreement with Warsaw.[15]

Litvinov was also informed of the Rumanian position. On September 2 he told Payart, the French chargé in Moscow, that tacit Rumanian agreement to the passage of planes was not enough. Since Warsaw and Bucharest were unwilling to agree formally to the transit of Soviet forces, the only way out was an appeal to the League of Nations. The Foreign Commissar also urged French-Soviet-Czech staff talks and a French-British-Soviet political conference to be followed by a joint declaration which would undoubtedly receive President Roosevelt's moral support. That same evening Maisky, the Soviet Ambassador to London, called on Churchill and elaborated in some detail on the Payart-Litvinov conversation. He failed to mention the Rumanian offer to close their eyes; according to his account Litvinov had stated that Rumanian-Soviet relations had recently improved and a mere majority vote of the League Council would induce Bucharest to allow the passage of Soviet ground and air forces. At the time, Churchill felt he was given the information because the Soviet

Government feared a rebuff in case a direct approach were made to the Foreign Office. But it is more likely that Litvinov hoped to provoke pressure in Commons for a stiffer attitude by the British Government.[16]

Bonnet saw Litvinov at Geneva on September 11 and urged taking advantage of Rumania's intention not to oppose the passage of aircraft. The Foreign Commissar remained adamant, however, and continued to demand a recommendation from the League and formal permission from Bucharest for the passage of air and ground forces. On the same day Bonnet approached Comnen personally. Even an appeal from the League, the Rumanian Foreign Minister declared, would not induce his government to give formal approval for the transit of air or ground forces, but Rumanian antiaircraft artillery was incapable of interfering with any flights of Soviet aircraft. As he later wrote, Comnen had several conversations with Litvinov at Geneva at this time, but the Foreign Commissar made no "allusion to the technical possibilities of coming to the aid of Czechoslovakia." Bonnet was the only one "who posed the question." [17]

Although yielding to French requests, the Rumanian Government much preferred that other powers be the first to "close their eyes." As Lord De La Warr of the British delegation to Geneva reported, Comnen informed him on September 15 that no definite agreement existed with Russia, but [18]

in case of war, supplies would probably pass through Roumania to Czechoslovakia and he thought there would be no difficulty in such a case in allowing transit, especially for aeroplanes. He stressed . . . difficulties . . . a single line railway entailed some 500 miles of devious route to borders of Czechoslovakia. . . . Roumanian Minister for Foreign Affairs went out of his way to emphasise that Polish help was the key to the whole situation in Eastern Europe. Russia's natural line of communication with Czechoslovakia lay through Poland and if the latter was willing to allow Russian aid to pass through her territory Roumania could then march and if she did so, so could Yugoslavia.

In this matter of transit of Soviet forces, the Rumanian Government pursued prudent but, considering Rumania's position, hardly dishonorable diplomatic tactics. While agreeing to honor their commitments to their French and Czechoslovak allies insofar as they dared, Rumanian spokesmen were careful in statements directed toward Berlin to say nothing that would place Bucharest on the wrong side of the fence before such action was absolutely necessary. At the same time they sought to create the impression that Rumania actually was militarily incapable of preventing the flight of Soviet aircraft over the country. As early as April 30, 1938, when questioned by the German Minister, Comnen gave his word of honor that no negotiations with the U.S.S.R. for the transit of ground and air forces had taken place. Some unarmed planes purchased by Czechoslovakia had flown across Rumania, he admitted, but this was fully in accordance with international usage.[19]

On June 24 the German Minister reported on a conversation with the Rumanian Court Minister who stated that King Carol had "violently rejected" a Czech request for the transit of planes (presumably with Soviet pilots). In view of the Polish-Rumanian treaty the King had ordered the general staff to prevent such transit, even though the planes should be disguised as Czechoslovak.[20]

When I asked what Rumania intended doing if, in spite of this, aircraft were to cross Rumanian territory in nonstop flights by night, the Court Minister replied: "In that case we will fire on them."

In reply to my discreet question as to whether Rumania possessed sufficient anti-aircraft guns on the frontier in order to open fire, he smiled and said that unfortunately this was not the case, and he was forced to admit that it was not easy for Rumania to shoot down foreign aircraft with her own fighters.

The Rumanian service attaché in Warsaw told the German air attaché on July 19 that Rumania would oppose the passage of Soviet troops and aircraft and cited the treaty with Poland. "Rumania, however, could only oppose the Russians with success if she were not alone. . . . if the potential war situation in Eastern Europe were not hopeless for Rumania from the start." And early in September, when the German chargé in Bucharest remarked on a press report that Rumania would side with the West in the event of war, Comnen expressed surprise that the matter was even mentioned. "The Foreign Minister then explained, pointing to the map, that there were practically no facilities for transport of Soviet troops through Bessarabia. Only existing railway would in combination with lateral road take a disproportionately long time to transport even a small number of Russian troops." [21]

On July 26, Szembek, the Polish Deputy Foreign Minister, had questioned Comnen regarding rumors that Bucharest would allow the passage of Soviet forces and would be content with lodging merely a formal protest. Comnen gave his "word of honor that there was not a single word of truth" in all the rumors. Should the "Soviets make the slightest attempt to cross the frontier," Rumania would rely on her alliance with Poland. The Rumanian Minister to Berlin told State Secretary Weizsäcker of the Auswärtiges Amt on September 9 that it "was in the most vital interest of his country that Russia should be prevented from interfering via Rumanian territory. In this connection Rumania was at one with Poland." And on the 20th the Rumanian Ambassador to Warsaw assured Szembek that "there was no question of allowing Soviet troops to traverse the territory of his country." [22]

In a conversation at Geneva on September 12 with the representative of a Balkan country friendly to Germany, Comnen denied any truth in a Havas report on Rumanian agreement to the passage of Soviet forces. No formal denial had been made, however, in order not to weaken the position of France, Czechoslovakia, and the U.S.S.R. vis-a-vis Germany. Upon being informed of the talk, the German Consul General at Geneva pointed out to Berlin that Comnen was "obviously at pains to steer clear of Franco-Russian efforts to secure the premature public declaration of Rumania's attitude." He also felt that the statement had been made in the hope that it would be passed on to the Germans. [23]

Finally, on September 27, following his return from Geneva, Comnen asked the German Minister to inform Berlin that Bucharest was bound by no secret treaties or agreements. He could give his word of honor on that. "When I [the German Minister] asked how matters stood regarding flight of Soviet Russian aircraft to Czechoslovakia, C replied that he had no information up to date; unfortunately Rumania did not yet possess the necessary instruments for detecting whether the aircraft were crossing over

Rumania and if so, how many. Neither had she enough antiaircraft guns." [24]

IN THE PERIOD following the Austrian *Anschluss* two doubts troubled Western diplomats and statesmen when they attempted to predict the action of the Soviet Government in the event of a German attack on Czechoslovakia. First, the Great Purge which had started on a small scale at the end of 1934 reached its high point during 1938. An estimate that one out of every eight adult male Soviet citizens was in a prison or forced labor camp may have been somewhat conservative for 1938 alone. The government, the economy, and the Red Army were rapidly becoming completely demoralized. Second, once hostilities had actually started the Soviet Union might furnish no assistance even if it were militarily capable of doing so.

As early as March 14, 1938, Léger, Secretary General at the Quai d'Orsay, told the U.S. chargé that "he had not received sufficient information concerning the effect of the recent trial and revelations in Moscow to determine whether the Russian Government was capable today or was willing if capable to furnish effective assistance to Czechoslovakia. . . . Frankly he did not know what Russia could or would do." Three weeks later, on April 5, Sir Alexander Cadogan, the Permanent Undersecretary at the British Foreign Office, told Czechoslovak Minister Jan Masaryk that British official circles deeply distrusted Russia and doubted that she could make a significant military effort beyond her own frontiers.[25] Colonel Firebrace, the British military attaché in Moscow, wrote down a detailed evaluation of the Red Army on April 18: [26]

A minimum of 65 per cent of all officers of the rank of divisional commander and above have been lost to the army. . . . The commanders of the military districts have been changed in every case except one . . . In many districts the command has changed several times during the past year owing to the liquidation of the commander, Central Asia leading the list with the proud record of five commanders in twelve months. Nearly all the more efficient higher commanders have disappeared, including all who had the benefit of higher training in Germany. The places of the liquidated officers have usually been taken by men of inferior merit, in many cases promoted for party faithfulness more than for military efficiency, and in others by the rapid advancement of quite junior officers, captains having been advanced directly to the rank of divisional commander. It may therefore well be doubted whether there are now available men who are capable of commanding armies in the event of war. . . .

From the military point of view there must be considerable doubt as to whether the Soviet Union is capable of fulfilling its obligations . . . by undertaking a war of offence. In defence of its territory, I still consider that the Red Army would be a formidable opponent.

In forwarding his military attaché's report to London the following day, Lord Chilston elaborated on several nonmilitary factors Colonel Firebrace had only mentioned in passing: Given the existing disorganization, the Soviet economy could hardly stand the strain of a war. Under the current conditions there seemed to be little danger of a revolt; one might well be expected in case of war, however. The complete isolation of the population could no longer be maintained; this, together with a complete economic collapse, mass executions on an even greater scale than in peacetime, and "the moral effect of possible military defeats," could easily topple the regime: [27]

It seems probable that . . . nothing short of an immediate threat to the integrity of Soviet territory would be held by the rulers of this country to justify entry into a war. . . . In my opinion the risk entailed from an internal point of view by going to war would in Soviet councils by far outweigh the purely potential menace constituted by any change in the European balance of power. . . . the Soviet Union must . . . for the time being, be counted out of European politics in so far as the exercise of a decisive influence one way or the other is concerned, though there is no reason why, with time and in changed circumstances, it should not play an extremely important role in world affairs.

These and other reports evidently had their influence upon Lord Halifax. During Anglo-French conversations in London on April 29, he observed that "recent events, such as the execution of many members of the Higher Command of the army, and the general state of internal unrest in that country, made it extremely doubtful whether Russia could be counted upon to make any great contribution, if, indeed, she could make any contribution at all." Daladier had to admit that the purge had weakened the Red Army. He pointed out, however, that the Soviet air force was still numerically the "strongest" in Europe and that the country's "potential war resources were extremely great." [28]

Subsequent reports to London from Moscow were in the same vein. On May 22 Vereker, the British chargé, supplied additional evidence to support Lord Chilston's evaluation of the previous month: The Soviet press had "consistently avoided suggesting that Red Army would march in the event of a German invasion of Czechoslovakia." Nor had there been any reference to the assurances Kalinin had given the Czech delegation to the May Day ceremonies. Vereker found the absence of any mention of the anniversary of the Soviet-Czech pact (May 16) especially significant; in earlier years it had been the "subject of more or less enthusiastic articles." In commenting on conversations with the Czech and German military attachés, Colonel Firebrace concluded a report of May 30 with the observation that the Soviet Government would avoid a war in 1938 if at all possible and would seek "any pretext" to evade its obligations to France and Czechoslovakia.[29]

These reports undoubtedly reinforced the impression already formed in London. In a June 15 talk with German Ambassador Dirksen, Prime Minister Chamberlain, according to Dirksen, "agreed in outspoken terms with my critical exposition of economic conditions in Russia and the growing internal tension, which had greatly weakened the country. His dislike for the Soviet Union was unmistakable." [30]

French Ambassador Coulondre probably sent similarly pessimistic reports to Paris. When Vereker and Firebrace called on him at his request on May 15,[31] he informed them that he had been called home for consultations by Bonnet, who had taken over as Foreign Minister the previous month. During his last visit to Paris, said Coulondre, he had given a very conservative opinion of the chances that the U.S.S.R. would actively oppose German moves. In the preceding month, however, he had felt, "in the vague and intuitive manner in which one senses such matters in Soviet Russia," that Moscow might adopt a more active policy. His two British colleagues, after admitting the difficulty of forming a valid judgment of the situation in Russia, repeated the warning they had dispatched to London against placing any reliance upon the Soviet Government.

Whatever opinions Coulondre may have expressed, on May 27 Bonnet told the Polish Ambassador to Paris that the pact with the U.S.S.R. was very "vague" and the French Government placed little reliance on it. In the event of a Polish-German war, however, it could have a certain value. Poland would not have to fight on two fronts and might be able to obtain Soviet war and raw materials. The French Foreign Minister gave his reasons for these views in a conversation with Bullitt and U.S. Secretary of the Treasury Morgenthau in Paris on July 26: He "believed that the recent 'purges' . . . had so weakened the . . . Red Army and the government that it would be impossible for the Soviet Union to contemplate war beyond its frontiers." [32] Finally, as the crisis approached its climax, French military leaders began to doubt openly even the worth of Soviet aid in the air. On the morning of September 24, General Gamelin observed to the British military attaché that aerial support, the only type feasible, would be hampered by the limited number of air bases in Czechoslovakia.[33]

Aside from doubting the worth of Soviet aid, Bonnet, some other French officials, and a few well-informed neutral diplomats (Bullitt especially) doubted that any would be extended if a war actually did break out. While not necessarily fearing a social revolution in the wake of any new world war, a favorite theme of Communist propaganda, they did suspect the Soviet Government was actively trying to provoke a war from which it expected to profit. In August Coulondre expressed this fear to the German Ambassador in Moscow, Count Schulenburg: "I hope from my heart that it does not come to a German-French conflict. You know as well as I do for whom we are working if we get at loggerheads." And a secretary of the German Embassy in Moscow reported a remark made to him by Payart, the French chargé, on August 30: "In case of war the Soviets would have the last laugh. Having no common frontier they had no need to expose themselves to any great danger." [34]

After a long talk with the U.S. Ambassador during the morning of September 2, British Ambassador Phipps (Paris) reported Bullitt's fear, "that Russia's great wish is to provoke a general conflagration in which she herself will play but little part, beyond perhaps a little bombing from a distance, but after which she will arise like a phoenix, out of all our ashes, and bring about a world revolution." That afternoon Bonnet told Phipps that Soviet Ambassador Suritz, acting on instructions from Litvinov, had recently been "pestering" him. Suritz had been pressing the French to adopt a firmer attitude with regard to Czechoslovakia and to urge the British Government to do the same: [35]

M. Bonnet replied that he had noticed, and approved, the caution showed by the Soviet Government vis-a-vis of their neighbour, Japan, and he proposed to display similar caution in regard to Spain and Germany. He enquired incidentally what help the Soviets would give in case of a German attack on Czechoslovakia. M. Suritz said he would enquire of M. Litvinoff, but so far nothing has come back. . . .

M. Bonnet says that Russia's one wish is to stir up general war in the troubled waters of which she will fish. He here confirms the opinion expressed to me by Mr. Bullitt.

Litvinov's conversations with Payart in Moscow and Bonnet in Geneva during September only served to reinforce the latter's doubts. During this period, the French Foreign Minister later wrote, he had felt his government was "running a grave risk," that Moscow would allow France to become involved in a conflict and draw Britain in after her and then justify its own inaction on the grounds of the attitude of Poland and Rumania.[36] Bonnet's efforts for peace with Germany at almost any price can hardly have been based on his suspicions of Soviet policy, but they certainly gave it a quite plausible justification.

GERMAN DIPLOMATS in Moscow and German leaders in Berlin also doubted that the U.S.S.R. would give the Allies any substantial aid in the event of war. In the case of the Germans, however, the doubts were for all practical purposes conviction. Reporting to Berlin on Litvinov's press statement of March 17, Tippelskirch, the German chargé, observed that the Foreign Commissar had given an "evasive answer" when questioned regarding the possibility of independent Soviet support of Czechoslovakia; "the Soviet Government is avoiding committing itself definitely and is leaving it to the other powers to decide upon practical measures." In a letter of March 28, Tippelskirch referred to rumors of pending Soviet-Rumanian negotiations regarding transit. He thought they would be held in Bucharest, "if they take place at all." In a second letter to Berlin a week later he mentioned another rumor, that Bucharest had denied any negotiations were under way, and suggested that Litvinov "only wished to provide himself with an alibi in order not to be forced to support Czechoslovakia." Tippelskirch went on to cite the passage of the Czech-Soviet pact requiring prior action by France and evidence that Moscow had no intention of supporting the Czechs: [37]

The Soviet press treats the Czechoslovak question with great reserve. As a rule the Soviet press mentions only France's obligations to Czechoslovakia. On one occasion only has Izvestia intimated in a weekly review that Russia, too, would do her bit toward creating a "lasting cordon of collective defense" against aggression. One can take this to mean whatever one likes. It has never yet been said that the Soviet Union will range herself with all her power behind Czechoslovakia.

Shortly after the middle of May, Ambassador Schulenburg wrote Berlin that under the existing political circumstances Rumania would never agree to the passage of Soviet troops. "Neither can I believe that the Russians are making great efforts to obtain this privilege. One is constantly seeing signs here of how little the Soviet Union wants war." [38]

The British Government had proposed that the League allow its members freedom of action regarding recognition of the Italian conquest of Ethiopia, and Litvinov made a rather lame speech on the subject before the League Council on May 12. In a dispatch to Berlin four days later Schulenburg pointed out that Litvinov's problem had been to create no great difficulties for Britain while at the same time maintaining Soviet prestige: [39]

Litvinov's attitude in the Abyssinian question is further evidence of the present weak position of the Soviet Union in international relations. As a result of the bloody domestic events, the specific gravity of the Soviet Union in international politics has been reduced to such an extent that any attempts by Litvinov to win over other countries to the Soviet viewpoint would have been doomed to failure from the very beginning.

These and other reports from Russia had their effect in Berlin—not so much upon Hitler, who in the final analysis believed what he wanted to believe, as upon the responsible officials of the Wilhelmstrasse and the generals. A directive for an attack on

Czechoslovakia (Operation Green) was issued on May 30. The directive (four printed pages) made only two references to the possibility of Soviet intervention: "In all probability attempts by Russia to give Czechoslovakia military support, particularly with her air force, are to be expected." On the next page the primary mission of the Luftwaffe was described as the "destruction of the Czech Air Striking Force and its supply bases" as soon as possible in order to preclude its use "and, should the case arise, that of the Russian and French Air Forces," against the German field forces and German cities. On the same day State Secretary Weizsäcker wrote a letter to the German Ambassador in China: "Russia hardly exists in our calculations today," he concluded. "As long as Stalin makes himself as useful as now, we need not particularly worry about him as regards military policy." [40]

Also on the same day, Schulenburg reported from Moscow the general opinion among foreign diplomats that the U.S.S.R. would avoid a conflict with Germany "at all costs" in view of domestic conditions and the threat of a Japanese attack in the Far East. The feeling was that the "Soviet Union will only intervene in a war if she herself is attacked, or if it became manifest that the outcome will be favorable to the side hostile to Germany." After a careful evaluation of Soviet press reaction during the "May Crisis" when a German attack on Czechoslovakia appeared imminent, Schulenburg felt justified in describing Moscow's policy in more precise terms: [41]

During the first days of the crisis of May 20 to 25, the Soviet press contained no reference to the standpoint of the Soviet Government itself in the problem of Czechoslovakia. . . . she only proclaimed her own policy when French intentions had become known . . . when the threatening war clouds seemed to have rolled away. . . .

The attitude of the Soviet Government during the May crisis thus showed that, in the event of a war between Germany and Czechoslovakia, it would at the start be unwilling to commit itself or to show its hand. . . .

The Soviet Government, with an eye on the internal situation in Russia and fearing a war on two fronts, must hold aloof from military enterprises for the time being . . . It follows, therefore, the proved tactics of mobilizing other powers, particularly France, against its foes, of fomenting those conflicts which do break out—as for example in Spain and China—by deliveries of war material, and of extending them as much as possible by political agitation and intrigues of all kinds.

Around the middle of June, the Moscow correspondent of the International News Service was instructed to check on a report from Prague that the German Government intended to approach Moscow with an offer of better political relations. The correspondent asked the press section of the Narkomindel what the Soviet reaction to such an offer would be. After waiting two days for an answer, the journalist presented to the press section the draft of a telegram stating that the Soviet reaction to such an approach would probably be negative. The head of the press section, acting in his capacity as censor, suggested a version stating that the Soviet Government would probably welcome any German proposal that contributed to world peace but would reject anything that weakened it as an attempt to disrupt the front of the peaceful countries. The correspondent informed the U.S. Embassy of the incident and Kirk, the chargé, in turn informed Schulenburg and queried him about the likelihood of such a German approach. A *rapprochement* was "out of the question," the German Ambassador replied. In their reports on the matter both he and Kirk pointed out that the two-day delay indicated the suggested revision had been approved by Litvinov. As Schulenburg reported, the incident showed "that the Soviet Union on its part did not intend to close the door to negotiations with Germany definitively." [42]

In his Leningrad speech a few days later on June 23, the Foreign Commissar hinted that the main reason for Moscow's opposition to Hitler's foreign policy was its strong anti-Soviet flavor:

It makes no difference to us that one power rather than another will exploit this or that colony, win this or that foreign market, subject to its rule this or that weak State. The point, however, is this, that Germany is striving not only for the restoration of the rights trampled underfoot by the Versailles treaty, not only for the restoration of its pre-war boundaries, but is building its foreign policy on unlimited aggression, even going so far as to talk of subjecting to the so-called German race all other races and peoples. It is conducting an open, rabid, anti-Soviet policy, suspiciously recalling those times when the Teutonic Order held sway in the Baltic countries, and publicly abandons itself to dreams of conquering the Ukraine and even the Urals.

Concluding his report to Berlin on the speech, Schulenburg observed that Litvinov had refrained from bellicosity and had tried to "leave open all possibilities. The attempt to arrive at an objective attitude toward the policy of the Third Reich is striking." [43]

Two months later, on August 22, Litvinov told the German Ambassador that should Germany attack the Czechs France would mobilize and Britain would have to stand by France, whether Chamberlain wanted to or not. The U.S.S.R. would do her best to fulfill the promise of support to Prague. When Schulenburg expressed doubt that the great powers would start a major war over Czechoslovakia, the Foreign Commissar replied that it was mainly a question of power politics. While the Soviet Government was not responsible for the creation and composition of Czechoslovakia, it feared the growing power of a violent and aggressive National Socialist Germany. If "the old democratic Germany had still existed," he added, "the Czechoslovak question would have assumed quite a different aspect for the Soviet Union. The Soviets had always been in favor of the right of self-determination of peoples." [44]

On the same day the German Ambassador's private secretary informed the third secretary of the British Embassy of the conversation. He stated that the members of his mission interpreted Litvinov's remark as clear evidence that Moscow was not unalterably opposed to any German-Soviet *rapprochement.* Such a development was out of the question, however, in view of Hitler's attitude. In fact, Schulenburg had not yet informed Berlin of this particular remark for fear of enraging the Führer.[45]

Schulenburg was probably correct on June 23 in suspecting that the Prague report of a pending German approach to Moscow was "not unwelcome to M. Litvinov; it gave him the opportunity once more to hold up before the French ally the specter of a German-Soviet understanding." The Foreign Commissar's remark of August 22, however, may possibly have been a very cautious attempt to sound out the Germans regarding a *rapprochement.* If such were the case, his statement that France, Britain, and the Soviet Union would stand by Czechoslovakia was intended to increase the attractiveness of an understanding. On August 27 Litvinov again expressed to Schulenburg his conviction that France would come to the aid of the Czechs. He also remarked that Rumania feared she would be next on the German list once Czechoslovakia were out of the way. In a letter to Berlin written two days after the conversation of August 27, Schulenburg observed that the Foreign Commissar was trying to create the groundless impression that Rumania might after all agree to the passage of troops. "But, of course, M. Litvinov likes to give others false impressions as much as he can." [46]

In the summer and fall of 1938 such tactics, if they were indeed consciously employed, were useless. Hitler had no reason for seeking an agreement with the U.S.S.R. since that country obviously posed no threat to Germany. After the interview of August 22, the German Ambassador reported that he had repeatedly tried to get Litvinov to say how the Soviet Union would aid Czechoslovakia. The Foreign Commissar had "avoided answering this question again and again. It would seem to be the 'mot d'ordre' here not to commit oneself on this point." The Soviet chargé in Rome was also evidently forced to admit on August 28 that his government could provide assistance only by air; Italian Foreign Minister Ciano noted that the chargé had "intimated" "in veiled terms" that there would be no all-out Soviet effort.[47]

Sometime during June or July a general German strategic directive for Operation Green (an attack on Czechoslovakia) was drafted. According to the draft, Soviet intervention, if it occurred, was expected to begin with "mere reinforcement of the Czech Air Force and armaments." The possibilities of direct air and naval operations against Germany and possibly an attack through the Baltic states were to be considered, however. This was the only reference to the Soviet Union in four printed pages. Hitler conferred with Generals Brauchitsch and Keitel on September 3 at the Berghof. According to the notes made by the Führer's adjutant, most of the conference was devoted to the actual invasion of Czechoslovakia. At the close Hitler ordered further development of the fortifications in the west; there was no mention of the possibility of Soviet action or of defensive measures against the U.S.S.R. Six days later at Nuremberg, Hitler,

Brauchitsch, Halder, Keitel and several others discussed details of the plans for the attack. The conference lasted from 10:00 P.M., September 9, until 3:30 the next morning. According to the adjutant's notes, no mention was made of the Soviet Union on this occasion either.[48]

In a letter to Berlin ten days after the signing of the Munich agreement, Tippelskirch pointed out two significant features of Soviet conduct during the crisis: [49]

How little confidence the rulers placed in the reliability of the population during the Czechoslovak crisis can be seen from the fact that the newspapers printed the most important events in comparatively small and unobtrusive type, mainly under the heading "Latest News," and without further comment. . . . the Soviet Union also neglected to take such preliminary measures for mobilization as was considered necessary, for instance, in Holland, Belgium, and Switzerland.

THE PUBLISHED British and German documents covering the months preceding Munich fill three fat volumes, and a number of memoirs have also appeared. But in 1958, twenty years after the event, the Soviet Foreign Ministry, using its own files and those of the Foreign Ministry in Prague, was able to assemble only a thin paperback volume.[50] And even this contained a number of previously published documents.

Soviet policy during the months preceding Munich was clearly to encourage French and British resistance to Hitler. Although no evidence indicates that Stalin ever thought of engaging the U.S.S.R. in such resistance, Moscow carefully maintained the ostensible purity of its position. Even in the small Soviet collection, several documents reflect this effort to avoid any appearance of responsibility for the Czech surrender.[51] But in the Soviet collection itself, assurances of aid to France and Czechoslovakia give the impression of evasiveness and insincerity. It would have been much more convincing had Litvinov frankly admitted that his government could furnish no direct and effective aid to Czechoslovakia without driving Poland and Rumania into the arms of Germany. Nevertheless, he might have added, significant forces could be sent to France without dangerously weakening the Red Army at home and inviting a German attack through Poland. Potemkin, then the ambassador to France, stressed this possibility in a discussion with Premier Blum on February 17, 1937.[52] But in 1938 this type of assistance was evidently never mentioned.

If the Soviet Government never intended to support France and Czechoslovakia in 1938, then distrust of the West instilled at this time can hardly have led to Stalin's pact with Hitler a year later. Nevertheless one consequence—and the basic cause—of the Munich agreement should be noted: From time to time within all societies, a psycopath will embark on a brief career of robbery and wanton murder. He may even kill a well-armed but unsuspecting policeman who halts him for a traffic violation. The killer is soon hunted down, but only after he has clearly demonstrated his true nature. The price of hunting down a criminal within a society is negligible, but in 1938 the price in lives and property of exterminating a mad dog who controlled a modern, well-armed state was astronomical and could only be paid, by democracies at least, when the mad dog was generally recognized as such. In 1938 the average citizen of France and Britain was dreadfully aware of the price. Some of the leaders, e.g. Daladier, had themselves fought in the trenches twenty years earlier.

In addition it was realized that the first World War had been, in a sense, an accident. In 1914, almost a century after the last general European war, responsible statesmen had not realized the consequences of their acts. Chamberlain and Daladier, Halifax and Bonnet were determined not to let this happen again. It is not too much to say that the British and French leaders did indeed avoid war in 1938 and even in 1939—World War I. Lord Halifax clearly revealed these attitudes in a conversation with the French Ambassador in London on September 9, 1938: [53]

At one point in our conversation [wrote the Foreign Secretary] M. Corbin said that if it was only a question of Czechoslovakia, it might be possible to judge the issue differently. The French Government, however, felt that if this contemplated aggression were allowed to pass unresisted, their turn would come next. I said that this really was an argument in favour of a certain war now, against the possibility of war, perhaps in more unfavourable conditions, later. With that argument I had never been able to feel any sympathy: nor did I think that the conclusion of it could be justified.

"What could France have done?" asked Bonnet as the title of the next to last chapter of his volume covering Munich. He was of course seeking to justify his own policies, but even if one joins in the favorite sport of diplomatic historians for over twenty years, beating a discredited foreign minister, the question still remains. It has been argued, and was argued at the time, that Hitler was bluffing. Indeed, had Britain and France maintained a firm attitude from the summer of 1938 or earlier it is quite possible that Hitler would never have allowed the crisis to develop. By September, however, his prestige was too deeply committed for him to back down. It has also been argued that had the Western powers not surrendered at Munich the German generals would have overthrown Hitler. Since they were unable to bring themselves to make the effort until July 1944, when Germany faced certain and utter defeat, and then botched the attempt, this argument commands little consideration. Had Britain and France supported Czechoslovakia in the fall of 1938, World War II would simply have started a year earlier.

But would the outcome have been the same? An all-out French attack in the fall of 1938 might conceivably have broken through the German defenses and ended the war before Hitler could raise and train the additional divisions needed to defeat France in 1940. Germany did have air superiority, however, and a comparatively narrow front to defend in the west. A determined French offensive could hardly have done more than attract from a Czechoslovak front the German divisions needed to hold in the west and thus enabled the Czechs to keep fighting until, perhaps, the summer of 1939.

It is not too much to say that the fate of the First Czechoslovak Republic was sealed at Verdun and Passchendaele. But that of the second was indeed sealed at Munich. In abandoning Czechoslovakia to Hitler in 1938, the French and British leaders also abandoned her to the U.S.S.R. ten years later. In February 1948, using the covert threat of Soviet support, Stalin's Czech puppets seized power in an unopposed *coup d'état*. Unlike Hitler in 1938, Stalin *was* bluffing in February 1948 as Tito demonstrated a few months later. But after Munich and six years of German occupation, too many Czechs had decided they could expect no support from the West and should join the Communist Party or otherwise come to the best terms possible with their most powerful neighbor. Not a very heroic decision perhaps and certainly a mistake, but hardly to be condemned by those who cheered Chamberlain or Daladier on the morrow of Munich—or preached isolation in the United States while Britain stood alone against Nazi Germany.

6

Stalin's Desperate Diplomacy

October 1938—March 31, 1939

After Munich Soviet propagandists declaimed, if possible, even more vehemently than before the agreement. But their only new theme was the disavowal of any responsibility. A TASS release of October 2 denied a United Press report that Moscow had authorized Daladier to represent it at Munich: The Soviet Government "had and has no connexion whatever with the Munich conference and its decisions. The said United Press report is a stupid fabrication from beginning to end." The Soviet ambassadors to London and Paris had received no information regarding the Munich negotiations which had not appeared in the press, declared TASS two days later. No conversations were held nor agreements made with the Soviet Government on the fate of Czechoslovakia and concessions to the aggressor. France and Britain merely informed Moscow of *faits accomplis*, and "the Soviet Government had and has nothing whatever to do with the Munich conference and its decisions." [1]

On the same day, October 4, *Pravda* stated that the great acclaim which greeted the Munich Agreement in the West was beginning to die down and people were beginning to realize an outrage had been committed. It disclaimed any Soviet responsibility for the event; Moscow alone had remained faithful to its engagements: [2]

The Soviet Government declares before the whole world that it was opposed to the aggressive intention of the fascist invaders towards the Czechoslovak Republic. . . .

99

The U.S.S.R. was the only ally which remained faithful to Czechoslovakia. . . . The Government of the Socialist State is the only one whose policy consists in a continual struggle for peace and for the independence and liberty of peoples against the aggressors and fascist invaders.

In a speech on November 6, 1938, Molotov cited the recent "repulse" of the Japanese at Changkufeng on the Manchurian-Siberian border as a warning to other aggressive powers. He roundly condemned the Munich Agreement, warned that it had merely whetted the appetites of the aggressors, and rejected any Soviet responsibility: [3]

While the French Government renounced its treaty with Czechoslovakia at the moment of the decisive test and came to an arrangement with England and German fascism, whatever the cost to democratic Czechoslovakia, the Soviet Union showed that its attitude to international treaties is utterly different. It demonstrated to the entire world that its fidelity to the treaties it has concluded for fighting the aggressor is unshakeable. Notwithstanding all the attempts, even the most scoundrelly, to portray the Soviet attitude to the Czechoslovak question as vacillating and indecisive, none, not even the most skilful, succeeded.

Hitler had completely bluffed France and Britain, declared Litvinov during an October 1 luncheon conversation with Bonnet at the Soviet Embassy in Paris. Had the two countries stood firm, together with Russia they would have made Hitler back down. In relating the conversation to British Ambassador Phipps, Bonnet "smiled when he referred to the probable extent of Soviet help had war broken out, and also at Russia's extreme valour from a safe and respectable distance from the scene of hostilities." [4]

One of the bitterest Communist attacks on the Governments of France and Britain for their part in the Munich Agreement was contained in the lead article of the *Communist International* for October 1938: [5]

German fascism had reached a deadlock. Its blackmailing sabre-rattling was doomed to collapse as soon as it was faced with a peace front including all great democratic powers. Nothing could have been easier than to establish such a peace front and force the fascist warmongers to their knees. But it was precisely such a capitulation of the Hitler government which the British and French reactionaries wanted to prevent at all costs. To them Hitler is the gendarme *protecting them from the democratic struggle of the peoples for liberty, from the working class and from the Soviet Union* [italics in original]. They would much rather sacrifice the interests of all nations than do without their policemen.

An editorial in *Izvestia* for October 24 claimed that Chamberlain had surrendered because he knew successful resistance was possible only with the help of the Soviet Union: [6]

> European reaction was perfectly aware that the victory of democracy over fascism, of the peace forces over the war forces is impossible without participation of the U.S.S.R., that bastion of peace and democracy. This is why Chamberlain was afraid of victory and beat a retreat before fascist Germany, which also feared the defeat which was menacing it.
> No informed politician could have any doubt of the power of the Soviet Union . . . Governments knew also that the U.S.S.R. will meet its obligations in Europe. That the leaders of British and French policy capitulated none the less is not due to self-deception, but to their preference for capitulation rather than victory. . . .
> The peoples will not forget the lessons of Munich. . . . Above shaken Europe stands the unscalable rampart of *the land of Socialism,* the only State which has come out of the recent European crisis with enhanced prestige.

British policy was to reduce France to the role of "junior partner," a second-class state, while Britain took the lead in reaching an agreement with Germany, declared *Pravda* in an article of November 21, 1938. The article also hinted that the British Government would be quite willing to appease Germany with French colonies and, in general, to let France make the greatest sacrifices to maintain Britain's world position. The writer concluded with the warning that "the London reactionaries will try energetically to take in hand the Government of the French Ship of State, steering it resolutely to the right not only in foreign policy, but also in internal policy and internal relationships." [7]

The lead editorial in the February issue of the *Communist International* condemned Chamberlain (and Daladier) as a conscious accomplice rather than a dupe of Hitler and Mussolini. Bourgeois leaders were not to be trusted, and new Munichs could be prevented only by vigorous and united action of the masses:

> The working class must realize from experience that large sections of the bourgeoisie in all countries are in league with the fascist aggressors, that they are prepared at any time to adopt a policy of open

treachery . . . in order to defeat and suppress the forces of their own peoples . . . the working class must realize that in no circumstances must they rely upon bourgeois or petty-bourgeois politicians, that these . . . even if not traitors, will, in the decisive hour, prefer surrender to struggle, that they remain firm only to the degree in which they are subject to the direct pressure of the working class and the masses of the people.

An article in the March issue severely criticized the British Labour Patry for not opposing Chamberlain, for adopting the thesis that he was being "hoodwinked" by Hitler. In reality he was following the policy of the City which was supporting fascism as a gendarme against socialism and freedom and desired to set up a fascist government in Britain. The leadership of the Labour Party "sabotages in every possible way the creation of a determined opposition against Chamberlain." [8]

Maisky called on the Foreign Secretary on October 11 and protested a speech by a minor cabinet member who had stated that Russia had offered no real help in the Czech crisis, but, because of military weakness, had given only vague promises. Three days later *Pravda* reported the protest and proclaimed the speech "a complete distortion of the Soviet Government's attitude. Its position was clear and precise, and left no room for doubt." Before he left Halifax, the Soviet Ambassador pointed out that the Balkans and Turkey would fall under the political and economic yoke of Germany and this would be more dangerous to Britain than to Russia. "He was at a loss to understand why we failed so completely to appreciate the necessity of checking these methods of aggression before it was too late." [9]

"The Munich agreement has sold out the most important strategic positions of Great Britain and France," declared the *Journal de Moscou*, the organ of the Narkomindel, in an October 1938 editorial. The agreement had not "saved" Czechoslovakia, and the writer cited Belgium and Serbia in the first World War as countries which had survived even though occupied. He condemned new guarantees to the republic as hypocritical and asked how Britain and France could defend it in the future when they were unwilling to support the country while it still had an effective army, industry, fortifications, "and most precious of all, the collaboration of the U.S.S.R., how can they defend her, disarmed?"

Germany would not have dared start a war, continued the article, but Britain and France were themselves isolated as a result of Munich. Will "the powers who still have their independence make a supreme effort for collective action? And will they be able to meet before Hitler forbids international meetings?" [10]

A lead article in the November 15 issue of the journal warned of a pending concrete military alliance among the anti-Comintern powers which would be directed primarily against England. At a farewell luncheon for departing British Ambassador Lord Chilston on November 17, Litvinov claimed "sure knowledge" that this was really the case. Discussing the agitation over the Ukraine in the German press, a December 27 editorial in the *Journal de Moscou* maintained Germany would be very foolish to abandon her moves against the Western powers, which had been so successful in the past, and embark on a campaign against the Soviet Union where she was sure to meet determined and succcessful opposition. The true aim of the press agitation was to distract the attention of public opinion in Britain and France from the danger of German westward aggression.[11]

The *Communist International* for January 1939 claimed that Munich had been proven a dismal failure and that the British and French people were becoming more and more disillusioned. The British Government were prepared to appease the aggressors with other people's colonies, even France's, warned another article in the same issue. A third writer pointed out that France was still the chief enemy in German school texts and in the youth press. Another editorial held German conquest of southeastern Europe an essential preliminary step in gaining strength to "finally and completely crowd France out of the European sphere of influence." [12]

THE RATHER FRANTIC TONE of Soviet propaganda after Munich undoubtedly reflected very real and quite understandable concern on the part of Stalin. In concluding the agreement, Britain and France seemed to have tacitly approved any expansion Hitler might care to undertake toward the east, and the international position of the Soviet Union appeared more serious than it had for seventeen years. Stalin can have had little hope of Anglo-French action to halt aggression which did not directly menace British or French interests or territories. But Germany could organize a serious campaign against the U.S.S.R. only from Polish territory. The Baltic states formed a narrow corridor, unsuitable for the deployment of large armies; Rumania alone was too distant and was separated from Germany by Hungary. Poland, on the other hand, directly linked Germany and Russia, and from her eastern frontier German armies could launch a determined attack along the traditional invasion road to Moscow. And Polish-German relations had been very close indeed during the Munich crisis.

Beck's actions had in fact strained Poland's ties with her French ally almost to the breaking point. At the height of the crisis Polish Ambassador Lukasiewicz, unwilling to appear personally at the Quai d'Orsay because of a previous exchange of words with Bonnet, requested Bullitt to transmit a message. As late as March 18, 1939 Léger was convinced that Poland would eventually be a German satellite: [13]

He strongly suspected that M. Beck had betrayed Roumania or was in the process of doing so, with the idea of deflecting Germany to the South East. M. Beck was entirely cynical and false. . . . the plan of the Polish Minister for Foreign Affairs was to ask His Majesty's Government to make an alliance with Poland . . . He knew that His Majesty's Government could not undertake a definite commitment of the sort . . . He would then return to Poland and report his request and its rejection . . . , say there had been two alternatives for Poland, viz. to lean on Great Britain or Germany, and that now it was clear that she must lean on Germany. . . . his was a hand-to-mouth policy . . . he only wanted to get off the difficulties of the moment even at the cost of being the vassal (perhaps the chief vassal) of the new Napoleon.

Beck seems to have really desired to form a bloc with Hungary and Rumania opposed to German as well as Russian expansion in Eastern Europe.[14] At any rate, the abject course envisaged by Léger was politically impossible for a *Polish* Foreign Minister. Public opinion would have forced his resignation. Aside from this any combination with Germany would have been ultimately disastrous. A prompt German victory would have left Poland a satellite of Germany; a German defeat would have left her under

Soviet sway. Most of the fighting in any indecisive campaign which had neither of these results would have been on Polish territory.

But Hitler and certain of his followers had long toyed with the idea of a German-Polish combination directed at Russia. As early as November 15, 1933, months after assuming power in Germany, Hitler had told Polish Ambassador Lipski that he desired good relations with Poland, that any war would only result in the communization of Europe, and that Poland was "an outpost against Asia." On January 22, 1935 he expounded to Lipski on the military danger which both Germany and Poland faced in the east and rejected as mistaken the policy of previous German governments and military leaders who desired a German-Soviet combination at the expense of Poland. Such "a policy, even if it resulted in territorial gains at Poland's expense, would lead to an intensification of the greatest danger of all to Germany, i.e., from the Soviets." In a conversation with Lipski on May 22, 1935 he restated his thesis and again condemned the policy of Reichswehr Generals Gröner and Schleicher, who "considered a militarily powerful Soviet Union a threat only to Poland, but not to Germany. This was a shortsighted policy." A *"rapprochement"* with Poland was more advantageous to Germany than uneasy relations with Russia. Russia is Asia" he added. On December 18 of the same year Lipski was told that Hitler favored European solidarity but considered it as ending at the Polish-Soviet frontier. "How could there be any association with Soviet Russia, which proclaimed world revolution?" When Beck visited Berlin in January 1938, the Führer told him his negative attitude toward communism was immovable and he saw no sign of Soviet communism evolving into nationalism. During a visit to Italy in the spring of 1938, Hitler remarked to the Polish Ambassador to Rome that he would like to extend the Polish-German nonaggression agreement of 1934 beyond its ten-year term. The danger of a war from which only communism would profit outweighed the large number of Germans still outside the Reich.[15]

Among Hitler's chief lieutenants, Göring supported most actively the idea of a German-Polish alliance. During a visit to Poland at the beginning of 1935 he repeated to Beck and Deputy

Foreign Minister Szembek Hitler's assurances of the complete change of policy toward Poland since the Weimar Republic and the Reichswehr:

A strong Poland was needed by Germany, to form a common barrier against Russia. . . . when powers were being transferred to Chancellor Hitler by General Schleicher at the beginning of 1933, the latter explained to Hitler what should be the main lines of Germany's policy in relation to Poland. His idea was to come to an understanding with France and Russia and, with the latter's help, to proceed to the elimination of Poland. . . . Hitler . . . did not utter one word during this exposition. Only after he had left General Schleicher did he say to M. Goering: 'Und ich werde das gegenteil machen.' [And I will do the opposite.]

Further discussing Polish-German relations, M. Goering pointed out that Poland formed a link between the Baltic and Black Sea, and that great opportunities were open to her on the Ukrainian side.

During the same visit Göring was especially frank when talking to Polish generals. He suggested extensive plans, hinting very strongly at a joint attack on Russia. Germany would take northwestern Russia and Poland the Ukraine. He even repeated these hints in a conversation with Marshal Pilsudski but received little encouragement.[16]

Göring spoke of the Soviet threat to both Poland and Germany in a conversation with Szembek in Berlin on August 12, 1936. He emphasized the common interests of Poland and Germany vis-a-vis Russia in a conversation with Marshal Smigly-Rydz, the head of the Polish Army, in Warsaw six months later (February 1937); it was necessary to align the policies of the two countries, he concluded. "On this assumption it would be desirable to determine how far a policy of collaboration could be worked out. . . . it would be desirable to influence the public opinion of both countries." In November of 1937 Göring made remarks of the same nature to Szembek when the latter visited Berlin.[17]

He emphasized the weakness of the Red Army when talking to Smigly-Rydz in Warsaw in February 1938, but felt it would [not?] be difficult to defeat. He also gave the Polish marshal evidence of Hitler's repugnance toward the Soviet Government: The Führer had received Moscow's latest ambassador, when the latter presented his credentials, at Berchtesgaden, so that a German honor guard would not have to present arms to a Soviet representative.[18] On August 10, 1938, Göring and Lipski had an informal conversation at a reception in Berlin: [19]

Goering said that he would like in the very near future to have a longer talk with me and to discuss—of course, confidentially and unofficially, as usual—the possibility of closer Polish-German contact on certain matters. . . . mutual cessation of espionage . . . and, further, a certain exchange of information on the Russian and Czech problems.

In reference to the Russian problem, he said in a general way that it would acquire actuality after the settlement of the Czech question. He reverted to his idea that in the event of a Soviet-Polish conflict Germany could not remain neutral and refrain from rendering assistance to Poland. He denied the rumour that Germany wanted to march against the Ukraine, and emphasized that the Reich's interest was concentrated primarily on putting an end to Bolshevik activities. On the other hand, Poland, in his opinion, might have certain direct interests in Russia, for example, in the Ukraine.

As we have seen in Chapter 2, as early as 1933 Moscow appeared worried over the possibility of a German-Polish combination. Beck was well received during his visit to Moscow in February 1934, but an article in the *Communist International* of July 1934 repeated the claim that certain circles in both Germany and Poland were plotting a joint attack on the U.S.S.R. The writer declared that "some influential circles of the Polish bourgeoisie, including those near to Pilsudski," were seeking "a common language with Germany on the basis of an anti-Soviet policy." These circles were speculating on "the chances of an attack on the U.S.S.R. by Japanese imperialism." The Nazis in Germany encouraged these ideas "because they know that the first stage of German-Polish military collaboration will under any circumstances be the occupation of Poland by the German Army." [20]

The lead editorial of the *Communist International* for April 20, 1935 flatly rejected any doubt of Germany, Japan, and Poland being "completely in unison in respect to a joint aggressive policy, which is supported by close military and technical cooperation." The writer went on to predict an early seizure of the Memel district from Lithuania. The Third Reich, "working hand in glove with Poland, will consolidate its positions in the Baltic countries." Under these circumstances the task of the Communist parties, "especially in Great Britain, Germany, Japan and Poland is to transform the ardent longing of the masses . . . for peace into a mass movement, into a gigantic force with which the warmongers . . . will have to reckon." The June 5 issue of the journal reprinted a talk given to a number of Communist Party propagandists from various Moscow factories. The speaker declared that Germany hoped to regain all she had lost to Poland at the end of World War I. But for the time being Berlin sought to lull Poland with disavowals of territorial aspirations and promises of territory in the Soviet Ukraine.[21]

In a report to the Central Executive Committee on January 10, 1936, Molotov also harped on the subject:

Reports recently appeared of the conclusion of a military agreement between Japan and Germany, and of Poland's complicity in this matter. . . .

The fascist rulers of Germany sometimes endeavour to divert the attention of simple people from their plans of conquest with regard to the Soviet Union by referring to the absence of common frontiers between Germany and the U.S.S.R. But we know, on the other hand, that Germany . . . is feverishly preparing to occupy a dominant position in the Baltic and has established special relations with Poland, which has fairly extensive common frontiers with the Soviet Union.

Stalin himself had something to say on the topic. In an interview on March 5, 1936, American journalist Roy Howard cited Warsaw statements regarding Poland's "unwillingness to permit any foreign troops to use its territory . . . against a third nation," and asked how Germany could attack the U.S.S.R. Stalin replied that when an aggressor needed territory for a base it could usually find it. He mentioned the case of Belgium in 1914 and the German offensive from Latvia toward Leningrad in 1918. "I do not know what specific frontiers Germany could use for her purposes, but I think that those willing to 'lend' her a frontier can be found."[22]

The occupation of the Rhineland, two days after Stalin's interview, allowed Germany to fortify her western frontiers. In a future war the Wehrmacht would no longer have to seize or defend unprotected territory west of the Rhine and could use more troops in an offensive toward the east. The tone of the Comintern journal became even more bitter:

The policy of Beck will inevitably lead to the enslavement of Poland by German imperialism. . . . Today Hitler Germany has an army twice as big as Poland has, while the equipment of this army and its potential . . . power is fifty times that of its Polish partner. The fact that an organization of German Storm Troopers was recently discovered in Upper Silesia showed that the German fascists intend at the first convenient opportunity to unite by force the province of Upper Silesia to the German Empire. . . .

The occupation of the demilitarized zone of the Rhineland by Hitler is a menace not only to the security of France and Belgium, but of Poland as well. . . . By sweeping its troops into the Rhineland and erecting fortifications there, German fascism isolates Poland from France.

In the October 1936 issue of the *Communist International* the same author warned of the danger of a German seizure of Danzig and Upper Silesia. Claiming that it represented the views of many important Polish conservatives, the writer went on to cite an article in a Polish journal which pointed out the foolishness of a war between two overpopulated countries like Poland and Germany and urged colonization of lands seized from Russia.[23]

Moscow may never have been seriously alarmed about a Polish-German alliance and may have regarded it only as a potential danger. Bullitt, while ambassador to the U.S.S.R., tended to discount the Soviet disquiet: "All Litvinov's propaganda trumpetings to the contrary, the Soviet Government knows very well that Germany can not be in a position to make war on the Soviet Union for many years. Every feasible route for German attack leads across Polish territory and the whole basis of Polish policy is never to permit the foot of either a German or a Russian soldier to be placed on her soil." [24] True enough, but why the "propaganda trumpetings"? The Kremlin may have merely desired some insurance. If Communist propaganda abroad had seriously embarrassed Poland during the war with Soviet Russia in 1920, it might well do so again.

In any event, 1936 marked the high point of the apparent Soviet anxiety. After the end of that year only scattered minor references to the subject appeared in the Communist press. Of course Japan's preoccupation with China after 1937 greatly reduced if it did not completely eliminate the danger to the U.S.S.R. of a two-front war. But we have a more direct explanation for the comparative quiet of Communist spokesmen on the subject of Poland after 1936: Soviet intelligence penetrated the German Embassy in Warsaw the following year. From 1937 until shortly before the outbreak of the war in 1939, a counselor of the embassy, Rudolf von Scheliha, was in the pay of a Soviet intelligence agency.[25]

But despite the inside information from the German Embassy after 1936, Stalin could not be absolutely sure no agreement existed or was pending. There were far too many fingers in the German foreign-policy pie. Before his appointment as Foreign Minister, Ribbentrop had maintained his own semiofficial foreign office which still existed. One of the most important advocates of the Polish alliance, Göring, had nothing at all to do with the Auswärtiges Amt. It was quite possible for a Polish-German agreement to be arranged without the knowledge of the Warsaw Embassy, and Polish actions at the time of Munich tended to support the view that some sort of an alliance existed.

The first direct diplomatic move by the Soviet Government following Munich was an effort to ease tension in relations with Poland and Germany. By the summer of 1938 the tone of the German press when referring to Stalin and the Soviet press when mentioning Hitler had created an intolerable atmosphere. Both parties agreed to moderate press references to the opposite leader, and in October 1938 Litvinov and Schulenburg reached an oral agreement extending this moderation of press and radio to remarks about the countries themselves.[26]

At about the same time the Narkomindel evidently made friendly overtures to Warsaw. On October 18 Beck ordered that Polish Ambassador Grzybowski in the U.S.S.R. should "continue to maintain the atmosphere of *détente* initiated by Potemkin." A joint Polish-Soviet communiqué released on November 26 stated that as a result of conversations between Litvinov and Grzybowski relations between the two countries would continue to be based on previous agreements, including the nonaggression treaty of 1932, which was not to expire until 1945. Both governments were in favor of trade expansion and "liquidating the frontier incidents which have recently occurred." [27]

Beck later told the British Ambassador to Warsaw that the

Polish Government had complained in Moscow after the military demonstrations on the frontier during the Czech crisis and an increase in the number of frontier incidents. Litvinov had suggested the joint communiqué and the Poles had agreed. Domestic economic conditions in Poland may also have played a part. Several factories in the Teschen district had previously exported a large part of their product to Russia. During conversations conducted between December 16 and 19, Foreign Trade Commissar Mikoyan and an official of the Polish Ministry for Industry and Trade agreed that commerce between the two states could reach a volume of 140 to 160 million zlotys per annum. They also agreed to start negotiations the following month for a trade treaty and agreements covering the volume of imports and exports for 1939 and the clearing of balances.[28] One of the most acute evaluations by a contemporary observer was that of German Ambassador Schulenburg: [29]

Prior to the meeting at Munich, the Soviet press launched heavy attacks against Poland almost daily, representing her as Germany's satellite. After Munich these press attacks became milder and less frequent, and about 2 weeks ago they ceased altogether. . . . The Soviet Union feels isolated since Munich. . . . that her mutual assistance pact with France has lost its value . . . By flirting with Poland the Soviet Union hopes to drive a wedge into German-Polish relations. The Soviet press has been trying to give an anti-German angle to the latest negotiations with Poland and to build up their significance in every possible way.[30] By normalizing her relations with Poland the Soviet Union hopes to be able to break Poland loose from the front of the aggressor states, which she imagines to exist. By revitalizing the pact relating to nonaggression and nonparticipation in hostile coalitions, the Soviet Union is seeking insurance against Poland's accession to the Anti-Comintern Pact. The fear of such a development—of a joint German-Polish action against the Soviet Union—has undoubtedly existed here. The Soviet Union believes that by improving her relations with Poland she has countered that threat and has pushed back any future German offensive in the East from the Polish-Soviet to the German-Polish frontier.

AFTER MUNICH few diplomatic cards remained in the Kremlin hand, but Stalin and Litvinov might still raise the bogy of a German-Soviet *rapprochement*, a second Rapallo, and with this threat secure support from Britain and France. As early as September 30 a high official of the Narkomindel remarked to a foreign diplomat, "We have failed to support ourselves on a rotten plank. We will go elsewhere." But the campaign had probably not yet been planned in detail on October 4 when the Deputy Foreign Commissar told French Ambassador Coulondre that France and Britain had deliberately kept the Soviet Government out of the Munich negotiations and left the U.S.S.R. no choice except a fourth partition of Poland. Although Potemkin did not bluntly say so, he was of course implying that his government had already received proposals from Germany for an agreement and a subsequent attack on Poland. At about the same time (early October) Potemkin made a similar remark to Italian Ambassador Rosso.[31]

On October 16 Litvinov repeated to Coulondre the prediction Maisky had made to the U.S. chargé in London two months earlier: Once France was neutralized and Germany supreme on the continent, Hitler had two choices: an attack on Britain or the Soviet Union. He would choose Britain as her defeat would make it possible to replace the British Empire with a German Empire. To accomplish this he would be willing to come to an understanding with the U.S.S.R. The Soviet Union had only to stand fast. Should the Western powers decide to oppose Hitler they would have to turn to Russia. Coulondre concluded his report on the conversation with a warning that tentative Soviet approaches to Berlin could be expected.[32]

Also during October, rumors of the pending resignation of Litvinov circulated in Moscow. They probably arose spontaneously but may have been nourished by judicious hints from Soviet sources. They served to emphasize the possibility of a change in Soviet policy. Since Litvinov had been the great champion of collective security in the League of Nations and elsewhere, his removal would indicate that Russia was turning toward a policy of isolation or even *rapprochement* with Germany. At the end of November the Central European correspondent of the Chicago *Daily News* was convinced that Hitler had offered a nonaggression pact to Stalin but that the latter had not yet given his answer. A week or so later the Bulgarian Prime Minister warned the French Minister in Sofia of the possibility of a Soviet-German understanding and subsequent partition of Poland. This had long been a dream of certain German General Staff officers, he reminded his listener. The new Czechoslovak Foreign Minister, Chvalkovsky, in a conversation with the U.S. Minister in Prague on December 29, 1938, also expressed concern over the possibility of German-Soviet cooperation.[33]

During discussions with Lispki at Berchtesgaden on October 24, Ribbentrop brought up the question of the restoration of Danzig to Germany and a German extraterritorial autobahn and railway across the Corridor. The ambassador carried the proposition to Warsaw and returned with Beck's reply on November 19. Although not absolutely ruling out German annexation of Danzig, the Polish Foreign Minister feared the domestic repercussions of such a step. He was less unfavorably inclined toward the idea of a corridor across the Corridor.[34]

At the beginning of January 1939, Beck accepted an invitation from Ribbentrop and visited Germany personally. At Berchtesgaden on January 5, Hitler dwelt on the desirability of settling the problem of Danzig. He also restated his familiar thesis: the Polish-German community of interest vis-a-vis Russia, whether tsarist or Communist, was complete; Germany needed a strong Poland; and "every Polish division engaged against Russia was a corresponding saving of a German division." He assured Beck that his interest in the Ukraine was merely economic, i.e. Poland was welcome to Ukrainian territory. The next day at Munich the two foreign ministers again discussed Danzig and the trans-Corridor rail and highway, and Beck again emphasized the strength of Polish public opinion.[35]

Beck returned home thoroughly alarmed. At Berchtesgaden he first realized a break was inevitable. During earlier conversations Hitler had always said, "ich möchte" (I wish). This time he said, "es muss sein" (it must be). From his listener's expression the Führer realized his mistake and tried, without avail, to change the impression he had given. In a conversation with U.S. Ambassador Biddle on January 10, "Beck emphasized Poland and France must meet at an early date to clarify their joint and respective positions vis-a-vis Germany. They were now both in the same boat and must face realities." [36]

But on the surface nothing indicated that the close relations between Poland and Germany were not closer than they had ever been. In fact, January 1939 probably marked the high point of the German effort to seek an alliance with Poland against Russia. Referring to German propaganda directed toward the Ukraine, Ribbentrop regretted the effect it also had in the Polish Ukraine:

In my [Ribbentrop's] opinion, however, this could be changed only if Poland and we would work together in every respect in the Ukrainian question. . . . in the course of a general, generous settlement of all problems between Poland and us we might very well be moved to regard the Ukrainian question as covered by a special Polish prerogative and to support Poland in every way . . . On the other hand, of course, this presupposed a more and more pronounced anti-Russian attitude on the part of Poland . . .

In this connection I asked Beck whether he did not want to accede to the Anti-Comintern Pact some day.

Beck explained that this was not possible at the present time . . . Poland would do everything to cooperate with us against the Comintern in police matters, but if she entered into a political treaty with Germany to this end, then she would not be able to maintain the peaceful neighborly relations with Russia which were necessary to her security. Nevertheless Beck held out the prospect that Poland's policy might be capable of future development in the direction desired by us.

I asked Beck whether they had given up Marshal Pilsudski's aspirations in this direction, that is, toward the Ukraine; he answered me laughingly that they had even been in Kiev, and that these aspirations were doubtless still alive today.

The Polish Foreign Minister agreed to consider all aspects of a possible German-Polish treaty. An exchange of views through the respective ambassadors during the following weeks was to be followed by a visit to Warsaw by Ribbentrop before the end of the winter. Ribbentrop seemed as hopeful as ever of securing the alliance with Poland and settling the problem of Danzig and the Corridor. Not until the conclusion of the visit to Poland, late in January, did he begin to realize that his hopes were unjustified.[37]

Any news of these exchanges which the Russians may have received from their agent in the Warsaw Embassy must have been quite alarming. Stalin and Litvinov apparently decided the rumors and hints of a German-Soviet combination were not being taken seriously enough in the West. Something concrete was needed—the visit of a German delegation to Moscow.

In negotiations with the Soviet trade delegation in Berlin early in 1938, German economic authorities had proposed that the U.S.S.R. liquidate in 1938 and 1939 by exports to Germany a debt of 183 million Reichsmarks which fell due during 1940–43. In return Germany would grant a fresh credit of 200 million Reichsmarks. The Russians were unwilling to pay the debt before maturity, however, and the Germans could secure only a new clearing agreement (of March 1, 1938) valid until the end of the year.[38] By November Germany's foreign-trade and raw-material situation was such that Göring's office and other economic agencies were emphatically urging an attempt to expand trade with Russia. The embassy in Moscow had also recommended this on several occasions. In a memorandum dated November 4, the Director of the Economic Policy Department of the Auswärtiges Amt, Wiehl, observed that talks which must be held soon with the Soviet trade delegation to extend the existing clearing agreement would furnish a good opportunity to sound out the Russians regarding resumption of the credit negotiations. But "a sounding out . . . does not promise much success as the Russians will hardly commit themselves to delivering larger quantities of raw materials to Germany, especially as, in view of the inordinate delay in delivery by German industry, they would have considerable difficulty in disposing of the proceeds of these deliveries by imports." [39]

The clearing agreement was renewed for another year on December 19, and on the 22nd the Germans proposed a credit of 200 million Reichsmarks and an increase in deliveries of Soviet raw materials during the following two years. On January 10, 1939, four days after the Ribbentrop-Beck talks in Munich, Soviet Ambassador Merekalov requested an interview at the Auswärtiges Amt and was received by Wiehl on the following day:

The Ambassador stated that the Soviet Government was prepared to resume the credit negotiations broken off in March of last year, on the basis of the proposal made by Germany on December 22, 1938 . . . The Soviet Government further desired that the negotiations should be resumed immediately and in Moscow, because it thus expected a speedier and more successful course of the negotiations. In

Moscow the German delegation would have the opportunity to become acquainted on the spot with the possibilities of the German-Soviet exchange of goods and the requirements of the Soviet economy.

It would be difficult for the Germans to carry on the negotiations in Moscow, Wiehl replied. Aside from the fact that such talks had in the past usually taken place in Berlin, the Economic Department of the Auswärtiges Amt was very busy and could hardly spare personnel for a delegation. In addition Counselor of Legation Schnurre, who would head such a delegation, was scheduled to carry on talks with the Poles during the current month. But Wiehl agreed to consider the request. Merekalov then emphasized the importance his government attached to the proposal; by holding the talks in Moscow, where they could be brought to a quick and successful conclusion, the U.S.S.R. intended to show consideration for Germany: [40]

The Soviet Government felt that the holding of the talks in Moscow must be symbolic of the desire of both sides to arrive at an improvement and a reactivation of German-Soviet economic relations. . . . that the previous economic talks between Germany and the Soviet Union had been conducted in Berlin . . . was rather an argument in favor of holding the negotiations in Moscow this time. He asked that the fact that he as Ambassador was personally concerned with the matter should be regarded as the expression of the Soviet Union's desire thereby to begin a new era in German-Soviet economic relations.

Wiehl expressed satisfaction over the desire for a reactivation of trade but refused to commit himself regarding the place at which the negotiations would be held. In submitting his recommendations to State Secretary Weizsäcker the following day, he pointed out that from the purely technical point of view it would be quite feasible to conduct the talks in Berlin, especially since the Soviet Ambassador was well versed in economic matters: [41]

The strong desire to have a German delegation come to Moscow can therefore only be interpreted in the sense that the Soviet Government would like to demonstrate to the outside world the value placed also by the Third Reich on the continuation of economic relations. On the other hand, because of the raw materials, our interest in the achievement of a favorable credit agreement is so great that it does not appear expedient to frustrate the negotiations in any way, or even to delay them or render them essentially more difficult by a refusal of the Russian request.

He therefore recommended that the chairman of the German trade delegation, Schnurre, together with possibly one other representative of another agency, be sent to Moscow. Together with Hilger, the head of the economic section of the Moscow embassy, they should be able to conduct the talks successfully.

The recommendation was approved, and on January 20 Wiehl informed Merekalov that Schnurre would proceed to Moscow from Warsaw on the 30th. He hoped all necessary preparations would be made as Schnurre had to return to Poland not later than the middle of February: [42]

> The Soviet Ambassador Merekalov replied that, though the German answer did not completely meet the wishes of the Soviet Government [no delegation with brass band], he saw with genuine satisfaction in this answer the intention of the German Government to take these wishes as far as possible into consideration. . . .
> The conversation closed with a repeated assurance by the Soviet Ambassador that he regarded the sending of Herr Schnurre as an accommodating gesture by Germany and as a good omen for the progress of the negotiations.

Litvinov immediately proceeded to exploit the forthcoming visit. In his first interview with the new British Ambassador, Sir William Seeds, on January 25, he mentioned the scheduled arrival within a few days of a German *delegation* which was to discuss a trade agreement. During a conversation with Soviet Ambassador Maisky two days later, Lord Halifax asked if it were true as reported that a German trade *delegation* (Halifax' word) was to visit Moscow in the near future. Maisky said the report was true and that the visit was being made on German initiative! [43]

At a public reception earlier in the month, Hitler had engaged in a friendly chat with Merekalov, and by mid-January reports were circulating of a pending meeting of German and Soviet representatives in Stockholm or Copenhagen. At any other time a TASS release would have officially denied such rumors, but when queried by correspondents in Moscow, Soviet officials stated they had no information on the subject.[44]

Ironically enough, the publicity that should have made Litvinov's plan successful wrecked it. Several sensational articles about a German trade delegation en route to Moscow for comprehensive trade talks appeared in the British and French press. The content of these articles was brought to Ribbentrop's attention in Warsaw on January 26 as he was preparing for an interview with the President of Poland. The German Foreign Minister was already in a bad mood; probably Beck's polite obduracy was finally beginning to raise doubts. He interpreted the news as an attempt to wreck his plan for a Polish-German alliance. Shouting that in the moment when he was trying to achieve the basic co-operation between Poland and Germany against Russia, he was attacked from the rear with a scandalous, disruptive report, he ordered that Schnurre (then in Warsaw) should return to Berlin immediately.[45]

The news of the cancellation of Schnurre's journey reached Moscow on January 28, but Litvinov did not despair. The campaign continued, although in a minor key. On the 31st *Pravda* reviewed an article from the London *News Chronicle* by Vernon Bartlett, who had stated that the Soviet Government did not intend to help France and Britain in a conflict with Germany and Italy but rather intended to conclude agreements which would leave it at peace with its neighbors. From Moscow, U.S. chargé Kirk reported the publication of the review without *Pravda* comment. The "obvious inferences," he wrote,[46]

are either that the views quoted actually represent Soviet policy or that the publication . . . is intended to serve only as a warning to other countries. Whatever may be the intention of the Soviet Government in ventilating such views in the press the fact of their publication is a marked departure to the previous treatment of rumors in regard to a possible *rapprochement* with Germany which have heretofore been publicly ignored and privately denied.

On February 3, at his own request, Maisky called on the British Parliamentary Undersecretary of State, R. A. Butler. Most of the conversation pertained to commercial relations between Britain and the U.S.S.R. However, "Mr. Butler gained the impression from M. Maisky that the Soviet Government would now pursue an isolationist policy." At the same time rumors of pending German-Soviet commercial negotiations sprang up anew in Moscow. Around the middle of February Litvinov told the French Ambassador that Schulenburg had officially suggested such talks. Speaking with British Ambassador Seeds on the 19th, the Foreign Commissar saw "no signs whatever that France and Great Britain would do anything but continue to capitulate; Soviet Union would therefore 'keep aloof' all the more readily as their interests were not directly threatened." During the latter part of the month, new reports again circulated in Moscow of the possible dismissal of Litvinov. It was said his previous anti-Nazi attitude would hinder a *rapprochement* with Germany.[47]

Although the attempt to raise the bogy of a second Rapallo was not nearly as successful as Litvinov must have hoped, it did cause some apprehension. As early as January 27, 1939, in reporting information from the German Embassy re Schnurre's journey, Seeds had concluded with the statement "There is as yet no indication of any impending political or military contacts." Cadogan, the Permanent Undersecretary at the Foreign Office, discussed the matter with the French Ambassador to London on February 1. "It seems to me," he concluded his minute of the conversation, "that we shall have to watch very carefully the development of any tendency towards a rapprochement between Germany and the Soviet." On the other hand Chamberlain told U.S. Ambassador Kennedy on the 17th that the possibility of such a combination was slight; the two parties were too distrustful of each other. Daladier and Lukasiewicz expressed the most acute judgment during a luncheon with Bullitt on March 9: [48]

Both Daladier and the Polish Ambassador were of the opinion that the Soviet Union was to be counted on for nothing. They both felt that it was certain that internal conditions in the Soviet Union would prevent the Red Army from taking any active part in any war anywhere and both agreed that no reliance could be based on any promises of Soviet support in the form of supplies to Poland or Rumania. Both agreed also that if Hitler should be willing it would not take a half hour to form an alliance between Germany and the Soviet Union. Stalin was panting for such an agreement.

IN A SPEECH to the eighteenth congress of the All Union Communist Party on March 10, 1939, Stalin himself delivered the finale of the post-Munich, pre-Prague propaganda symphony. This has frequently been cited as the first approach to Hitler which led to the treaty of August 23. But no evidence supports such an idea.

The chief target of German aggression was still the Soviet Union, and serious Polish-German friction was not yet evident. What hope could Stalin have had that an approach to Hitler would succeed? In reality the speech merely repeated the main themes of the existing Communist propaganda line: [49]

That the Anti-Comintern Pact was really directed against Britain and France:

. . . the fascist rulers decided, before plunging into war, to frame public opinion to suit their ends, that is, to mislead it, to deceive it.
A military bloc of Germany and Italy against the interests of England and France in Europe? Bless us, do you call that a bloc! 'We' have no military bloc. All 'we' have is an innocuous 'Berlin Rome axis'; that is, just a geometrical equation for an axis. (*Laughter*)
A military bloc of Germany, Italy and Japan against the interests of the United States, Great Britain and France in the Far East? Nothing of the kind! 'We' have no military bloc. All 'we' have is an innocuous 'Berlin-Rome-Tokyo triangle'; that is, a slight penchant for geometry. (*General laughter*)
A war against the interests of England, France, the United States? Nonsense! 'We' are waging war on the Comintern, not on these states. If you don't believe it, read the 'anti-Comintern pact' . . . It was not hard to see how preposterous this whole clumsy game of camouflage was; for it is ridiculous to look for Comintern 'hotbeds' in the deserts of Mongolia, in the mountains of Abyssinia, or in the wilds of Spanish Morocco. (*Laughter*)

That the governments of France and Britain were not being duped by the aggressors but were deliberately encouraging them because of fear of their own people and with the intention of dictating terms when all the belligerents had been bled white. This particular passage is material for the psychologist rather than the historian; Stalin was accusing the Western powers of the very policy which he longed to be in a position to follow:

To what then are we to attribute the systematic concessions made by these states to the aggressors? . . . the first imperialist world war led to the victory of the revolution in one of the largest countries. They are afraid that the second imperialist world war may also lead to the victory of the revolution in one or several countries. . . . The policy of non-intervention reveals an eagerness, a desire, not to hinder the aggressors in their nefarious work; not to hinder Japan, say, from embroiling herself in a war with China, or, better still, with the Soviet Union; not to hinder Germany, say, from enmeshing herself in European affairs, from embroiling herself in a war with the Soviet

Union; to allow all the belligerents to sink deeply into the mire of war, to encourage them surreptitiously in this; to allow them to weaken and exhaust one another; and then, when they have become weak enough, to appear on the scene with fresh strength, to appear, of course, 'in the interests of peace,' and to dictate conditions to the enfeebled belligerents.

That the Western powers needed the Soviet Union to erect any serious barrier to further Axis expansion; that they had better be careful or Soviet aid would not be forthcoming:

The tasks of the Party in the sphere of foreign policy are:
1. To continue the policy of peace and of strengthening business relations with all countries;
2. To be cautious and not allow our country to be drawn into conflicts by warmongers who are accustomed to have others pull the chestnuts out of the fire for them.

On March 15, 1939, five days after Stalin's speech, Hitler occupied Bohemia and Moravia, and within weeks the international situation of the U.S.S.R. had changed completely—from serious to safe. But this change only became apparent early in April; during the last half of March, the German threat to the Soviet Union seemed greater than ever before. The occupation of the Czech lands was ominous enough, but a week later Hitler seized additional territory almost on Stalin's doorstep. En route home from Rome, the Lithuanian Foreign Minister had an interview with Ribbentrop in Berlin on March 20. The latter in effect demanded the immediate return of the Memel territory, occupied by Lithuania after World War I, and backed the demand with not too covert threats. A Lithuanian delegation arrived in Berlin two days later (the 22nd), and a treaty embodying the terms of the transfer was signed late that evening.[50] After Munich Stalin had attempted to impress the West with the danger of a German-Soviet agreement; after the seizure of the Czech lands and Memel, he apparently tried to impress Hitler with the possibility of a tacit Anglo-Soviet understanding.

MR. R. S. HUDSON, a member of Parliament and Secretary of the British Department of Overseas Trade, accompanied by his wife and three assistants, arrived in Moscow on the morning of March

23 for the purpose of conducting tentative commercial negotiations with Soviet trade authorities. Accompanied by Seeds, he made his first call on the Foreign Commissar the same afternoon. Litvinov took the opportunity to present his views in detail. They were on lines familiar to the ambassador: a summary of previous mistakes of the "capitulating" Western democracies and the Soviet efforts to guide Europe to salvation. Litvinov's exposition was very comprehensive and went back to 1934. He again urged a conference of all the large and small powers: [51]

Touching but lightly as he generally does in conversation with me [Seeds] on British weakness (in contradistinction to his habit when conversing with a French representative), he said that France was practically done for: she was, as he put it, full of German agents, disaffected and disunited, at the mercy of certain leading politicians whom he profoundly distrusted. He foresaw in the not far-distant future a Europe entirely German from the Bay of Biscay to the Soviet frontier and bounded, as it were, simply by Great Britain and the Soviet Union. Even that would not satisfy German ambitions but the attack, he said smiling happily, would not be directed to the East.

On the 25th Seeds reported the mission was being received "in most friendly atmosphere and accorded lavish hospitality." He also noted that it was not being "featured" in the press in any manner. For a week or so, however, there had been considerably fewer sneers in Soviet newspapers over the "capitulating policy" of Britain. At the same time, in his conversations Litvinov did not conceal his suspicions that the British Government still, in their hearts, wished to pursue further the policy of appeasement.[52]

No hard and fast agreements were reached during the course of the discussions in Moscow. But at lunch on the 27th, the day of the delegation's departure, Foreign Trade Commissar Mikoyan informed Hudson that he and Litvinov had agreed that the trade negotiations should be continued later in London. At 5:00 P.M. Hudson was received by Molotov, Litvinov and Mikoyan. It had been hinted that Stalin himself might be present, but an attack of sore throat prevented his appearance. A Soviet communiqué on the discussions was presented and approved by Hudson. In a message telephoned to London before the afternoon meeting, he had mentioned Litvinov's desire to issue a communiqué which contained some mention of political matters. Halifax immediately telephoned Moscow: "While nature of press communique is not clear to me, it is most desirable that there should be no mention of any political questions therein." But the next day the release appeared in the Moscow papers, and Seeds reported he had been unable to stop publication: [53]

Despite strenuous efforts I was unable to get into touch with M. Litvinov until after communique had been issued to the Provincial press . . . M. Litvinov points out any attempt to stop publication everywhere would be impracticable and would also defeat its own ends. He was extremely surprised that His Majesty's Government should apparently wish it to be pretended that no exchange of views on international situation had taken place with Mr. Hudson who was a member of the Government and an Under-Secretary of State for Foreign Affairs: moreover statements made by Mr. Hudson in the London press just before his departure had led public opinion here and abroad to attach political importance to his mission.

On March 29 Maisky told Cadogan, the Permanent Undersecretary at the Foreign Office, that Halifax' attempt to delete mention of political matters from the communiqué had created an "unfortunate impression" in Moscow. Before his departure Hudson had told him (Maisky) that he intended to discuss political affairs. Cadogan had also given this impression and such talks had, in fact, taken place. The British request had therefore come as a "surprise and something of a shock to the Soviet Government." Cadogan explained that Halifax had only objected to the mention of political matters because he had not expected such a reference and had not seen the text. He had found it "quite unexceptionable" when he read it later. The communiqué itself mentioned Hudson's conversations with Litvinov and Mikoyan, his reception by Molotov, and the intention to continue the trade talks in London. The last part related to political matters: [54]

A friendly exchange of views also took place concerning international affairs, which served mutually to acquaint both parties with the attitudes of the Governments of the two States, and brought out the points of contact of their positions in the cause of peace. The personal contact established between the authorized representative of the British Government and members of the Soviet Government will doubtless assist the consolidation of Soviet-British relations and also international collaboration in the interests of the solution of the problems of peace.

On March 28, 1939, the day after the departure of the British delegation, Litvinov handed the Latvian and Estonian Ministers identical notes: [55]

. . . no matter what kind of agreements were signed, "voluntary" or concluded under outside pressure, should they result even only in the abatement or restriction of the independence and sovereignty of the Republic of Latvia [Estonia], permitting in it the political, economic or other domination of a third state, and granting to the latter any exceptional rights and privileges, both within the territory of Latvia [Estonia] and its ports, this would be recognized by the Soviet government as insufferable and contradictory of the stipulations and spirit of the . . . treaties and agreements regulating at present its mutual relations with Latvia [Estonia], and even as a violation of these agreements with all the consequences arising therefrom.

This declaration is made in the spirit of sincere benevolence toward the Latvian [Estonian] people, with the purpose of enhancing in the Latvian [Estonian] nation a feeling of security and confidence in the readiness of the Soviet Union to prove with deeds, in case of need, its interest in preserving in its entirety for the Republic of Latvia [Estonia] its sovereign existence as a state and its political and economic independence, as well as confidence in the inability of the Soviet Union to remain an idle bystander of open or masked attempts to destroy this sovereignty and independence.

At any other time the Soviet notes to the two Baltic republics could be accepted as what they apparently were, an attempt to stiffen the two governments to resist Nazi infiltration or threats. At this time and later, Stalin seems to have been genuinely concerned over the problem of small states which, succumbing to threats and despairing of effective aid from abroad, became more or less unwilling accomplices of the aggressors. The Soviet emphasis upon "indirect" aggression through the Baltic states in subsequent negotiations with the British and French may have reflected an earlier and genuine anxiety. Two states, Austria and Czechoslovakia, had already fallen without firing a shot, and six more, Estonia, Latvia, Lithuania, Hungary, Rumania and Bulgaria, were to become satellites or subjects of one aggressor or the other within little more than two years. Stalin's apparent fear was not without justification.

Even earlier, on February 2, 1939, the Soviet Government had, in effect, broken off diplomatic relations with Hungary. It had closed its legation in Budapest and requested the closing of the Hungarian Legation in Moscow. Hungarian submission to German pressure was the reason given for this action. In the eyes of the Soviet Government, Hungary had, "to a considerable degree lost its independence." Hungarian adherence to the Anti-Comintern Pact was also cited.[56]

Around March 15 the Soviet Ambassador in London had assured the Rumanian Ambassador, unofficially, that the Soviet Union would afford all possible aid to Rumania should the Germans ever attempt to make trouble through Hungary. Seeds in Moscow, commenting on the Soviet move, pointed out that Rumania bordered directly on the Ukraine "and it is clearly to the interest of the Soviet Union to encourage Roumania to offer such resistance as she can to German penetration . . . The Soviet Government no doubt argue that . . . hope of assistance from the Soviet Union would make Roumania less likely to give in without a struggle . . . What Soviet assistance would amount to in actual fact is another matter." [57]

Approaches had been made to Finland as early as the spring of 1938, following the *Anschluss*. At first Soviet representatives had stated that the U.S.S.R. desired a military agreement with Finland covering the case of a German attack on that country. They had also expressed fears of a fascist *coup d'état* in Finland in the event of such an attack. Later the Soviet Government had attempted to get the Finns to cede certain islands in the Gulf of Finland. Fortified and in Soviet hands they would have been valuable in the naval defense of Leningrad. These Russian efforts lasted until April 1939.[58]

If the Soviet notes were what they seemed to be, then Latvia and Estonia had been singled out because they were (1) small, weak states likely to succumb to German pressure, (2) close enough to Germany for such pressure to be applied, and (3) close enough to the Soviet Union to be dangerous as German satellites. The German reannexation of Memel on March 23, when Hitler landed from the warship *Deutschland* and delivered a speech from a balcony, was disturbing enough. But Lithuania, unlike Latvia and Estonia, had no common frontier with the U.S.S.R. Litvinov knew better than to attempt a similar approach toward

Poland. At best it would have provoked an embarrassing "mind your own business!" reaction from outraged Polish dignity; at worst it might have driven Poland toward closer relations with Germany.

Approaches were made, however, which the Polish Ambassador to Moscow, Grzybowski, termed "marked advances." Sometime in March, probably after the transfer of Memel, Moscow offered to furnish Poland with certain material aid. On March 23, the French Ambassador to Warsaw commented on the Franco-Soviet Pact and assured Deputy Foreign Minister Szembek that in case of war Poland could determine the extent of Russian participation, i.e. could limit Soviet aid to the furnishing of war materiel. The ambassador also declared that "Soviet Russia will not act against you." In his diary Szembek commented that Litvinov had evidently authorized the French Government to assure Warsaw that he "would undertake nothing against Poland as long as she did not place herself in the German camp." Grzybowski attributed Moscow's apparent desire to arrive at an understanding with Warsaw to fear of German expansion in the Baltic states. Three months later he remarked to Szembek that the approaches had ceased and that the Russians were very slow in fulfilling their earlier promises.[59]

Stalin undoubtedly wished to encourage the Baltic states to resist German aggression, but an additional motive may have inspired the Soviet notes: a desire to impress the Germans with the possibility of a tacit Soviet-British agreement. Suspicions of a British understanding with Russia did, in fact, exist in Estonia. On April 21 the head of the political department of the Estonian Foreign Ministry, Kaasik, asked the British Consul at Tallinn if any discussions between London and Moscow affected the Baltic states. The latter replied that he knew nothing: [60]

It was alleged [reported the consul] that the Soviet declaration had been made as a result of conversations with Mr. Hudson at Moscow. . . .

I told M. Kaasik that . . . I had an impression that there was a sort of 'whispering campaign' going on. . . . that a report was being spread among the lower classes that Mr. Hudson had offered the Soviet Government a free hand in the Baltic States as an inducement to act with Great Britain against Germany. M. Kaasik said that there was undoubtedly Soviet propaganda going on among the working classes . . . He said that there was considerable nervousness, even among well-informed Estonians, regarding the Anglo-Russian consultations, and fear that the interests of the Baltic States might be overlooked.

The Latvian Government, for reasons of its own, preferred not to publicize the Soviet notes. Although the Estonians wished to do so, Litvinov cited the Latvian stand and also refused to agree to publication. He was, however (according to Kaasik), willing to have the text given to other governments. Litvinov may have desired a small amount of leakage, enough to come to the ears of the Germans, and at the same time wished to avoid obvious publicity which might raise the suspicion that the notes were primarily a diplomatic trick.[61]

On March 31, in summarizing the course of the visit of the British delegation, Seeds noted that, except for a brief announcement of Hudson's arrival, no mention of the discussions had been made in the Soviet press. The communiqué of March 28 was the only mention since the delegation's departure.[62] If Litvinov was trying to impress the Germans, he was proceeding with considerable finesse. The lavish hospitality (special railway coaches, two autos with Intourist guides assigned for sight-seeing during the whole stay, a special performance of the ballet *Swan Lake* for which the prima ballerina, Ulanova, had come down from Leningrad, a performance of the opera *Eugene Onegin,* a "magnificent bouquet" for Mrs. Hudson at the time of arrival and again upon the departure of the delegation), the interview with Molotov— one with Stalin himself had evidently been considered—together with the meager mention in the press may have been designed to attract German attention and rouse German suspicions.[63]

In evaluating the motives behind this Soviet move, it might be well to go back to December 21, 1933, when Litvinov had a long conversation with Bullitt, then the newly appointed Ambassador to Moscow. At that time the Soviet Government was genuinely concerned over the possibility of a Japanese attack: [64]

We discussed ways and means of preventing such an attack [reported Bullitt]. Litvinov suggested . . . the institution by the United States of proposals for non-aggression pacts between the United States, the Soviet Union, China and Japan. I explained to him the difficulties in the way of any such proposal. He then said that he felt that *anything that could be done to make the Japanese believe that the United States was ready to cooperate with Russia, even though there might be no basis for the belief, would be valuable* [italics supplied]. He asked whether it might not be possible for an American squadron or an individual warship to pay a visit during the spring to Vladivostock or to Leningrad.

7

The Last of Litvinov

March 15—May 3, 1939

"I knew it. In fourteen days no one will talk about it anymore," remarked Hitler on March 16 as he stood on the walls of the Castle of Prague. German troops had occupied the city the day before, and an aid had just informed him that Britain and France had not mobilized.[1] But as Weizsäcker later wrote, the occupation was truly a "cardinal" and "irreparable" blunder. There was absolutely no justification in the state of German-Czech relations. The Czechs, after Munich, seemed resigned to their inevitable status as a German satellite. The move caused a complete about face on the part of governmental and public opinion in France and Britain. Hitler had broken an agreement he had made less than six months previously. Unlike Versailles this agreement had not been imposed by force but had been freely entered into by the German Government. Less than a month before the march into Prague, Chamberlain had remarked to U.S. Ambassador Kennedy "that the only hope of doing business with Hitler is to take him at his word . . . it is by no means certain that the word will be kept, but up to date he has no reason personally to disbelieve it." On June 6, 1939 a Swedish industrialist presented Chamberlain with some rather vague proposals from Göring. The Prime Minister cited the general lack of faith in Hitler and rejected the proposals out of hand: [2]

The only thing Göring contemplated offering to us in return for our concessions [minuted Chamberlain] was a series of fresh assurances, but since Hitler had already broken his word and brushed aside the assurances which he had given on numerous occasions, of what value could fresh assurances be? . . . the very fact that he [Hitler] could so completely convince himself of the rightness of an action which to everyone else appeared completely wrong, rendered it impossible to place any reliance upon new assurances since it would be equally easy for Herr Hitler to convince himself that he was justified in throwing these over-board also.

The second factor was the matter of nationality and self-determination. As long as purely German districts had been occupied and regions with a German majority demanded, a democratic generation, imbued with the idea of self-determination and the rights of peoples, found it difficult to deny these apparently just aspirations. With the occupation of Bohemia and Moravia, with their overwhelming Czech majority, Hitler destroyed the last justification of his *Heim ins Reich* slogan. Had he demanded Danzig and a corridor across the Corridor before his annexation of the Czech lands, the British guarantee to Poland (of which more later) might not have been forthcoming.

The first whispers of the storm that was to level the "Thousand Year Reich" six years later were voiced by Chamberlain at Birmingham on March 17, 1939:

What has become of this declaration of 'No further territorial ambition'? What has become of the assurance 'We don't want Czechs in the Reich'? What regard had been paid here to that principle of self-determination on which Herr Hitler argued so vehemently with me at Berchtesgaden when he was asking for the severance of Sudetenland from Czechoslovakia and its inclusion in the German Reich?

Does not the question inevitably arise in our minds, if it is so easy to discover good reasons for ignoring assurances so solemnly and so repeatedly given, what reliance can be placed upon any other assurances that come from the same source? . . . Germany, under her present regime, has sprung a series of unpleasant surprises upon the world. . . . Yet, however much we might take exception to the methods which were adopted in each of those cases, there was something to be said, whether on account of racial affinity or of just claims too long resisted—there was something to be said for the necessity of a change in the existing situation.

But the events which have taken place this week in complete disregard of the principles laid down by the German Government itself seem to fall into a different category, and they must cause us all to be asking ourselves: 'Is this the end of an old adventure, or is it the beginning of a new?'

'Is this the last attack upon a small State, or is it to be followed by others? Is this, in fact, a step in the direction of an attempt to dominate the world by force?'

ON THE AFTERNOON of the same day (March 17) the Rumanian Minister to London, Tilea, informed Halifax that the Germans had made economic demands on his country amounting practically to an ultimatum. He emphasized the urgency of the situation and asked if the British Government could "give a precise indication of their position in the event of Roumania becoming victim of German aggression." Halifax immediately wired Ambassador Seeds in Moscow to ask if the Soviet Government could "give any indication that they would, if requested by Roumanian Government, actively help the latter to resist German aggression." [3]

Russia's diplomatic isolation had ended. From this time on she was courted by the West. To the Germans, the object of Stalin's own affections, she could offer a repetition of the two-front war which Germany had lost in 1918 or neutrality and raw materials for the hungry German war economy. The British and French Governments considered Soviet aid to Poland invaluable. A neutral Russia would also be the equivalent of a second Brest Litovsk and would mean the blunting if not the complete nullification of the chief British weapon, the blockade. But in the final analysis the Western leaders saw in a pact with the Soviet Union a means of overawing Hitler and preventing, or at least delaying, the outbreak of the second World War. And to Hitler himself a pact with Russia eventually represented a way to completely discourage the Western Allies and secure a second Munich.

Two concepts were to guide British policy in the following months. On March 26 Chamberlain expressed the first: [4]

I must confess the most profound distrust of Russia. I have no belief whatever in her ability to maintain an effective offensive, even if she wanted to. And I distrust her motives, which seem to me to have little connection with our ideas of liberty, and to be concerned only with getting every one else by the ears. Moreover, she is both hated and suspected by many of the smaller States, notably by Poland, Roumania, and Finland.

On the other hand, as mentioned above, an alliance with Russia could be expected to have a deterrent effect on Hitler. In a report of March 25 the British military attaché in Berlin gave the reasons for this view: [5]

Germany risks defeat only if confronted by two-front war and blockade. Such blockade can only be *rapidly* effective if Germany's eastern front is on or close to her present frontiers and if she has to fight to gain and hold resources essential to her powers of resistance. . . . Furthermore unless the countries on her eastern border are certain that we will permit no further German aggression . . . these countries will almost inevitably slide into Germany's camp . . . Regarded *purely from the point of view of the German army* [italics in original] I consider that provided we can now secure the eastern front that we desire the present would be the most unfavourable moment for them becoming involved in general hostilities.

Upon receiving Halifax' instructions, Seeds asked Litvinov if the Soviet Government, upon a Rumanian request, would promise active assistance. The Foreign Commissar promised to consult his government. Meanwhile what was the position of the British Government; did they wish the Soviet Government to commit itself while retaining their own freedom of action? What was the British reaction to the occupation of Prague? The ambassador cited Chamberlain's speech of March 17 which did not seem to satisfy Litvinov. The most awkward question was why the Rumanian Government had not approached Moscow directly in the matter.[6]

Seeds's first interview took place during the afternoon of March 18. At 10:00 that evening the two met again. It would be rather pointless, said the Foreign Commissar, for the various governments to inquire regarding the attitudes of the other governments before making up their own minds. The Soviet Union therefore suggested that British, Soviet, French, Polish, and Rumanian delegates discuss the "possibilities of common action." He himself thought Bucharest would be the best meeting place for such a conference.[7] The next day Ambassador Maisky gave Halifax additional arguments for a conference. Litvinov, he said, felt this would be the quickest method of achieving a concrete result, and the psychological effect of holding such a conference at Bucharest would be helpful in both Berlin and Rumania. The Foreign Secretary agreed that his government had no desire to "waste time in prolonged and argumentative diplomatic exchanges." But he considered it dangerous to hold a conference without any assurance of its success. He stated that the British Government were considering a new proposal which they believed would have the same result as a successful conference.[8]

Of course this was not the first time Litvinov had urged a conference in connection with an international crisis. At the time, however, the menace of a German attack had never seemed greater; on the surface Polish-German relations were still cordial. The Foreign Commissar wished to do everything possible to encourage Anglo-French resistance to Hitler; at the same time he wished to deter the Nazi regime from any rash move. A conference would have accomplished all of these things, to a greater or lesser degree, without committing Moscow to any subsequent course of action. If nothing else, a conference would have served as a soap box for the dissemination in Britain and France of propaganda designed to inspire a popular demand for resistance to Germany.

During the same evening of March 18 Litvinov addressed a note of protest regarding the occupation of Bohemia and Moravia to the German Ambassador:

The Soviet Government cannot recognize the incorporation of Bohemia and also, in one form or another, of Slovakia in the German Reich to be legitimate and in conformity with the generally accepted standards of international law and justice or the principle of national self-determination. . . . the actions of the German Government, far from eliminating any danger to the general peace, have on the contrary created and enhanced such danger, disturbed political stability in Central Europe, enlarged the elements contributing to the state of alarm already created in Europe, and dealt a fresh blow to the feeling of security of the nations.

Articles in *Pravda* and *Izvestia* on the 20th also called the German action illegal. One article compared the new "protectorate" over the Czech lands to the colonial regimes established in Africa in the nineteenth century. Both articles pointed out that the German action was the direct result of Munich and nonintervention, and *Pravda* stated that the Soviet Union could not remain indifferent to fascist aggressive acts which poured oil on the fires of the "second imperialist war" which was already underway.[9]

But Litvinov's remarks to Schulenburg, at an Italian Embassy reception during the evening of the 18th, belied even the rather mild tone of the note. The Soviet Government felt that it too must "clarify its position," said the Foreign Commissar, since Britain and France had protested and President Roosevelt had made a statement on the occupation. When Schulenburg asked what was the "practical import" of the note, Litvinov replied that his government "had simply wished to make their point of view clear." [10] In other words the Soviet note was merely for the record.

DURING THE WEEK following the seizure of Prague on March 15, Chamberlain conceived the first considered move to halt German expansion: "to get a declaration signed by the four powers, Britain, France, Russia, and Poland, that they would act together in the event of further signs of German aggressive ambitions. I drafted the formula myself." And on March 20 Lord Halifax wired the ambassadors in Warsaw, Paris, and Moscow. Citing the annexation of the Czech lands as an indication that Hitler had gone beyond mere irredentism and was embarking on a program of domination which threatened every state in Europe, he instructed the ambassadors to obtain the views of the governments to which they were accredited regarding the draft of a four-power declaration: [11]

We the undersigned, duly authorised to that effect, hereby declare that, inasmuch as peace and security in Europe are matters of common interest and concern, and since European peace and security may be affected by any action which constitutes a threat to the political independence of any European State, our respective Governments hereby undertake immediately to consult together as to what steps should be taken to offer joint resistance to any such action.

Seeds presented the proposal to Litvinov on the afternoon of the 21st. The latter's attitude was negative. He continued to press for a conference and informed the ambassador that misleading press reports abroad had forced him to publish a communiqué: The Soviet Government had suggested a conference but the British Government had found the proposal premature. The Foreign Commissar also doubted that Warsaw would agree to a four-power declaration. But the following evening Litvinov sent for Seeds and informed him that the Soviet Government was willing to sign the declaration as soon as France and Poland had accepted. He further suggested that the prime ministers as well as the foreign ministers sign and that the Baltic and Scandinavian countries should be invited to adhere to the action after publication.[12] The German demands on Lithuania probably caused the Soviet about-face. Litvinov apparently learned of them after his interview with Seeds on the 21st.

For their part the Poles unequivocally rejected a joint declaration with Russia. The British Ambassador presented the proposal to an undersecretary of the Foreign Ministry on the 21st (Beck was indisposed). The Polish official's first fear was of the effect such a declaration would have on the German attitude toward Poland; aside from that any Polish cooperation with Russia would be difficult. That evening Beck had recovered sufficiently to dine with the ambassador and discuss Halifax' proposal. "His [Beck's] chief preoccupation was the suggested participation of Soviet. Hitherto Poland had kept the balance between Germany and Soviet Russia and had avoided coming down on one side or the other. The proposed declaration would definitely place Poland in the Soviet camp and the reaction in Germany, especially given the Fuhrer's mentality, would undoubtedly be serious." The Foreign Minister implied, however, that his government might join Britain and France in such a declaration if the U.S.S.R. were not involved.[13]

Beck considered the matter and two days later instructed the Polish Ambassador in London to inquire if the British Government might not be willing to conclude a bilateral agreement "in the spirit of the proposed declaration." He cited the difficulties of multilateral negotiations and the swift march of events.[14] The Polish Ambassador took the matter up with Halifax on March 24, but on the 30th the British Government asked the Poles if they would object to a unilateral British guarantee. Warsaw agreed, and on March 31, 1939 Chamberlain made a declaration in Commons: [15]

Certain consultations are now proceeding with other Governments. In order to make perfectly clear the position of His Majesty's

Government in the meantime before those consultations are concluded, I now have to inform the House that during that period, in the event of any action which clearly threatened Polish independence, and which the Polish Government accordingly considered it vital to resist with their national forces, His Majesty's Government would feel themselves bound at once to lend the Polish Government all support in their power. They have given the Polish Government an assurance to this effect.

I may add that the French Government have authorized me to make it plain that they stand in the same position in this matter as do His Majesty's Government.

Thirteen days later the Prime Minister made a similar declaration covering Rumania and Greece. Although Stalin at first did not believe his ears, the most pressing and immediate danger to Russia, Western acquiescence to German conquest of Poland and Rumania, had disappeared. The Polish and Rumanian Governments, overawed and terrified by a German threat of force, might still allow their territory to be used as a base for an attack on the U.S.S.R., but the British guarantees had minimized even this possibility.

Once the guarantee to Poland had been given, it became apparent that support from the Soviet Union would be invaluable in any Polish-German conflict. But military support was not primarily desired. In fact, while British and French military circles felt the Red Army might prove to be a formidable opponent fighting defensively on its own territory, they considered its offensive ability strictly limited. In the matter of military supplies, however, Russia could play a crucial role. Even if she furnished no supplies herself, most of the war materiel sent to Poland from France and Britain once hostilities had started would have to cross Soviet territory. The Baltic would be closed; railway connections with Rumania were meager and easily interdicted. Any significant aid from the West could arrive only via Murmansk and Archangel or Odessa and other Black Sea ports.

Here the anti-Soviet attitude of Poland and Rumania was to provide an apparent obstacle to any agreement with Russia. Although Beck had never committed himself or his government, the numerous German approaches were not without their effect. He was convinced that Hitler's anti-Communist attitude was immuta-

ble; as long as Poland refrained from any agreement or cooperation with Russia, Germany would never destroy the buffer
against Bolshevism on her eastern frontier.

During a formal conversation with Halifax at the Foreign Office in London on the morning of April 4, Beck declared that any
mutual-assistance pact between Poland and Russia would immediately provoke a hostile reaction in Berlin. "Poland had succeeded
in 1934 in putting Polish-German relations on a normal and
satisfactory basis . . . in spite of the existence of the Polish-
French Treaty . . . if they similarly engaged themselves towards
their eastern neighbour, matters would be brought to a breaking
point." Halifax then asked if a mutual assistance agreement between Poland and Britain would not have a provocative effect
upon Germany. Beck was uncertain, but he thought the effect
would not be as great as one produced by a Polish-Soviet agreement. He cited the Polish-French Treaty as an analogy: "Hitler
himself had said that he had nothing to say against that Treaty, as
he had no intention of attacking either Poland or France."

During a conversation with Chamberlain and Halifax that afternoon, Beck maintained the same position. Chamberlain pointed
out that if Poland were already at war, there would be no danger
if Russia were involved. If the British Government could arrange
for assistance—war materiel—beforehand, would the Poles welcome such assistance? Beck remained adamant and recalled "a
remark of Marshal Pilsudski to the effect that, even if we have to
fight some day, that is no reason for our sleeping with our rifles in
our beds. For the present, he had no authority to express any
opinion about possible relations between Great Britain and Soviet
Russia, but he was not in a position to accept any agreement
which would have the effect, if even only indirectly, of linking
Poland with Soviet Russia." [16]

In Berlin two days later, Ambassador Lipski told Weizsäcker
that Beck would sign nothing in London which would conflict
with the German-Polish agreement of 1934. Polish-British relations were of a bilateral defensive nature. "We are not joining any
blocs, but are negotiating in London directly on the basis of a
certain reinsurance." The same assurance was given to the Ger-

man Embassy in Warsaw. The Rumanian Foreign Minister, Grigore Gafencu, visited Berlin, Paris, and London in the spring of 1939. Passing through Poland en route to Germany on April 17, he was joined on the train by Colonel Beck. The latter asked Gafencu to emphasize, in his forthcoming interview with Hitler, that the Poles had made no agreement featuring Russia. Beck also stated he was prepared to give a formal assurance that Poland would never become a member of any bloc or alliance of which Russia was a member. But sometime between March 27 and 31, Hitler had already ordered preparations for the attack on Poland.[17]

Although not quite so strongly opposed to being linked with Russia, for all practical purposes Bucharest's attitude was identical with that of Warsaw. On April 10 the Secretary General of the Rumanian Foreign Ministry, in London for confidential discussions of the proposed British guarantee to Rumania, called on Halifax. He feared a formal four-power treaty or agreement (Britain, France, Poland and Rumania) might provoke Hitler. Because of the existing Franco-Soviet treaty it would actually be a five-power pact which included Russia.[18]

Gafencu spoke with Hitler, Göring, and Ribbentrop on April 18 and 19. In a telegram dispatched to Bucharest on the 20th, he warned against seeking assistance from Russia. Germany might react by increasing its support of Hungary. On the 28th he had a long talk with Bullitt in Paris:[19]

He said that he had small belief that any promise that the Soviet Union might make to France and England would be respected. He could not possibly enter into any direct defensive agreement with the Soviet Union. Hitler had stated to him a few days ago that if Rumania should enter into a pact with the Soviet Union it would be the end of friendly relations between Germany and Rumania and had implied that Germany would attack Rumania at once.

Gafencu added that Rumania would be most embarrassed if either England or France should make pacts with the Soviet Union guaranteeing Rumania against attacks as such pacts might be in themselves sufficient to provoke Hitler to attack Rumania. . . .

He added that he did not believe that the Soviet Union had any intention of sending the Red Army under any conditions across any frontier in Europe. The policy of the Soviet Union would remain to become involved as little as possible in any European war in the hope that at the end of such a war in an atmosphere of complete destruction and exhaustion the Red Army might sweep the Continent in the interest of Bolshevism.

AT THE BEGINNING OF APRIL Chamberlain opposed a formal alliance with Russia and made a number of comments on the subject in his private correspondence with his sisters. He sympathized with Beck's opposition to any cooperation with the U.S.S.R.: "I confess I very much agree with him, for I regard Russia as a very unreliable friend . . . with an enormous irritative power on others . . . I can't believe that she has the same aims and objects as we have, or any sympathy with democracy as such. She is afraid of Germany and Japan, and would be delighted to see other people fight them." The Prime Minister felt an alliance with Russia would not necessarily be welcomed by the Dominions. It would tend to weaken resistance to Germany in the Balkans and might even force Spain into the Axis. In addition he disliked Soviet tactics in negotiating, which "include the publication in the press of all their despatches and continuous close communication with the Opposition." According to his biographer, Chamberlain stated his deepest objection when he wrote that "the alliance would definitely be a lining up of opposing blocs." In other words it would re-create the alignment of powers which had caused the Austrian ultimatum to Serbia to swiftly develop into a general European war. The majority of the cabinet, however, were inclining more and more toward an outright alliance with the U.S.S.R.[20]

A telegram of April 13 from Seeds in Moscow strengthened this inclination. Concerned over the reaction of Poland and Rumania, and the consequent delay in further proposals to Russia, he warned Halifax of the danger that the Soviet Government might be tempted to adopt an isolationist attitude, especially since the danger from Germany had declined considerably. The British guarantees to Poland and Rumania meant that a German attack in the east would involve Germany in hostilities with Britain and France. Even if Germany should overrun Poland and Rumania, it was unlikely that she would then gratuitously attack Russia and add her to the sum of Germany's enemies:[21]

While not going all the way with those foreign observers who believe that the situation is now developing [into?] the Soviet idea of a war where all capitalist Europe will destroy itself for the benefit of Soviet Russia, it does seem to me that as things are now this country can quite properly be tempted to stand aloof and in case of war confine its advertised support of the victims of aggression to the profitable business of selling supplies to the latter. . . .

I am bound however to point to a possible danger arising either now or in case of war at the stage where Germany had reached the Soviet frontier through Poland, namely an offer by Germany to the Soviet Union of Bessarabia and parts of Poland not to mention perhaps Estonia and Latvia. I do not myself think the danger is more than "possible". . .

But I do emphatically agree . . . in the hope that some means may be found . . . to prevail on Poland and Roumania to accept the idea of some form of Soviet military assistance. Such acceptance to be notified *now* and not put off until an outbreak of war when this country might be tempted to follow counsels of prudence or worse.

Although the British Government were not yet prepared for a full alliance with Russia, a new proposal, which also had the backing of Paris, was sent to Seeds on the following day. He presented it to Litvinov on April 15. Britain proposed a unilateral Soviet declaration "that in the event of any act of aggression against any European neighbour of the Soviet Union which was resisted by the country concerned, the assistance of the Soviet Government would be available, if desired, and would be afforded in such manner as would be found most convenient." Halifax thought such a statement would have a "steadying effect upon the international situation," in other words it might make Hitler stop and think.[22]

In the meantime German-Soviet relations were developing in a manner which was destined, eventually, to produce a very unsteadying effect upon the international situation. Hitler issued the first general directive covering the possibility of an attack on Poland on April 3. At about the same time he jokingly remarked to General von Brauchitsch that his next step would be a state visit to Moscow. On April 7 Ribbentrop telephoned Dr. Peter Kleist, a member of his semiofficial private foreign ministry, the *Dienststelle Ribbentrop*, and a specialist in East European affairs. The Foreign Minister first inquired regarding Kleist's acquaintance with members of the Soviet mission to Berlin. The latter replied that he had had some official contact and, being requested to do so, gave his impressions of the Soviet Ambassador and the leading personalities of the embassy. After a slight pause, Ribbentrop suddenly instructed Kleist to cultivate his Russian acquaintances and report anything significant.[23]

Around the middle of April, the Counsellor of the Soviet Embassy, Georgi Astakhov, invited Kleist and another German specialist in East European matters to tea. Contrary to the usual practice of Soviet officials, Astakhov received the two Germans alone. After some polite preliminary small talk, the Soviet diplomat launched on a survey of the history of German-Soviet relations. He pointed out the senselessness of Germany and Russia fighting over "split hairs" instead of working together as they had frequently done in the past. The two countries should adopt a common policy instead of fighting one another to the ultimate benefit of third powers. His listeners, of course, remained noncommittal. When Kleist reported on the conversation, Ribbentrop was alarmed rather than pleased. He accused his aid of having exceeded his instructions and ordered him to avoid, for the time being, further contact with Astakhov. He doubted that Hitler desired any development of the conversation.[24]

At approximately the same time Chamberlain was remarking to U.S. Ambassador Kennedy that he felt he could conclude an agreement with Russia at any time.[25] Stalin, however, had other ideas. He was prepared to conclude an agreement with the West only if one with Hitler could not be secured.

On April 17, 1939 the Soviet Ambassador to Berlin visited State Secretary Weizsäcker for the first time since the ambassador had assumed his post in July 1938. The ostensible reason for the visit was the fulfillment of certain Soviet contracts with the Skoda works: [26]

Towards the end of the discussion I threw in a remark to the Ambassador that, even given good will on our side, the atmosphere was not exactly favourable at the present moment for making deliveries of war material to Soviet Russia owing to reports of a Russian-Anglo-French air pact and such like. M. Merekalov took advantage of this interjection to pass on to politics. He asked about the views held here on the present situation in Central Europe. . . . he asked me about our relations with Poland and about alleged military clashes on the German-Polish frontier. After I had denied the latter and made a few fairly dispassionate remarks on German-Polish relations, the Russian Ambassador asked me point-blank what I thought of German-Russian relations.

I replied . . . we had always wished to live in a mutually satisfactory condition of economic exchange with Russia. Recently the Russian press appeared to me not to have lent their full support to the anti-German tone adopted by the American, and partly also by the British newspapers. As regards the German press, M. Merekalov doubtless scrutinized it closely and could form an opinion for himself.

The Ambassador then spoke somewhat as follows: Russian policy had always followed a straight course. Ideological differences of opinion had had very little adverse effect on relations between Russia and Italy and need not disturb those with Germany either. Russia had not exploited the present friction between Germany and the Western Democracies against us, neither did she wish to do that. As far as Russia was concerned there was no reason why she should not live on a normal footing with us, and out of normal relations could grow increasingly improved relations.

With this remark, towards which he had been steering the conversation, M. Merekalov ended the talk.

AT FIRST Stalin feared the British guarantees to Poland and Rumania were not bona fide, that Britain and France would not go as far as actual military action in the event of a German attack in the east. On April 1, the day after the guarantee to Poland, Litvinov complained to Seeds that he was in the dark as to what the British were planning and that his government would in the future "stand apart free of any commitments. . . . he expressed doubts whether we would regard attack on Danzig or Corridor as threatening Poland's independence. In any case we could pursue our own policy; Soviet Government would stand aside—a course which might possibly be in their best interests." [27]

On the afternoon of April 14, the day after the British guarantee to Rumania, Maisky called on Halifax and stated that his government was also prepared to aid Rumania: "The Soviet Government wished to learn the views of his Majesty's Government as to the best methods by which such assistance could be given and as to the part the various Powers concerned could play in helping Roumania." [28] Litvinov later claimed that Maisky's statement was in reply to an earlier direct question on the part of Halifax. The Foreign Secretary could not remember asking such a question, and no evidence in the published documents indicates that it was asked. In other words, Maisky's declaration was "out of the blue."

During the last half of April several important Soviet diplomats were ordered home to give their views and observations in person. On the 15th Litvinov remarked to Seeds that he had just ordered Maisky to report to Moscow for consultation. On the 17th Merekalov told Weizsäcker he was going to visit Moscow in the next few days. And toward the end of the month Deputy Foreign Commissar Potemkin was ordered out on a diplomatic reconnaissance to Ankara, Sofia, Bucharest, and Warsaw.[29]

In a conversation with Seeds on the 16th Litvinov dwelt at length on the type and extent of the assistance which Britain intended to give Rumania and which she wished other powers to give. The Foreign Commissar was rather obviously "fishing."[30]

He said that the Soviet Government wished first of all to have reply to enquiry made by their Ambassador . . . as to nature of assistance which would be required from the various powers concerned for protection of Roumania. . . . Soviet Government . . . were ready in principle to come to Roumania's assistance but that they wanted to know how far Great Britain and other countries were prepared to go when it came to the point . . . He said when pressed it might come to a public declaration but repeated that at present they must have the facts to go on.

In a telegram to Halifax on April 17, Seeds stated that the Soviet Government had some grounds for believing it was to be "manoeuvred into holding the baby," particularly the tone of the opposition press in Britain and the lack of response to Maisky's approach re aid to Rumania. "Hence M. Litvinov's questions to me (which I only summarize in my telegram): how do we know that Great Britain will declare war in case of armed aggression? Will she only lodge protest or not even that? Hence M. Potemkin's statement recently to French Charge d'affaires that the Soviet Government were hampered by apparent British reluctance to be bound down to anything definite."[31]

Developments in the next few days, however, clearly reflected the changed attitude of the British Government: On the 19th Lord Halifax delivered a firm speech in the House of Lords, and the next day in Commons Chamberlain announced that a Ministry of Supply, responsible for raw materials and arms production, would be established. But the most significant act—in a country which had never had military conscription in peacetime—was the introduction on April 27 of a motion in Parliament for the approval of compulsory military training. Although opposed by Labour and Liberal members in the debates, the motion was adopted late that evening by a vote of 376 to 145. And the next day Hitler must have convinced Stalin that German relations with Poland and the West had deteriorated beyond repair: In a speech to the Reichstag, the Führer denounced the British-German Naval Treaty of 1935 and the Polish-German nonaggression agreement of 1934.

The following day Halifax wired Seeds that Litvinov's doubts of the genuineness of the British guarantees were unfounded: [32]

I do not understand why . . . Soviet Government should affect to believe that His Majesty's Government are not committed by the declarations they have made to Poland and Roumania. The language of those declarations . . . make it clear that in the event of any action being taken which clearly threatened the independence of these countries and which the latter considered it vital to resist, His Majesty's Government would feel themselves bound at once to lend them all the support in their power.

Because of the May Day holidays Seeds was unable to see Litvinov until May 3. The interview took place in the morning; the Foreign Commissar had stated he could not receive the ambassador that afternoon, and Seeds received the impression that he was scheduled to report to Stalin. Litvinov "again asked whether there would be a declaration of war by His Majesty's Government in the event of aggression. I said that declarations of war were rather out of fashion these days but that under promises made to Poland and other countries an aggressor on such a country which resisted a clear threat to national independence would find himself in at any rate a state of war with Great Britain." [33]

Late in the evening of the same day, the news leaked out that Litvinov had been replaced by Molotov as Commissar of Foreign Affairs. Probably he was dismissed immediately after reporting that the British and French really intended to fight. It is not difficult to imagine several reasons for the action: Stalin had long disliked him but since no other policy was feasible had never quite dared sack the champion of "collective security." Litvinov, a Jew, would have been the person least likely to secure an agreement with Nazi Germany. The dismissal of Litvinov would serve as a hint to Hitler of Stalin's real intentions and desires.

What is significant is that he was dismissed immediately after reporting that France and Britain would fight. Until May 3, 1939 Stalin still had lingering fears that no effective aid would be given to Rumania and Poland, that after a short campaign, or even a political surrender by the Poles and Rumanians, a powerful German Army, uncommitted in the west, would be deployed on the Russian frontiers from the Black Sea to the Baltic. Once this had come to pass there would have been little hope of avoiding a conflict with Hitler. If unwilling to fight for Poland and Rumania, France and Britain would certainly not lift a hand for the Soviet Union. Instead of the capitalist world bleeding itself white for the ultimate benefit of communism, the two greatest totalitarian systems would have devoured one another.

Developments in the Far East furnish the most conclusive evidence of Stalin's newly formed conviction that he was safe in the west. As early as April 1939 Soviet and Outer Mongolian patrols were probing into what the Japanese claimed as Manchukuoan (Manchurian) territory. At the same time Soviet aircraft began reconnaissance flights over Manchuria. Incursions of sizeable units, including motorized troops and tanks, finally provoked a savage if restricted border war. According to a Japanese account, large-scale fighting started on May 8. Another source gives May 4, the day after Litvinov's dismissal.

Hundreds of tanks and planes were involved; the Japanese admitted 18,000 casualties, and, in view of its subsequent tactics in Finland and in World War II, the Red Army's losses must have been just as great. By June Soviet troop reinforcements were being sent to the Far East from the Urals and the southern and southeastern military districts of European Russia. An armistice was finally arranged in September 1939, probably as a result of Japanese discouragement in the wake of the Soviet-German pact of August 23.[34]

8

Stalin Coaxes Hitler

May 4—July 22, 1939

Immediately after Litvinov's dismissal, and presumably with Hitler's approval, Göring attempted to discourage Poland and the Western powers with the threat of a German-Soviet combination. As early as April 16 during a visit to Rome, he told Mussolini that he intended to recommend cautious feelers aimed at a *rapprochement* with Russia. Such a development would arouse anxiety in Poland, i.e. weaken that country's determination to resist German demands. Mussolini stated that better relations depended upon the attitude of Japan, but he was favorably inclined toward the idea and emphasized the possibilities of foiling British efforts to "encircle" Germany.[1]

On May 3 General Bodenschatz of Göring's Luftwaffe staff told the Polish military attaché in Berlin that war was inevitable before the end of the year and that Britain and France would be unable to prevent a quick German conquest of Poland. Germany and Italy were making approaches to Moscow, he warned, and important results could be expected. On the 6th, two days after Litvinov's dismissal was announced, Bodenschatz had a long conversation with the assistant French air attaché in Berlin: "Do you think that Hitler would be prepared to fight without holding all the trump cards?" asked the general. "Were you not struck, in his last speech, by the fact that he made no reference whatever to Russia? Have you not noticed the understanding manner in which this morning's newspapers—which incidentally, had received precise instructions on the subject—speak of M. Molotov and of

146

Russia?" Bodenschatz then referred to the journey to Moscow of the Soviet Ambassador and military attaché and claimed they had been received before their departure by Ribbentrop and at the Oberkommando of the Wehrmacht and briefed on German views. "I can really tell you no more," said the general, "but you will learn some day that something is underway in the East." Ideological differences would prove no bar to an agreement, he warned, and "just as Hitler did not consider himself in a position to settle the question of Austria and of Czechoslovakia without Italy's consent, he now would not dream of settling the German-Polish difference without Russia." Becoming more and more aroused, the general finally declared: "There have already been three partitions of Poland; well, believe me, you will witness a fourth!" [2]

Göring's moves aroused comparatively little anxiety at this time in the West. Commenting on General Bodenschatz' statement in a report to Bonnet of May 7, Coulondre, who had been appointed ambassador to Berlin, pointed out that Hitler might be approaching the U.S.S.R. with the idea of using the threat of a *rapprochement* to force concessions from Poland. The ambassador hit very close to the truth when he speculated that Hitler had not yet decided "between a real understanding with the U.S.S.R., or a simple diplomatic manoeuvre intended to reverse the situation in his favor. One would be rather inclined to adopt the latter conjecture." Coulondre informed British Ambassador Henderson of the claims of a German-Soviet understanding, and the information was duly reported to London where a Foreign Office official in a minute of May 9 pointed out that "the Germans and Italians have every interest in putting such stories about and the Russians might not be overhasty to contradict them as they might well enhance the value of the Soviet connexion in our eyes." And in a conversation with Szembek in Warsaw on the 12th, French Ambassador Noël expressed the opinion that German propaganda was currently emphasizing the possibility of an agreement with the U.S.S.R.[3]

On May 21 Cadogan wired Halifax at a League meeting in Geneva: According to a secret German source Schnurre was to leave Berlin for Moscow the following day to negotiate a far-reaching commercial agreement. Cadogan suggested it might be well to let Maisky know that London was aware of the rumor. Questioned by Seeds in Moscow the next morning, Potemkin denied the report and stated that, according to the Soviet chargé in Berlin, the Germans were busy spreading such rumors.[4]

Göring himself fired the last recorded shot in this particular diplomatic skirmish during a conversation with Henderson on June 7: In "talking about what he described as Poland's blindness to realities, Göring somewhat ominously observed that Germany and Russia would not always remain on unfriendly terms." [5]

Although the situation had not developed nearly as far as Göring and his spokesmen pretended, both parties continued to make very cautious and tentative feelers. On May 5 Schnurre informed Astakhov that the German Government had decided to carry out the contracts between the U.S.S.R. and the Skoda works. The chargé was "visibly gratified" and inquired about the resumption of Soviet-German economic negotiations broken off in February. Schnurre replied that the problems raised by the last Russian answer were still being studied. "Then Astakhov touched upon the dismissal of Litvinov and tried, without asking direct questions, to learn whether this event would cause a change in our attitude toward the Soviet Union."

Four days later the chargé introduced a newly arrived TASS representative to Braun von Stumm of the Information and Press Department of the Auswärtiges Amt. He also mentioned the recent absence of attacks on the U.S.S.R. in the German press and, upon von Stumm complaining of the lack of reciprocal action in Moscow, stated that his government evidently feared the new German attitude was only a tactical move. Asked about the significance of Litvinov's dismissal, Astakhov said no change was involved as the former Foreign Commissar had always followed broad directives. "Therefore, one could hardly speak of a reorientation of Policy at present, particularly since Soviet Russian policy depended on that of others, and not least on that of Germany."

The Soviet chargé called on Schnurre again on May 17 and stated that his government wished to retain its trade commission in Prague as a subordinate agency of the Soviet trade delegation

in Berlin. Schnurre promised a prompt decision and the conversation turned to Soviet-German relations generally. Astakhov again
mentioned the recent reserve of the German press with regard to
Russia and expressed the fear that it might be only a temporary
measure. He "stated in detail that there were no conflicts in
foreign policy between Germany and the Soviet Union and . . .
no reason for any enmity between the two countries." In reply to
an incidental question regarding Anglo-Soviet negotiations, the
chargé declared that "the result desired by Britain would hardly
materialize." He "repeatedly referred to Italy and stressed that
the Duce even after the creation of the Axis had let it be known
that there were no obstacles to a normal development of the
political and economic relations between the Soviet Union and
Italy." Throughout the conversation Schnurre maintained a reserved attitude.[6]

Litvinov's dismissal had aroused intense interest in Berlin. On
May 6 Ribbentrop ordered Schulenburg and the assistant military attaché (General Köstring, the military attaché, was travel-
ing in eastern Siberia) to report to Munich for discussions on the
9th. The ambassador was then in Teheran as the official German
representative at the wedding of the Crown Prince of Iran, and
Hilger, the embassy's economic expert who had been born in
Russia and had served on the embassy staff for almost twenty
years, reported instead.

After a briefing by Hilger at Munich on the 9th, Ribbentrop
reported to the Führer that afternoon. The next day the two
were unexpectedly summoned to Berchtesgaden where Hilter
personally questioned Hilger and, contrary to custom, allowed
him to do most of the talking. The Führer's first question was
why had Stalin ousted Litvinov. Hilger replied that he was convinced it was because Litvinov had urged an agreement with the
West whose intentions in case of war Stalin distrusted. In answering the second question, was Stalin prepared for an understanding
with Germany, Hilger hardly knew where to start: He was
"tempted to give Hitler a résumé of German-Soviet relations
since 1933, and to remind him how often the Soviet government,
during the first years of his rule, had expressed the desire of
maintaining the old friendly relationship" but only mentioned a

statement in Stalin's March 10 speech that there were no grounds for a German-Soviet conflict. To his surprise neither Ribbentrop or Hitler could remember the substance of the speech.

The Führer then asked "how things looked in Russia." Hilger declared that Bolshevism presented a very real danger but could be neutralized by reasonable political and economic ties. He emphasized the growing economic strength of the U.S.S.R. but pointed out the damage done by the great purges of 1936–38. Touching on the growing conservatism in Russia, Hilger stated that "Stalin realized that a healthy and strong political structure could not be erected on the basis of Communist doctrines." He mentioned the resurrection of the old tsarist military heroes and Stalin's efforts to encourage a new Soviet patriotism, the strengthening of parental authority and school discipline, and the trend away from experiments in the arts. Although he made no comments, Hitler listened attentively and urged the speaker to continue when he made a short pause.

The Führer's first reaction was negative. "This Hilger is himself half Russian," he exclaimed after his visitor had left. "One possibility is that Hilger has fallen victim to Soviet propaganda. In that case his description of conditions in the Soviet Union is worthless. But if he is right, then we have no time to lose in taking measures to prevent any further consolidation of Soviet power." [7]

On the other hand the assistant military attaché at Moscow had stated in Berlin that the U.S.S.R. was no stronger and in no better position to launch an offensive than in September of the previous year. Thus when Schulenburg arrived in Berlin from Teheran, shortly after Hilger had reported at Berchtesgaden, Ribbentrop informed him that communism no longer existed in the Soviet Union, the Comintern was no longer significant in Soviet foreign relations, and therefore no real ideological barrier remained between Russia and Germany. Upon his return to Moscow, the ambassador should very discreetly inform the Soviet Government that Germany was not hostile to the U.S.S.R. and try to determine the current Soviet attitude toward Germany. But the Foreign Minister emphasized the necessity for caution in view of the probable reaction of Japan to a German approach to the Kremlin. He discounted the likelihood of an agreement between Russia and the West since Britain and France were unlikely to render any significant military assistance to any East European country. Ribbentrop also said that in the event of a conflict with Poland, Germany did not intend to occupy all of that country. The Foreign Minister presented no written instructions, but Schulenburg received the impression that, without committing his government in any way, he should indicate the change in attitude and reassure the Russians that Berlin desired an independent Poland—i.e. no common frontier with the U.S.S.R.[8]

After his return from Germany, the ambassador's first interview with Molotov took place at 4:00 P.M. on May 20. Schulenburg mentioned the more friendly attitude toward the Soviet Union in Berlin and stated that his government was now able to resume the economic negotiations suspended in February. It intended to send Schnurre to Moscow in the near future to discuss new German proposals with Mikoyan. Citing the cancellation of Schnurre's journey in January, Molotov replied that his government felt that Germany was not in earnest. For this reason Moscow could only resume the economic negotiations if the necessary "political basis" were established. The ambassador declared that Germany had always regarded the economic negotiations seriously and asked what was meant by "political basis." "M. Molotov then declared that the way in which a better political basis could be constructed was something that both Governments would have to think about. All my determined efforts to bring M. Molotov to make his wishes definite and more concrete were in vain. M. Molotov had obviously determined to say just so much and not a word more."[9]

Molotov's, or rather Stalin's, reluctance to make any definite proposals was natural enough. He was afraid of falling between two stools. Berlin might reject any concrete advances and inform Paris and London of their details. The British and French would thus be forced to conclude that any agreement with the U.S.S.R. was worthless.[10] From the German point of view the danger was equally great. "We must, I think, be extremely cautious," wrote Schulenburg to Weizsäcker, "as long as it is not certain that any possible proposals from our side will not be used by the Kremlin only to exert pressure on Britain and France." Should a proposal from Berlin be rejected and then published in Moscow, it would also destroy the legend of Hitler's implacable anti-Communist orientation. On May 21 the State Secretary wired Schulenburg to "sit tight and see if the Soviet Russians will speak more openly." [11]

Although Weizsäcker allegedly feared a Soviet-German pact would have catastrophic consequences, he and others in the Auswärtiges Amt and army wished to prevent any Soviet agreement with the West directed against Germany. In a memo to Ribbentrop of May 25 he pointed out that Germany could probably "prevent Anglo-Franco-Russian relations from assuming a still more binding character" but warned that any approach must be definite enough to be taken seriously, "otherwise it would be worthless or even dangerous: that is, Moscow would *inter alia*, forthwith play it off against us in Tokyo." The State Secretary suggested three tactical possibilities: (1) a statement by Hilger to Narkomindel officials in connection with economic matters, (2) a strong hint as to Germany's attitude delivered by the Italian Ambassador in Moscow, or (3) a conversation between Ribbentrop and the Soviet Ambassador to Berlin. [12]

Ribbentrop was favorably inclined toward a concrete approach. A draft of a telegram instructing Schulenburg to make a frank statement of Berlin's attitude was submitted to Hitler on the 26th, and the Foreign Minister discussed the matter with Japanese Ambassador Oshima, apparently the same day. Why should Germany and Japan stand by with folded arms, asked Ribbentrop, and watch the consummation of an Anglo-French-Soviet accord? Why has Moscow lent a friendly ear to Britain and France, he continued, why has it feared Germany and Japan? Would not the Soviet Union abstain from an agreement with the West if it were merely made known in Moscow that there was no reason to fear Germany and Japan? One must act at once, said the Foreign Minister, but a German *démarche* alone would certainly not suffice. A Japanese assurance was absolutely necessary, was perhaps the main factor. For this reason Ribbentrop had broached the matter with Oshima and now requested that he wire Tokyo in this sense.

The Japanese Ambassador flatly refused and gave two reasons: (1) Because of Soviet distrust any advance would produce an effect opposite to that desired. (2) Such a proposal would destroy all sympathy for the Axis in Tokyo, even on the part of the military, and render forever impossible a three power pact, i.e. Germany-Italy-Japan.

Ribbentrop then telephoned Italian Ambassador Attolico, informed him of the gist of the conversation, and asked his opinion—not as ambassador but as an expert on Soviet affairs. (Attolico had been ambassador to Moscow from 1930 until his assignment to Berlin in 1935.) The ambassador immediately declared that he agreed with Oshima. Any Axis approach would merely help the Kremlin to "sell more dearly its own goods" in Paris and London. Instead one should take the opportunity to bind Japan, and inform her that now was the time to reach an agreement with the Axis. Ribbentrop replied that, unless he reconsidered, he was not inclined to insist on an approach to Russia at present.

That evening Weizsäcker wired Schulenburg that the earlier instructions still stood and he should make no move without further orders; "nor is Herr Hilger to seek contact, nor finally, is it intended to send Herr Schnurre to Moscow shortly." The next day the State Secretary wrote the ambassador in Moscow: The success of any open approach had always been doubted in Berlin; frank language might even "call forth a peal of Tartar laughter. . . . a factor of some importance was that one link in the whole chain, namely a gradual conciliation between Moscow and Tokyo, was said by the Japanese to be extremely problematical. Rome also was somewhat hesitant." [13]

But on the 29th, from his country house outside Berlin, Ribbentrop called Attolico again. On the Foreign Minister's insistence, the ambassador joined him; Weizsäcker and the legal expert of the Auswärtiges Amt had also been summoned. Ribbentrop gave the details of Molotov's latest statement. Although "direct intervention" by Germany was not feasible, he still wished to disrupt the Anglo-French-Soviet negotiations and proposed "indirect intervention" by the Italian Ambassador in Moscow. Attolico doubted that a German move, of necessity cautious, could achieve any success before the conclusion of a Soviet agreement with the West. The situation could only be altered slowly, up to a certain point at least. Ribbentrop and Weizsäcker admitted the apparent soundness of this view, and the Foreign Minister then decided that Weizsäcker should talk to the Soviet chargé the next day. Hitler approved the move, and Astakhov called on the State Secretary the following morning at the latter's request. After some preliminary discussion of the status of the Soviet trade delegation in Prague, Weizsäcker got down to business.[14] He pointed out that developments in Polish-German relations gave Germany a freer hand in the east.

We had given short shrift to Communists and would continue to do so; on the other hand we did not expect from Moscow any predilection for National Socialism either. At this point the Charge d'Affaires interposed with accounts of how Russian relations with Italy and particularly Turkey, as well as with other countries, could be normal or even very good although, in those countries, Communism found no mercy. . . . Whether there was still room at all for any gradual normalization of relations between Soviet Russia and Germany, after Moscow had perhaps already listened to the blandishments of London, I did not know. However, after both the Charge d'Affaires and his Ambassador had used such open language in the Foreign Ministry, I wanted to avoid the reproach that we on our side had concealed and preserved silence on our own attitude. . . .

The Charge d'Affaires, who had followed the talk attentively . . . stated in conclusion that the ideological barrier between Moscow and Berlin had been, in reality, erected by us. Before our treaty with Poland we had rejected a Russian offer of alliance and until very recently there had been little comprehension here for the Russian thesis that foreign and domestic policy need not disturb each other. He believed that his Government had not wavered in this point of view and were still faithful to it today. In conclusion the Charge d'Affaires stated that he would report home on our conversation.

The same evening Weizsäcker wired the embassy in Moscow and suggested that Hilger contact Mikoyan. He should not indicate that the move was made on instructions; he had just spent two and a half weeks in Berlin discussing German-Soviet economic relations and this would be excuse enough. Hilger was to confine himself to generalities and not repeat the offer to resume negotiations. At the same time he should try to reassure the Foreign Trade Commissar as to the sincerity of German intentions. Hilger made the suggested approach on June 2. He assured Mikoyan that Germany really desired an economic agreement

and that possibilities for exports to the U.S.S.R. had improved
since February. German procrastination and failure to give a
definite answer in February had placed him "in a very awkward
position vis-a-vis his Government," replied the Commissar, and he
was no longer interested in negotiating. He promised to consider
the matter, however, and give a definite reply later.[15]

Six days later Mikoyan told Hilger that his government was
willing to receive Schnurre in Moscow if Berlin would accept in
substance the last Soviet economic proposal of February. The
Foreign Trade Commissar further stated that the Soviet Government would consider the dispatch of Schnurre proof that Berlin
was serious in the matter of "politics."

Six days after this interview, on June 14, Astakhov in Berlin
visited Bulgarian Minister Draganov, with whom he had no particularly close relations. The Soviet chargé stated that his government was hesitating before three choices: to conclude a pact with
France and Britain, to continue to draw out the negotiations for
such a pact, or to seek a *rapprochement* with Germany. Moscow
was inclined toward the third course which would not necessarily
involve any change in its ideological orientation. Other factors
were also involved: such as the refusal of the Soviet Government
to recognize the Rumanian occupation of Bessarabia. The
U.S.S.R. still feared a German attack through the Baltic states or
Rumania. Should the German Government agree to a nonaggression pact, however, or declare that it would not attack the Soviet
Union, Moscow would probably abandon the idea of a treaty
with Britain and France. Unfortunately, aside from some vague
allusions, Berlin had given no indication of its real wishes in the
matter. At the same time there was much to commend the second
course, to draw out the negotiations. Should a conflict break out
in the meantime, the U.S.S.R. would have a free hand.[16]

The Bulgarian Minister informed Woermann, the Director of
the Political Department of the Auswärtiges Amt, the next day.
"At the end," wrote Woermann in his memo of the conversation,
"M. Draganov repeated again that he had no indications why M.
Astakhov had made this disclosure to him. He was weighing the
possibility [!] that this must have been done with the intention
that M. Draganov should report it to us."

Schulenburg, in Berlin from June 12 to 24, called on Astak-hov on the 17th. The Soviet chargé again complained that Weizsäcker's remarks had been rather vague and very general. The ambassador replied that they appeared perfectly clear to him; the State Secretary's statement had been intended as an answer to Molotov's demand that the necessary "political basis" for eco-nomic talks be established. Germany did not intend to attack the U.S.S.R. and indeed wished to normalize German-Soviet rela-tions; thus Moscow had no grounds for becoming involved in Britain's "encirclement" policy. Astakhov emphasized the distrust which still existed in Moscow and would have to be overcome. He "stated quite frankly that good German-Soviet relations could not but be advantageous to both countries, for the whole course of history had shown that Germany and Russia had always done well when they had been friends, and badly when they had been enemies." [17]

Informed of the statement to the Bulgarian Minister, Hitler remarked that if Britain and France indeed secured a pact with the Soviet Union he would abandon the plans for an attack on Poland. "But should the Western powers fail and return home with empty hands, I can smash Poland without the danger of a conflict with the West." On the 15th or 16th Ribbentrop told Kleist that "It is now not a problem of Poland but rather of smashing the classical East-West coalition." [18]

Although encouraged by the new Soviet approach, Hitler could not decide on a positive reaction or did not yet consider such a reaction necessary. Ribbentrop spoke with Schulenburg several times during the latter's stay in Berlin but gave no precise instructions regarding a fresh approach in Moscow. He seemed worried about the effect a rapprochement with Russia might produce in Japan. Although Britain and France would probably eventually secure a pact with the U.S.S.R., said the Foreign Minis-ter, the German Government did not particularly fear such a development. In any event German-Soviet political discussions would have to follow the current economic negotiations, but Schulenburg might make a reassuring statement. The ambassador concluded that his foreign minister could not make up his mind and that future developments were uncertain.[19]

On June 11 Hilger was ordered to report to Berlin. Presumably he arrived on the 14th and started back the following day. On instructions from Berlin, the embassy had arranged an appointment, and Mikoyan received Hilger on the day of his arrival in Moscow, the 17th. Hilger had returned with a written answer to the Foreign Trade Commissar's offer and in opening the conversation pointed out that his trip to Berlin and the written reply should be considered additional proof of German earnestness. He then read the answer: [20]

The German Government are willing to send Counsellor Schnurre to Moscow with full power to negotiate on expanding and strengthening economic relations . . . and, if a common basis is found, to conclude an agreement. From the fact of our sending a German plenipotentiary as negotiator we beg the Soviet Government to conclude that the German Government expect and desire a positive conclusion on a broadened basis. We should have to refuse acceptance in advance of the Soviet counter proposal of February 1939, however, since it is precisely this counter proposal which is to be the subject of the negotiations. . . . in the meantime we have endeavoured to remove obstacles which in February still appeared to us as insurmountable. However, we expect the Soviet Government also to re-examine Soviet raw material deliveries in the light of German desires.

Mikoyan listened attentively and seemed impressed. When Hilger had finished, however, he declared that the answer did not meet his conditions. He still suspected "a political game in which the Germans had an interest just at the present moment, and from which they apparently expected to reap advantages." Hilger then stated that he had no idea as to what the commissar really wanted, to which Mikoyan replied that he had expected a concrete declaration accepting or rejecting specific points in his proposal. Hilger pointed out that the German answer had covered the main points explicitly enough and minor questions would have to be left to the negotiations. In conclusion Mikoyan expressed regret that the German answer was "not entirely favorable" but promised to present it to his government.

Hilger called on the Foreign Trade Commissar at the latter's request on June 25 and received a formal reply. Mikoyan again declared that he must know the specific points on which German and Soviet views differed. Hilger repeated his earlier arguments, but Mikoyan cited the fact that the Germans had placed him in an "awkward position before" and insisted that Hilger query Berlin about the existing differences of opinion.[21]

Schulenburg arrived back in Moscow on June 26; on the 28th he requested an interview with Molotov and was received three hours later. As a result of his talks in Berlin, the ambassador declared, he could give further assurances that Germany did not intend to attack the U.S.S.R. As evidence he cited the complete absence of anti-Soviet articles in the German press, acquiescence in Hungary's annexation of Ruthenia which proved that Germany had no designs on the Ukraine, and the nonaggression pacts recently concluded between Germany and the Baltic states.[22] Molotov remarked that these treaties were not with the Soviet Union to which Schulenburg boldly asked if the Soviet Government wished a similar treaty. But Molotov avoided answering this question. The ambassador also stated that the 1926 German-Soviet neutrality treaty (Treaty of Berlin) was still in force and had not been superseded by any later treaties between Germany and other countries.

The conversation then turned to the economic negotiations. Molotov agreed with Mikoyan's attitude and suggested that the Germans furnish the required information. Schulenburg pointed out that even armed with this information it would be difficult for him or Hilger to conduct the negotiations since it would still be necessary to consult Berlin frequently. He urged that Schnurre, who had the necessary authority, knowledge, and experience, be allowed to come to Moscow. Molotov replied that the cancellation of Schnurre's journey earlier in the year had displeased the Soviet Government. "It should be left to Mikoyan, who was well versed in the subject, to ask for what he considered right. When we had given the information desired by Mikoyan, a visit by Schnurre to Moscow might perhaps prove useful." [23]

After Hilger's interview with Mikoyan on the 25th, Schulenburg had sent Berlin an evaluation of Soviet motives: [24]

Mikoyan does not want to see the talks with us broken off, but wishes to keep the negotiations firmly in hand, in order to determine their course at any time. Obviously it would not at present fit into the framework of the Soviet Government's general policy if a sensation were to be created by a resumption of the economic negotiations and in particular by repeated journeys of a special plenipotentiary to Moscow. The Soviet Government apparently believe that, by resuming economic negotiations at this particular moment, we intend to influence the attitude of Britain and Poland, and thereby expect to gain a certain political advantage. They are afraid that, as soon as we had gained this advantage, we might let the negotiations peter out again.

In order to dispell these suspicions, the ambassador suggested that the Germans offer to receive a special Soviet delegate with plenary powers in Berlin. Should the offer be rejected Schulenburg and Hilger could carry on the talks in Moscow.

But in Berlin, Schnurre, in a minute of June 28, doubted that either course offered reasonable prospects of success. Mikoyan himself was the only Soviet official able to make decisions and any subordinate in Berlin "would have no latitude whatever for decisions or even for discussions" and "would consult Moscow on every question however insignificant." In addition discussions in Berlin could hardly be expected to disrupt the Anglo-French-Soviet negotiations: There "would be a vast difference between negotiations conducted here with a minor Soviet official . . . and those conducted, through a special German delegate in Moscow, with Mikoyan himself, who is not only Commissar for Foreign Trade but also Deputy Chairman of the Council of People's Commissars." The same objections applied to negotiations through the embassy in Moscow. If Mikoyan rejected negotiations in Moscow by a special German representative, Schnurre thought "it would be better to postpone the question of the negotiations entirely, since any other way will neither produce the political advantages expected by us nor bring us the clarity necessary for a decision on the economic possibilities existing vis-a-vis the Soviet Union."

On the 29th Hitler decided to suspend the negotiations indefinitely on the grounds that the Russians insisted on acceptance of their last proposal, but the Soviet authorities were not to be notified for a few days. The next day Weizsäcker wired Schulenburg that Ribbentrop had read the report of the latest interview with Molotov and felt that "in the political field enough has been said until further instructions and that for the moment the talks should not be taken up again by us." The ambassador was also to await further instructions regarding the economic negotiations.[25]

In a letter to Weizsäcker of July 10, Schulenburg agreed that it was best to make no more political advances for the time being. He felt, however, that certain minor steps might be taken. "Experience shows that it is not treaties and agreements which create a good or a bad atmosphere in international intercourse, but the way everyday things are handled." The ambassador suggested a somewhat more friendly attitude toward Soviet diplomats and attachés in Germany. "There will certainly often be other opportunities in Berlin of obliging the Soviet Russians and thereby proving our good will to them. I believe it would serve our purpose if we grasped every such opportunity and turned it to good account." [26]

Moscow evidently had the same idea. At the end of June the Soviet air attaché in London told the German assistant air attaché that his government did not really desire a pact with Britain and France and passed on some information he had gathered regarding British air rearmament. At the beginning of July Potemkin offered to release seven German nationals held in Soviet prisons in return for the release of ten Soviet citizens held in Spain. As Schulenburg noted, this was "the first sign of any accommodating disposition to speak of for a long time." Also early in July a Soviet officer, for the first time in years, attended a cocktail party given by the German military attaché, General Köstring. Finally, on July 24, Astakhov informed Weizsäcker that the Society for Cultural Relations with Foreign Countries wished to invite a German scientist and an official of the German Ministry of Agriculture to Moscow for the opening of an all-union agricultural exhibition and act as their host during a ten-day stay.[27]

Although opposed to economic negotiations with a Soviet representative in Berlin or by the regular German Embassy personnel in Moscow, Schnurre and Weizsäcker evidently felt that Hitler's decision to break off the negotiations completely was premature. A telegram giving the German position on various aspects of the economic negotiations and instructing Schulenburg to convey this information to Mikoyan had been drafted as early as June 28, the day before Hitler's order. In a memo of June 30 Schnurre recommended that the telegram be sent, pointing out that in his last conversation with Hilger the Foreign Trade Commissar had not mentioned the earlier demand for German acceptance "in substance" of the Soviet proposals of February. On July 2 Ribbentrop urgently requested Schulenburg to send further details, a verbatim report if possible, of his last conversation with Molotov. The Foreign Minister subsequently submitted the draft telegram containing the details of the German position to Hitler. The latter approved it, and the instructions were dispatched on July 7. But the Führer was still unwilling to make additional political advances. Tippelskirch, then on leave in Germany, wrote Schulenburg on July 12 that the authorities in Berlin evinced great interest in the problem of the U.S.S.R. "Opinions, however, fluctuate and are undecided. The will to take a definite political stand has not yet asserted itself." [28]

The detailed German views were made known to Mikoyan on July 10. Five days later he told Hilger that the information was helpful but several points were still not clear. For this reason he had called home Babarin, the trade representative in Berlin, had informed him regarding Soviet views, and instructed him to discuss the unclear points with Schnurre in Berlin. Mikoyan's attitude confirmed Schulenburg's earlier conclusion that Moscow intended to maintain contact but "at the moment, they are still chary of entering into actual economic negotiations which could not be concealed from the public." [29]

Babarin and two other members of the Soviet trade delegation called on Schnurre on July 18. The trade representative read a formal statement covering the Soviet interpretation of the latest German concessions and offering several Soviet concessions in turn. He stated that he was authorized to discuss the points covered in the statement and, if agreement could be reached, to sign a treaty in Berlin. Schnurre reserved his answer but objected that this method was just the opposite of the German plan to conduct the negotiations in Moscow which had been proposed by Mikoyan himself. The place of signature could be decided later, Babarin replied; the important thing was to clarify the points still in dispute. "It could, however," wrote Schnurre in his memo of the conversation, "quite obviously be gathered from his communications that the Soviet Government preferred unobtrusive negotiations by Babarin in Berlin to any negotiations by us in Moscow with People's Commissar Mikoyan, which would have the widest publicity."

But Schnurre was inclined to accept the offer. Babarin had made some significant concessions and the positions of the two parties were closer on a number of points. "A chance of eventually attaining an economically sound treaty undoubtedly exists so that, from a purely economic point of view, the negotiations should be continued, even though the conditions in Berlin are inconvenient for us." Although negotiations in Berlin would have no great political effect, a treaty on the basis desired could, if nothing else, produce closer German-Soviet cooperation "which will not fail to have its effect at least in Poland and Britain." [30]

Ribbentrop and Hitler evidently agreed with Schnurre, and Babarin was informed, probably on July 21, that the Germans were willing to conduct the discussions in Berlin. At the same time Stalin and Molotov were apparently taking what steps they could to insure against the Germans using the talks in Berlin to disrupt negotiations with the British and French in Moscow. On the 21st the Soviet Ambassador to Ankara told the Turkish Foreign Minister that there was no truth in any reports that his government was negotiating (on political matters?) with Germany. The ambassador gave the impression that he wished the conversation to be reported to the British. The news of German acceptance of Babarin's proposal presumably reached the Narkomindel the same day or evening, and to preclude any false rumors an announcement appeared in the Soviet press the next morning: "During the last few days negotiations with regard to trade and credit have been renewed between Germany and the U.S.S.R. Comrade Babarin . . . is conducting negotiations on behalf of the People's Commissariat of Foreign Trade, and Herr Schnurre on behalf of Germany." [31]

Weizsäcker officially informed Schulenburg on the 22nd and stated that the German authorities in Berlin would "act in a markedly forthcoming manner, since a conclusion, and this at the earliest possible date, is desired for general reasons." He also authorized the ambassador to again "pick up the threads" of the political feelers "without in any way pressing the matter; and for this purpose to avail yourself of, *inter alia,* conversations on current matters." [32]

9

. . . and Beats the Anglo-French Team

On April 15 Seeds presented Halifax' proposal for a declaration that Soviet assistance would be available if desired in the event of a German attack on one of Russia's neighbors. Litvinov's first reaction was that such a statement would bind the U.S.S.R. without committing others. He promised, however, to present the suggestion to his government. During the evening of April 17, 1939, only hours after Ambassador Merekalov had extended the first Soviet feeler through normal diplomatic channels in Berlin, the Foreign Commissar presented Seeds with a written Soviet counter proposal, a full military alliance: [1]

Under Article 1 of the draft, the U.S.S.R, Britain, and France were to conclude a five- to ten-year agreement obligating themselves to give all possible assistance in case of aggression in Europe against a signatory.

Article 2 required the same sort of assistance for the states which bordered on the Soviet Union from the Baltic to the Black Sea.

With Article 3, Stalin's designs began to unfold: "England, France and U.S.S.R. to . . . discuss and to settle within shortest period of time extent and forms of military assistance to be rendered by each of these States in fulfilment of paragraphs 1 and 2."

Article 4 required the British Government to declare that the guarantee to Poland was meant to apply only in the case of aggression by Germany.

According to Article 5, Poland and Rumania were to declare that their existing alliance (drafted originally with Russia in mind) applied to aggression from any quarter.

Article 6 bound the signatories to make peace only with the consent of their allies.

Article 7 revealed Stalin's intentions: "An agreement on above lines to be signed simultaneously with the terms of [military] convention which has been described above under paragraph 3." This meant that the treaty would not be effective until the military details had been agreed upon.

Litvinov's explanation of item seven was that "difficulties arose when military agreements were only negotiated subsequently to political conventions." The real explanation was, of course, that even if France and Britain should immediately agree to the political terms, the military staff talks could be drawn out indefinitely. If, contrary to Stalin's hopes, an agreement with Hitler should not be forthcoming and a German attack on the U.S.S.R. seemed imminent, the political treaty could always be signed at the last moment. With actual military discussions under way, Stalin would also be, psychologically at least, in a somewhat better bargaining position vis-a-vis Hitler.

Both the British and French Governments feared consummation of the full alliance proposed by Moscow would take too long. It might also have a bad effect upon the countries of Eastern Europe. Halifax, on April 28, summarized the factors governing the formulation of British policy: "(a) not to forego the chance of our receiving help from the Soviet Government in case of war; (b) not to jeopardise the common front by disregarding the susceptibilities of Poland and Roumania; (c) not to forfeit the sympathy of the world at large by giving a handle to Germany's anti-Comintern propaganda; (d) not to jeopardise the cause of peace by provoking violent action by Germany." [2]

Litvinov had objected to Halifax' original plan for a declaration by the Soviet Government on the grounds that it bound Russia but not other countries. Halifax felt there was little danger Russia would be "left out on a limb"; if the Germans attacked Poland or Rumania, France and Britain would automatically be at war. At the end of April, however, he was considering a modification of his original proposal to meet Soviet objections: [3]

The Soviet Government should make a public declaration . . . in which, after referring to the . . . statements recently made by His Majesty's Government and the French Government accepting new obligations on behalf of certain Eastern European countries, the Soviet Government would undertake that in the event of Great Britain and France being involved in hostilities in fulfilment of these obligations, the assistance of the Soviet Government would be available, if desired, and would be afforded in such manner as would be found most convenient. [in the final version, "afforded in such manner and on such terms as might be agreed."]

Seeds explained the British objections to the proposed full alliance and presented a Russian translation of the revised proposal to Molotov on the afternoon of May 8. After Molotov had studied the document carefully, the ambassador emphasized that such a declaration could only bind the U.S.S.R. if France and Britain were already engaged in hostilities and this had been the idea when the British Government had first approached Moscow: [4]

M. Molotov enquired [evidently his first question] whether it was intended to start military conversations. I said that this would depend on the course of events and was provided for in the words 'in such manner and on such terms as might be agreed'. To his question whether it was not intended that military conversations should begin at once, I answered that I thought on the whole such talks were envisaged only as a later development if events called for it . . . M. Molotov persisted in questioning the attitude of His Majesty's Government to military conversations and I finally said I was sure that, if friendly consideration were given by the Soviet Government to the proposal I was now presenting, His Majesty's Government would be glad to discuss any question arising out of the final line.

After some additional discussion, or rather questioning of Seeds, Molotov stated that the Soviet Government would consider the revised proposal carefully; "his government's policy had not changed, but, of course, it was liable to modification if other Governments changed theirs." In conclusion he pointed out that Moscow had replied to British proposals within three days while in this instance London had required three weeks.

The next afternoon Maisky called on Halifax, on instructions, and stated that his government still felt it might be drawn into a conflict either before France and Britain or alone. The Foreign Secretary cited the passage "in the event of Great Britain and France being involved in hostilities" which had been added expressly to meet Soviet objections on this point. The ambassador replied that the strategical position could develop in many ways and Halifax had not completely removed his doubts.[5]

A TASS communiqué released late that evening (the 9th) claimed that the latest British proposal, although it contemplated Soviet aid to Britain and France, made no mention of reciprocal aid should the U.S.S.R. likewise "be drawn into hostilities in carrying out the obligations it has assumed in regard to any eastern European State." Similarly an article in *Izvestia* of May 11 declared that only a full tripartite pact offering full reciprocity to the Soviet Union could prevent aggression. In a conversation with Halifax the same day, Maisky stated he had not yet received any instructions but claimed that Russia might become involved in a war as a result of commitments to the Baltic states. In such a case Britain would be under no obligation to furnish support: [6]

In connexion with his general argument M. Maisky mentioned military conversations and sought to establish the case that, under our proposal, the date of Anglo-French intervention would be uncertain, inasmuch as this would depend on the decisions of the French and British General Staffs . . . To this I replied that our guarantee to Poland and Roumania involved us in coming immediately to their assistance, if our conditions were fulfilled, and that, if words meant anything, it was impossible for us to give any assurance more complete.

Molotov gave Seeds the official Soviet answer on the night of May 14. The note stated that the British proposal did not cover the possibility of a direct attack on the Soviet Union. This loophole, together with the absence of any Western guarantee to Finland, Estonia, and Latvia, might "serve to provoke aggression in the direction of the Soviet Union." The Soviet Government felt that at least three conditions would have to be met in order to provide an effective barrier against further aggression in Europe: [7]

(1) The conclusion between England and France and U.S.S.R. of an effective pact of mutual assistance against aggression; (2) The guaranteeing by these three Great Powers of States of Central and Eastern Europe threatened by aggression including also Latvia, Estonia, and Finland. (3) The conclusion of a concrete agreement between England, France and U.S.S.R. as to forms and extent of assistance to be rendered materially to each other and to the guaranteed States,

failing which . . . as experience of Czecho-Slovakia proved, pacts of mutual assistance may be ineffective.

In discussing the note, Molotov told Seeds that its main feature was the need for "reciprocity" but evaded a definite answer as to whether or not this was more important than the question of the Baltic states.

In a letter to the Foreign Office two days later, the ambassador expressed doubts as to "what these people are actually up to. The recent article in the 'Izvestiya' . . . , their latest reply to our proposal, &c., might show that they mean to go on 'raising' us higher than we can possibly go." [8] The course of the negotiations to this point, however, did not justify Seeds's suspicions. The three conditions laid down in the Soviet reply corresponded to the first three articles of the treaty proposed by Litvinov on April 17. Although Stalin and Molotov eventually did bring up fresh demands, they were primarily concerned with drawing out the negotiations and for the time being contented themselves with securing British and French acceptance of the main demands already made.

The first step was to justify the Soviet demand for a treaty covering the eventuality of a direct attack on the U.S.S.R. As early as the beginning of May, commenting on the proposed declaration, the French Government had pointed out to London that the Soviet Government might still distrust Poland and might fear a Polish decision to accept an armistice and limit losses after a rapid and successful German action against Danzig and the Corridor.

During lunch with Maisky on the 16th, Sir Robert Vansittart dwelt on the difficulty and delay involved in securing the agreement of the Baltic states to any guarantee and the impossibility of a German attack on the U.S.S.R. through such a narrow corridor. The Soviet Ambassador finally admitted the possibility of an agreement which left out the Baltic states "but which must in any case include military conversations to decide how assistance would in fact be given on the more restricted but more practical basis of attacks via Poland and Roumania." [9]

At about the same time Potemkin told the Turkish Ambassador to Moscow that the Soviet Government desired an Anglo-French guarantee covering the possibility of a direct attack on Russia after the Polish-German issue had been settled by force or otherwise. On May 22 Léger informed Bullitt that Moscow had expressed fear regarding the possible assassination of King Carol and a reversal of the political situation in Rumania. An Iron Guard (Rumanian fascist) government might not resist a German occupation and German troops could thus attack the U.S.S.R. through Rumania without Britain being under any obligation to assist the Soviet Union. The same day at Geneva, where both were attending a League meeting, Maisky told Halifax that the weakness of the British plan was its complete dependence on the guarantees to Poland and Rumania. Should Rumania compound with Germany and allow an attack on the U.S.S.R. from Rumanian territory, Britain would have no obligation to act. The same was true of Poland. The Baltic states might also be bribed or intimidated into allowing the passage of German troops or the establishment of German air fields. Maisky used similar arguments in a conversation with Bonnet the same day and declared his government would accept no agreement unless it featured a promise of direct British assistance.[10]

As early as April 24 the French Government had proposed to London a regular tripartite agreement with Russia on the grounds that Moscow would accept nothing less. Daladier and Bonnet had no objections in substance, however, to the declaration urged by London. Should the Soviet Government accept the idea, so much the better.[11] With the definite Soviet rejection of the declaration on May 14, Halifax was forced to consider seriously the idea of a formal treaty. En route to the League meeting in Geneva, he conferred with Daladier and Bonnet in Paris on May 20. The Foreign Secretary saw two alternatives: (1) a direct triple alliance which would require mutual assistance in the event one of the signatories was directly attacked or became involved in hostilities as a result of assistance furnished to another state; the British Government and public opinion, however, were unlikely to accept such a step; or (2) a formal pact requiring the parties to act together should one of them become engaged in a war on behalf of another state. He presented drafts embodying both concepts. Although Daladier considered the second scheme an improvement over earlier ideas, he doubted that Moscow would still be willing to consider it. The first type of treaty, however, should prove acceptable. Reporting to London on his conversation with Maisky two days later in Geneva, Halifax wrote that the choice was "disagreeably plain": a breakdown in the negotiations or a full and formal alliance.[12]

Bonnet told Bullitt on May 8 that he had no faith in any promise Moscow might make to support Poland, Rumania, or Turkey. Eight days later Daladier admitted to Bullitt that he had as few illusions as the ambassador regarding the U.S.S.R. Nevertheless only an alliance which included Russia would be imposing enough to deter Hitler. The next day (the 17th) the British military attaché in Berlin concluded a report on rumors of German-Soviet feelers with a warning: "However much the Higher Command may dislike the prospect of a *major* war on *two* fronts in the German Army's present state of evolution, I believe that they might well be expected to go so far as to press for war if Russia should play their game even only to the extent of remaining neutral." Queried by Halifax during the talk in Paris on the 20th, Daladier said he felt there was a serious danger that Moscow might drop the whole project for an Anglo-French-Soviet agreement, and if such an agreement were not secured a Soviet-German combination was quite possible. From Berlin on the 22nd Coulondre warned that Germany "would do its best to take advantage, to the detriment of France and Great Britain, of any failure, howsoever veiled, in the conversations now taking place in Moscow." On the same day a memo presenting in detail the advantages and disadvantages of a pact with the U.S.S.R. was prepared in the Foreign Office: [13]

Germany is impressed only by a show of strength, and Italian policy has always been to reinsure with the stronger side. . . . if the eastern front, built up on Poland, were to collapse, Germany would be freed from the fear of a two-front war. Therefore, it might be claimed that a tripartite pact with the Soviet Union, if that is the only means by which we can be assured of the latter's support, is a necessary condition for the consolidation of the front which we have been trying to create. . . . Even though we may not be able to count implicitly on the Soviet Government either honestly wishing to fulfil, or being capable of fulfilling, their treaty obligations, nevertheless, the alternative of a Soviet Union completely untrammelled and exposed continually to the temptation of intriguing with both sides and of playing off one side against the other might present a no less, perhaps more, dangerous situation than that produced by collaborating with a dishonest or an incompetent partner.

In Parliament on May 24 Chamberlain announced that the British Government were now able to make fresh proposals, and the same evening Halifax wired Seeds that the government had decided on a mutual guarantee covering the possibility of a direct attack. The following day he cabled the draft of such a treaty: [14]

The Governments of the United Kingdom, France and the U.S.S.R. desiring to give effect, in their capacity of Members of the League of Nations, to the principle of mutual support against aggression which is embodied in the Covenant of the League, have reached the following agreement:

I. If France and the United Kingdom are engaged in hostilities with a European Power, in consequence of either (1) aggression by that Power against another European State which they had, in conformity with the wishes of that State, undertaken to assist against such aggression, (2) assistance given by them to another European State which had requested such assistance in order to resist a violation of its neutrality, or (3) aggression by a European Power against either France or the United Kingdom, the U.S.S.R., acting in accordance with the principles of Article 16, paragraphs 1 and 2, of the Covenant of the League of Nations, will give France and the United Kingdom all the support and assistance in its power.

Article II was identical except that it provided for Anglo-French aid to the Soviet Union should the latter become engaged in hostilities. Halifax explained to Seeds that the various points of the League Covenant had been carefully selected so as to justify the action contemplated and at the same time require no recourse to the League machinery and arouse no fears among neutrals that passage through their territory would be required for the troops of League members. Contingency (1) of Articles I and II was meant to apply to countries with which an agreement already existed or to which a guarantee had already been given: Poland, Rumania, Belgium, Greece, and Turkey. Contingency (2) was meant to apply to states which were not guaranteed but asked for assistance when attacked.

Article III was designed to meet the Soviet demand for a military agreement: "The three Governments will concert together as to the methods by which such mutual support and assistance could, in case of need, be made most effective."

Article IV could also be construed as providing for staff talks: "In the event of circumstances arising which threaten to call their undertakings of mutual support and assistance into operation, the three Governments will immediately consult together upon the situation. The methods and scope of such consultation will at once be the subject of further discussion between the three Governments."

Article V was meant to indicate that the mutual assistance contemplated would not involve crossing the territory of other states without their agreement: "It is understood that the rendering of support and assistance in the above cases is without prejudice to the rights and position of other Powers."

Article VI, together with the phrase "in conformity with the wishes of that State" in Articles I and II, was designed to avoid arousing fears among the small neutrals that Moscow might guarantee countries against their will: "The three Governments will communicate to each other the terms of any undertakings referred to in I (1) and II (1) above which they have already given. Any of them which may in future be considering the giving of such an undertaking will consult the other two Governments before doing so, and will communicate to them the terms of any undertaking so given."

Seeds and Payart, the French chargé d'affaires, called on Molotov together on the afternoon of May 27 and presented English and French texts of the latest plan. Potemkin, who acted as interpreter, translated aloud from the French text. Molotov appeared to be checking the translation from a paper on his desk and when the Deputy Foreign Commissar had finished declared that he had already received a text from Paris and that the proposal seemed "unacceptable." Payart and Seeds could hardly believe their ears and thought they had misunderstood the Russian term, "but M. Potemkin's translation put it beyond a doubt. We looked our astonishment" as Molotov continued that the British and French Governments clearly intended to draw out the conversations indefinitely and not allow themselves to be tied down by concrete engagements. Asked upon what he based his statement, Molotov replied that dependence upon the League and its cumbersome procedure meant that the agreement would never be effective; "he put it that the British and French were prepared to visualise Moscow being bombed by the aggressor while Bolivia was busy blocking all action in Geneva." The British Ambassador then carefully explained that the emphasis was meant to be upon the principles rather than the procedures of the League and that the articles mentioned had been selected with the idea of avoiding any recourse to the League machinery. But "quite palpably my words produced not the slightest effect; they seemed not to be heard or understood, although I could check M. Potemkin's interpreting as being excellent; M. Molotov had his mind made up, and at intervals again told us about Bolivian obstruction and the defects of League procedure."

Molotov then cited the words "without prejudice to the rights and position of other Powers" in Article V and pretended to believe that this passage referred to the rights and position of the aggressors. Seeds "patiently explained" that the article had been drafted to protect the rights of neutrals. Molotov finally declared that the British and French were merely drafting formulae; mention of the League made Articles I and II worthless, but, above all there was no provision for "effective action." Payart referred to Article III as providing for staff talks, to which Molotov objected that the article was vague and could only result in endless talks in the distant future. Britain and France were evidently avoiding the effective and immediate action desired by the Soviet Government; "we had evaded the third of the three essential points, the conclusion of a concrete agreement as to the forms and extent of assistance to be rendered mutually." After some additional argument, Molotov stated that his opinion remained the same. He would, however, deliver the proposal to his government.[15]

Acting on instructions from Halifax, Seeds spoke with Molotov again two days later and attempted to remove the "misunderstandings" under which the latter was laboring. The ambassador felt that he had eventually convinced Molotov of the actual nature of the reference to the League and reduced his suspicions of British intentions regarding military conversations. Molotov, however, still insisted on a prompt and concrete arrangement and repeated what Litvinov had told Seeds several weeks earlier, "that the Franco-Soviet Pact had turned out to be merely a paper delusion; experience in that respect had taught the Soviet Government the absolute necessity in practice to conclude, simultaneously, both a political and a military agreement." Seeds replied by pointing out the difficulties and delays involved in concluding such an agreement. Molotov then brought up the case of a country which, like Czechoslovakia, might not ask for aid. "Was British policy, as interpreted by our draft agreement, directed to allowing such aggression to proceed with no regard to neighbouring States who might find the aggressor on their frontier?" Under such circumstances German forces might be moved up to within a few miles of Leningrad. According to the proposed treaty, Seeds replied, an aggressor could still not attack the Soviet Union without involving Britain. "I said bluntly that neither His Majesty's Government nor British public opinion were prepared to consider forcing guarantees of protection on independent nations which did not desire them; such unwanted guarantees were menaces, not assurances of protection." After some additional discussion of this topic and "wranglings" on others, the ambassador departed hoping that the worst "misunderstandings" had been removed. He feared, however, that the question of the Baltic states might constitute an irreconcilable difference of opinion.[16]

In a speech to the Supreme Soviet two days after this interview (May 31), Molotov expounded on the international situation at length. After repeating the three Soviet conditions in the note presented to Seeds on May 14, he admitted that the latest Anglo-French proposal was a "step forward" but one "hedged round with so many reservations, including one referring to certain clauses of the League of Nations Covenant, that it may turn out to be a fictitious step forward." In addition the Anglo-French draft made no mention of aid for Finland, Estonia, and Latvia "which may prove incapable of defending their neutrality in the event of aggression." The same day Molotov told French Ambassador Naggiar that the three countries and perhaps even Lithuania, which had no common frontier with the U.S.S.R., should receive the same protection as Poland and Rumania. His government might have to "come to the assistance" of these states whether assistance were requested or not.[17]

On June 2 Molotov presented Seeds and French Ambassador Naggiar with a Soviet "modification" of the Anglo-French draft: The preamble declared that the three governments had concluded the agreement "with the object of making more effective the principles of mutual assistance against aggression adopted by the League of Nations."

Article 1 required mutual aid in the event a signatory became involved in a war resulting from: (1) a direct attack by a European power; (2) "aggression by that Power against Belgium, Greece, Turkey, Roumania, Poland, Latvia, Estonia and Finland, whom England, France and USSR have agreed to defend against aggression"; or (3) assistance to another European state which had requested such assistance in order to resist a violation of its neutrality.

Article 2: "The three States will come to an agreement within the shortest possible time as to methods, forms and extent of assistance which is to be rendered by them in conformity with paragraph 1."

Article 3 provided for mutual consultations in case of a threat of aggression in order, if necessary, to decide when and how to put the mutual assistance machinery into operation, "independently of any procedure applied by the League of Nations."

Article 4 required the three powers to reveal to one another the details of guarantees already given and consult with one another before giving new guarantees.

Article 5 ruled out a separate armistice in the event of hostilities.

Article 6: "The present agreement enters into force simultaneously with agreement which is to be concluded in virtue of paragraph 2."

Seeds merely stated that his government would give the text careful consideration. Naggiar made a personal suggestion, that the list of guaranteed countries might better be embodied in a separate and unpublished protocol. Molotov was dubious and the matter was not discussed at any length.[18]

Three days later, on the afternoon of the 5th, Bonnet showed Bullitt the latest Soviet draft and declared that it was unacceptable for two reasons, the matter of the Baltic states and the military conversations. The Foreign Minister then handed the ambassador a copy of the Soviet note of March 28 to Estonia. In view of this note, he said, the term "aggression" could mean that Moscow reserved the right to establish a protectorate over the Baltic states—with Anglo-French consent and support. His other objection was that once the political agreement was settled the Soviet Government would probably make impossible military demands. "To sign the proposed political accord as a document subjected to the conclusion of a future military accord therefore would be to sign a blank check that the Russians could fill in or not fill in as they might choose." Daladier had already told the Soviet Ambassador that France would not agree to make the political treaty dependent upon the conclusion of the military agreement nor agree to the Red Army invading a country with the excuse of protecting it from "aggression." [19]

The following day still another draft treaty was drawn up at the Foreign Office, and on June 7 Chamberlain told the House of Commons that the government were sending a Foreign Office representative to Moscow to give the ambassador "full information as to the attitude of His Majesty's Government on all outstanding points" and thus "more rapidly to complete the discussion that is still necessary to harmonise the views of the three Governments and so to reach final agreement." The government had wished to call Seeds home for consultations but the ambassador was confined to bed with influenza. As the next best alternative it was decided to send William Strang to Moscow. Strang, the head of the Central Department of the Foreign Office and later Permanent Undersecretary, was fully acquainted with the desires and reservations of the government and well qualified to furnish the advice and information Seeds might have received in London.[20]

Acting on instructions, Maisky called on Halifax on June 12 and declared that any agreement must cover the possibility of direct or indirect aggression against the Baltic states. Should the parties agree to this concept, the ambassador thought it would be fairly easy to work out a formula agreeable to all. Referring to point six of the Soviet draft, the simultaneous conclusion of political and military agreements, Maisky "observed that this matter could be discussed in the negotiations." The next day *Pravda* expounded at length on the necessity of a guarantee for the Baltic states and hinted that "reactionary circles" in the West were inspiring these states to oppose such a guarantee.[21]

Strang arrived in Moscow on the morning of June 14 bearing the latest British draft, a detailed memo on the British position, and written instructions for the ambassador. French Ambassador Naggiar, who had been instructed to consult with Seeds and support his moves, conferred with his British colleague that afternoon and the next morning. French translations of the more important points of the memo on the British position were prepared. The same afternoon (the 15th) Molotov received the two ambassadors and Strang in the Kremlin. During this and subsequent talks, Molotov sat at a desk on a raised dais with the others below him in a semicircle: Seeds, Strang, Naggiar, and Potemkin who acted as interpreter. No one suggested using a conference table which was in the room and the diplomats had to hold their papers on their knees and write notes as best they could. Neither of the two Soviet officials took notes, but from time to time Molotov busied himself with what Strang thought was a switch under the desk top. The talks may have been taken down verbatim elsewhere.[22]

Seeds began the conversation by stating that the British Government were pleased at the extent of agreement already reached and then read that part of the Foreign Office memo listing the agreed points. But "unfortunately M. Molotov was inclined to fear an attempt at compromising the Soviet position, and to examine with some distrust whether my allegation that we were basing this declared measure of agreement on the Soviet Government's own proposals was justified by the Russian text." Seeds then declared that his government hoped for agreement without undue delay on a treaty as short and simple as possible. The points still in dispute could be examined one by one without submitting complete drafts. The most important British objection concerned the naming of the guaranteed countries. At this point Seeds handed over a French translation of the pertinent part of the Foreign Office memo which argued that states already guaranteed could be covered in the treaty without naming them. In the case of states not already guaranteed, e.g., the Baltic states, "it should be agreed that the three Powers should consult together if one of them considered that its security was menaced by a threat to the independence or neutrality of any other European Power. If the other two Powers agreed that such a menace existed, and if the contracting Power in question was involved in hostilities in consequence, the other two Powers would go to its assistance."

When Potemkin had finished translating the document, Molotov expressed disappointment; from the tone of the British and French press he had expected something more positive. He then closely questioned Seeds in a manner the ambassador found "somewhat irritating" regarding British and French willingness to guarantee Finland, Estonia, and Latvia if these countries were willing, the attitude of Poland and Rumania toward the negotiations in Moscow, and the details of the arrangements with the states Britain had guaranteed. After some additional discussion, Molotov said he would meet with the ambassadors after studying the material given him.[23]

The following day, June 16, *Izvestia* announced that the conversation and "the Anglo-French formulae are considered in Narkomindel circles as not wholly favourable." That afternoon Molotov handed over an official Soviet reply: The U.S.S.R. was being asked to come to the aid of Poland, Rumania, Belgium, Greece, and Turkey if these countries were attacked, but Britain and France refused to support the Soviet Union should she become involved in a war as a result of an attack on Latvia, Estonia, and Finland. The U.S.S.R. could not accept this proposal since it would place the Soviet Union in a "position of inequality." Since no agreement seemed possible on this subject, the Soviet Government proposed a simple treaty providing only for a direct attack on one of the signatories. At the same time in "view of the existence of differences of opinion further discussion is necessary on the question of simultaneous entry into force of general agreement and military agreement." [24]

After Potemkin had translated the reply, Molotov declared that every time his government had made suggestions one of its conditions had been rejected. The British and French evidently considered his government as being composed of naive or foolish persons: "M. Molotov was most emphatic in his anxiety to make us understand that, in his view, the British and French Governments were treating the Russians as simpletons ('naivny') and fools ('duraki'). It became necessary for M. Potemkin to assure him that he had well and truly rendered the word 'duraki' as 'imbeciles'." [25]

Three days later, on the 19th, Halifax instructed Seeds to assure Molotov that the British Government were quite willing to take part in a guarantee of the Baltic states if this could be done without naming them or appearing to thrust a highly distasteful guarantee upon them. The two ambassadors should therefore try to thresh out in discussion with Molotov a formula acceptable to both sides. But the simple three-power treaty proposed by Moscow would not help Poland or any other state immediately menaced, and "I would not therefore be prepared to consider it except in the last resort." [26]

The two ambassadors met with Molotov again on June 21 and presented a written statement embodying the British position on the Baltic states. They also agreed that the problem of staff talks would require further discussion but an agreement on the question of a separate peace should present few difficulties. After Potemkin had translated the statement, the ambassadors presented Halifax' latest draft of Article 1: The other two countries would immediately furnish all possible support should one of the three become involved in a war with a European power as a result of: "(1) aggression by that Power against any one of these three countries, or aggression by it which, being directed against another European State, thereby constituted a menace to the security of one of these three countries, or (2) aggression by that Power against another European State which the contracting country concerned had, with the approval of that State, undertaken to assist against such aggression." [27]

Commenting on the new version in a telegram to Seeds, Halifax had earlier observed that there was no actual change since the question of what constituted a menace would "really have to be settled by consultation." Although Paris had thought the Russians would find the wording more acceptable, Potemkin immediately asked who would decide whether aggression against a European state menaced the security of one of the signatories. Seeds and Naggiar replied that the point could be left undefined or some definition could be sought. "We asked whether M. Molotov had any views as to these alternatives. To this question we received no reply."

The ambassadors explained that the wording was designed to meet Soviet views and at the same time avoid enumerating other states. Molotov felt his government must insist on naming the eight countries concerned. According to staff calculations, the U.S.S.R. would need a hundred divisions to fulfill the contemplated guarantees. Thus the guarantees which Moscow would receive in return should be precisely stated and not left vague as in the British draft. Should this prove impossible, a treaty providing for direct aggression against the signatories was the logical answer. Naggiar then repeated his earlier personal suggestion, that the countries concerned be listed in a separate and unpublished document. Molotov thought the idea might be discussed and asked Seeds's opinion. The latter agreed that the matter might be investigated, but the subject was not pursued further at this time.

In conclusion Molotov expressed doubt that the latest proposal represented any progress. He would submit it to his government, however. "We said that we should be glad to see any counter draft that the Soviet Government might wish to suggest. His only response was to reply that the proposals of the Soviet Government had already been embodied in the draft already submitted to us."

The next morning the Soviet press announced that the latest proposals contained nothing new, and that afternoon Molotov presented the two ambassadors with the official Soviet answer, "these proposals must be rejected as unacceptable." Seeds and Naggiar then asked how Article 1 of the Soviet draft of June 2 could be changed to meet British and French views. Molotov replied that since Britain and France could not agree to a limited treaty, his government reverted to its draft of June 2. "We asked whether the text of Article 1 of their draft of June 2 was to be regarded as *ne varietur*. He replied that it had been submitted to the two Governments for discussion." !!!

Naggiar then reverted to his personal suggestion of the previous day, that the guaranteed countries be listed in an unpublished protocol. Molotov replied that his government would be ready to discuss such a proposal if made officially. He also expressed the opinion that it would be better to settle the text of the first article before proceeding to the other points.[28]

In a telegram to Halifax of June 1, Seeds had referred to Molotov's speech the previous day and observed that the British draft handed over on May 27 gave the U.S.S.R. all that could be expected. It almost offered more than Russian aid would actually be worth: [29]

Soviet assistance is not worth purchasing at the price of extra hostility on the part of the Baltic States and other countries (not to mention the effect on British and probably American public opinion) which we should earn by yielding to the Soviet demands for what amounts to compulsory guarantees imposed on States who violently object to Soviet help. . . .

If, on the other hand, as many observers here believe, they are playing with us and are really out for isolation, no further concessions on our part will serve any useful purpose except to German propaganda.

As regards the risk of their compounding with Germany in the political sphere I have never thought it more than just a possibility at any time and I now think that the Soviet Union is sufficiently covered by our commitments in the matter of Poland and Roumania and Turkey to remove any serious temptation to indulge in so remarkable a volte face if our present negotiations broke down.

A week later Chamberlain told U.S. Ambassador Kennedy that quite possibly the Russians had absolutely no intention of concluding a pact. Should they reject the latest proposal, he was inclined to call a halt to the whole matter. On June 23 Halifax asked Maisky "point-blank whether the Soviet Government wanted a treaty at all . . . throughout the negotiations the Soviet Government had not budged a single inch and we had made all the advances and concessions. . . . I said that saying 'no' to everything was not my idea of negotiation, and that it had a striking resemblance to Nazi methods of dealing with international questions." [30]

At the same time there were weighty arguments against abandoning the talks. On June 1 Coulondre had reported information received through a "reliable intermediary" from a "senior official of the Wilhelmstrasse." Questioned by Hitler, General Keitel was reported to have declared that Germany would win a war in which Russia remained neutral; General von Brauchitsch had said she would "probably" win. Both generals reportedly agreed that Germany's prospects would be much worse if opposed by Russia. "The prevalent opinion at the Wilhelmstrasse," wrote the ambassador, "is that, if Poland does not yield, Herr Hitler's decision will depend upon the signature of the Anglo-Russian pact. It is believed that he will risk war if he does not have to fight Russia, but that if, on the contrary, he knows that he will have to fight Russia as well, he will give way." A week later General von Reichenau, in London as a member of the International Olympic Committee, assured Ivone Kirkpatrick of the Foreign Office that Hitler's motto was that of Moltke, "Erst wiegen dann wagen" (First weigh then wager). The Führer would make no reckless attempt to overcome Poland; he was willing to take risks but only if convinced that they offered good prospects of success. The same day Daladier mentioned Coulondre's report to British Ambassador Phipps who wired London that the premier felt "further delay may even be dangerous and encourage Herr Hitler to seize Danzig before we reach an agreement with the Soviet. . . . M. Daladier therefore feels that we must rope in Russia as soon as possible." [31]

Five days later (June 13) Coulondre reported again: According to someone in Ribbentrop's "immediate entourage," the Foreign Minister was convinced that the only feasible "solution" of the Polish problem was the partition of the country between Germany and Russia. "Herr von Ribbentrop has not given up this idea," wrote the ambassador. "He will not abandon it until the Anglo-Russian pact is signed. Until then he reserves all decisions, while continuing to show every consideration to the Soviets." [32]

On June 15 Erich Kordt of Ribbentrop's secretariat arrived in London on vacation. The next day he warned the Foreign Office through a French journalist friend that Berlin and Moscow were definitely in contact: [33]

According to Herr Kordt the Germans feel a degree of encouragement at the reception given to their first approaches. It is not clear, however, whether the Russians have done more than to lead the Germans on. Herr Kordt's conclusion is that if we want an agreement with Russia we had better be quick about it!

His view, like that of his brother [Theo Kordt, Counsellor of the German Embassy in London], is that an Anglo-Russian agreement would be a strong deterrent to war, and that a failure of the negotiations with Moscow would be a great temptation to the Central Powers [*sic*] to risk another move.

Toward the end of the month the Kordt brothers spoke at length with Vansittart. Erich Kordt considered the British guarantees in Eastern Europe a mistake. They would not deter Hitler but rather provide him with an argument that Britain was seeking to encircle Germany. A British-Soviet-French agreement could also be cited as preparation for a war against Germany. He and the (actually some) other members of the anti-Nazi opposition felt, however, that if such a heterogeneous coalition were ever formed it could never serve offensive purposes; moreover they were convinced of Britain's peaceful intentions. At the same time, since London had initiated negotiations with the U.S.S.R., it was unfortunate that they had not yet borne fruit. Despite the personal insults exchanged between Soviet Russia and Nazi Germany, Hitler would not hesitate to sit down at the same table with the Russians or make great concessions to Stalin. He had, in fact, already taken steps toward talks with Moscow and the approaches had not been rejected. "If you cannot now form your heterogeneous coalition," warned Kordt, "and instead Hitler unites with Stalin, it means war. I got it straight from the horse's mouth [*sic*], Hitler said a short time ago, 'Should Chamberlain close with Stalin, I will undertake nothing but rather summon a party congress of peace in the fall. If not I can smash Poland since the Western Powers will not stir and I will have my back free.' " Vansittart assured the two German diplomats that this time Hitler would not come out ahead; he would not find the British asleep: "Put your mind at ease. We are definitely concluding the agreement with the Soviet Union." [34]

In a letter of June 21 to the Foreign Office, Strang in Moscow wrote that the Soviet Government doubtlessly felt they could secure the terms desired simply by standing fast—"our public will force us to give way to them." Two days later Seeds wired that apparently there were only two choices: a list of the guaranteed states as in the Soviet draft of June 2 or a simple treaty covering only direct aggression against the three parties. The ambassador thought Moscow wished the mutual obligations "set down in black and white and to be clear beyond dispute." He also suspected that the Soviet Government wished to enumerate the Baltic states in order to have some excuse for going to their assistance, even if such assistance were not requested. "They pretend to fear, and perhaps they do genuinely fear, that the Baltic States may voluntarily, or under pressure, move into the German orbit . . . They therefore have it in mind to secure our assistance or at the least apparent connivance should they ever find it expedient to intervene in the Baltic States." [35]

Four days after this telegram (June 27), Halifax told Kennedy that the government had finally decided to agree to a list of guaranteed states. The Foreign Secretary and the rest of the cabinet, Kennedy reported, were inclined "to tell Russia to go jump into the Baltic Sea or any other sea they can find, except that they have been under constant pressure from all their friends who say that the failure of a Russian pact would be psychologically bad for England." That evening Halifax cabled still another draft of Article 1 to Seeds: [36]

The United Kingdom, France and the U.S.S.R. undertake to give to each other immediately all effective assistance should one of these countries become involved in hostilities with a European Power as a result of aggression by that Power against any one of these three countries, or aggression by it against another European State which the contracting country concerned felt obliged to assist in maintaining its independence or neutrality against such aggression. [At the suggestion of Paris, before being presented to Molotov, the final part was changed to "another European State whose independence or neutrality the contracting country concerned felt obliged to defend against such aggression."]

The Foreign Secretary pointed out that this draft gave Moscow the right to decide on intervention. Should Molotov still insist, the British Government would even accept a published list of states if such a concession secured final agreement and no other points were raised. The list must, however, include the Netherlands and Switzerland. The Foreign Secretary hoped this offer would demonstrate British sincerity. "If he can be convinced of this, we have a right to ask him to meet us on a matter of form and to have some regard for the considerations we have urged against public mention of States in question." Upon publication of a list of states as part of an agreement, "Germany will at once ask all the countries mentioned whether they welcome such undertakings and will quite likely elicit the response that they did not." Such replies would certainly embarrass the guarantors. Halifax therefore much preferred an unpublished list.[37]

Seeds and Naggiar submitted the latest proposal to Molotov on July 1. The latter declared the draft was too vague and needed a list of states. The ambassadors in turn suggested an unpublished list, and Molotov said he thought his government would agree. When the list was then handed over, however, Molotov objected strenuously to the inclusion of Switzerland and the Netherlands. The Soviet Government had no diplomatic relations with the two countries and they represented an additional obligation for his government. Since Britain and France proposed to extend the scope of the treaty, the Soviet Government would have to reconsider the situation. There were two possibilities: (1) establishment of normal Soviet diplomatic relations with Switzerland and the Netherlands or (2) compensation for the increased Soviet obligation elsewhere, e.g., Soviet-Polish and Soviet-Turkish mutual-assistance agreements. Molotov raised still another point: the Anglo-French draft did not cover "indirect aggression" as in the case of Czechoslovak President Hácha's surrender in March. This was especially important with respect to the listed states: [38]

We told him that this was a new point. There was nothing about such indirect aggression in the Soviet draft of June 2; and indeed our new draft gave the Soviet Government everything they had asked for in their own draft. He replied that the question of indirect aggression had been discussed during conversations and that the Soviet Government were as much entitled as were His Majesty's Government and the French Government to raise new points during discussions. He suggested that the point might be met if the words 'direct or indirect' could be inserted . . . We told him that we should have to refer this suggestion to our governments.

Molotov delivered the official Soviet reply on July 3: His government was willing to list the eight original states but not Switzerland and the Netherlands in an unpublished protocol: "Article 1 . . . will apply to following European States in the event either of direct aggression or indirect aggression, under which latter term is to be understood an internal *coup d'etat* or a reversal of policy in the interests of the aggressor: Estonia, Finland, Latvia, Poland, Roumania, Turkey, Greece and Belgium." The term "direct or indirect" would also have to appear in the published Article 1 which should specify that the contemplated assistance would be "given in conformity with the principles of the League of Nations but without it being necessary to follow the procedure of or to await action by the League." [39]

In the subsequent discussion Seeds pointed out that after all the Soviet complaints regarding the alleged lack of sincerity in the British proposals and their unfairness, Moscow now expected British and French support against direct or indirect aggression anywhere on the European frontier of the U.S.S.R. At the same time the Soviet Government refused to support Britain and France should they be attacked through Switzerland or the Netherlands. Molotov replied that his government had no objection in principle to extending its obligation to the two countries, but it must have compensation, i.e. mutual-assistance treaties with Poland and Turkey.

Naggiar then made a personal suggestion: Britain and France might promise to use their best efforts to secure Polish and Turkish agreements with the U.S.S.R. "M. Molotov said that promises and efforts were not enough: agreements with Poland and Turkey would have to be concluded at least simultaneously with the signature of our agreement. He only mentioned the absence of diplomatic relations with the two countries [Switzerland and the Netherlands] as a technical difficulty but we feel that we cannot be sure that that obstacle will not be raised later." [40]

Léger had told Bullitt on June 30 that a very grave crisis was inevitable before August 15 and could develop any day. Four days later the French Consul General in Hamburg reported commercial circles in that city thought that if an Anglo-Soviet-French pact were not concluded in the near future, Moscow would sign a five-year nonaggression pact with Germany. "It is felt moreover that such co-operation would aggravate the risks of an early aggression by the Reich against Poland and thus precipitate a general conflagration." The next day (July 5) Daladier told Bullitt he had no specific information but feared serious German-Soviet negotiations were in progress. The French Premier was convinced that only the belief that Britain, France, and the U.S.S.R. would fight at once in the event of an attack on Poland could deter the Führer. "He felt that Hitler would certainly decide to make war unless the Soviet Union should agree in the immediate future to an alliance with France and England and unless our Neutrality Act should be changed to permit the export of arms and munitions." After a conversation with Halifax the same day, Kennedy reported that the agreement sought with the U.S.S.R. was clearly "a negative agreement rather than a positive one. In other words they would like to tie up Russia so that there is no possibility of the Russians considering a deal with Germany." [41]

Nevertheless the British and French were still unwilling to accept Soviet terms on indirect aggression. In the conversation of July 5, Daladier told Bullitt he could never agree to this demand; in the event of a change of government in one of the Baltic states or any other development which Moscow found displeasing, the U.S.S.R. would have advance approval from France and Britain for an invasion. The following day Halifax wired Seeds: although Switzerland and the Netherlands could be dropped in the last resort, the Soviet definition of indirect aggression was "completely unacceptable": [42]

We could not possibly defend it either to the countries concerned or to public opinion here. Questions as to the meaning of 'indirect aggression', if this term is employed in the published Agreement, are bound to be raised, and if so we should either have to reply in the sense of the definition in the unpublished Protocol, or give an untrue statement of the position. . . . The use of the term 'indirect aggression' would confirm the worst suspicions of the Baltic States, whose objection to the proposed Treaty rests largely on their fear of Russian interference in their internal affairs. M. Molotov seems impervious to the argument that it is undesirable to drive the Baltic States gratuitously into the arms of Germany, but we cannot overlook this consideration.

At the same time the British Government were prepared to cover cases such as Czechoslovakia the preceding March. The Foreign Secretary therefore proposed another definition for the unpublished protocol: The "word 'aggression' is to be understood as covering action accepted by the State in question under threat of force by another Power and involving the abandonment by it of its independence or neutrality." Since the British Government considered it necessary to secure some concrete results as soon as possible, a simple three-power pact might be the best answer if agreement on indirect aggression proved impossible. This pact should, if possible, include a provision for further negotiations to extend the treaty to other states. Seeds's opinion was requested on the chances of securing such an agreement quickly. In conclusion Halifax expressed the hope that the ambassador would "now be able to bring negotiations to an end without further reference home."

The next interview with Molotov took place on July 8. He still insisted that his government could not agree to the inclusion of Switzerland and the Netherlands unless offered compensation elsewhere. He did, however, propose a new definition of indirect aggression: "the use by a European Power of the territory of one of the undermentioned States for purposes of aggression either against that State or against one of the three contracting countries." Seeds and Naggiar felt this formula was acceptable as long as the term "indirect aggression" was not used in the published Article 1. This was merely his own personal idea, Molotov replied, which he could recommend to the Soviet Government only if the term were retained. In concluding his report of the interview, Seeds observed that both he and Naggiar doubted that the Soviet Government would now be willing to conclude a more limited agreement should the talks on the general agreement break down.[43]

The following evening Molotov and the two ambassadors spent almost three hours going over the same ground again. The Soviet Government officially insisted on "direct or indirect" in Article 1, and Molotov proposed still another definition of indirect aggression in the unpublished protocol: "action accepted by any of the above mentioned States under threat of force by another Power, or without any such threat, involving the use of territory and forces of the State in question for purposes of aggression against that State or against one of the contracting parties, and consequently involving the loss of, by that State, of its independence or violation of its neutrality." As an example of the use of the "forces of the State in question," Molotov suggested the attachment of German officers or instructors to the Estonian or Latvian armies.

Article 6, covering the relation between the political and military agreements, was discussed in detail. His government, Molotov declared, considered it absolutely essential that the agreements be signed as well as enter into force simultaneously. Differences of opinion existed within the Soviet Government [!] regarding some features of the agreement but none on this point. By persistent questioning the ambassadors determined that Molotov would be willing to initial each of the seven articles of the political treaty once agreement had been reached on the text. Staff talks would then start immediately and on their conclusion the texts of the political and military agreements would be signed and become valid simultaneously. The political agreement would exist merely as a series of articles without force until both instruments were signed: [44]

We expressed our astonishment and pointed out to M. Molotov with the greatest emphasis our objections to this course but he was quite immovable. He said that without a military agreement the political Agreement would be a mere empty declaration, and the Soviet Government were not prepared to sign any political agreement unless they could at the same time sign a military agreement which would form an organic whole with the political Agreement. The only suggestion he was apparently prepared to make was that a date should be fixed in Article 6 for the conclusion of the military agreement.

In these circumstances my French colleague and I think we can carry the negotiations no further without further instructions.

Halifax' reaction to Molotov's latest definition was unequivocally negative. It "is impossible in the scope of any formula to cover all eventualities," he wired Seeds on July 21, "and to try to do so is bound to lead to nothing but suspicions and misunderstandings, both between the signatories themselves and among the other countries concerned." Such an attempt would serve no useful purpose but would undermine the whole moral position of Britain and France and give German and Italian propaganda an invaluable opportunity in the smaller countries: [45]

The words 'or without any such threat' would, as you have realised, allow each signatory to decide whether any voluntary arrangement which the State in question might make with a potential aggressor was to be interpreted as being 'for purposes of aggression' even though no aggression had taken place. Such a claim to interpret and pass judgement upon the actions of an independent State is one to which His Majesty's Government could not possibly be a party. . . . reference to aggression against the State in question . . . no doubt is intended to cover the case of a civil war or *coup d'etat* in which foreign forces were participating, but I do not think that this eventuality can be safely covered by any form of words and it ought not to be attempted. . . . The test still remains whether or not the country concerned has lost its independence or neutrality, and that is provided for in our formula.

Seeds should therefore explain the reasons and inform Molotov that his draft could not be accepted; at the same time he should urge him to study the British definition of indirect aggression very carefully since London would go no further. If the Russians were willing to accept the British formula, Halifax preferred to write it into the published Article 1. This would make reference to "direct or indirect" aggression unnecessary but the term could be retained if Molotov wished.

British opposition to the Soviet definition of indirect aggression stemmed from no hypothetically adverse reaction on the part of the smaller states. As early as May 23, the Secretary General of the Rumanian Foreign Ministry, in discussing the Moscow negotiations with Halifax at Geneva, had declared that his government considered two points essential: Rumania must not be mentioned by name in any agreement and would only accept assistance it had requested. The Rumanian Minister called at the Foreign Office on June 1 and repeated the request that his country should not be named. Ten days later the Polish Ambassador called, on instructions, and told Strang that Paris had informed Warsaw of the terms of Molotov's draft of June 2. The Polish Government could not agree to Poland being specifically mentioned in the treaty, nor could it agree with the idea that the U.S.S.R. would provide assistance without Polish consent. With respect to other countries, his government considered this concept a danger to the security of Eastern Europe.[46]

Two days after this *démarche* (June 12) the Latvian Minister left a note at the Foreign Office: Because of her policy of neutrality, Latvia desired no guarantees similar to those given certain other states. "The Latvian Government . . . trust that no disposition will be framed which could be interpreted as prejudicing without knowledge their liberty of action . . . to uphold the sovereign rights, the political independence and the security of Latvia." [47] In a circular letter of July 4 to its missions abroad, the Latvian Foreign Ministry denied a rumor allegedly circulating in London: that the British Government had promised that Soviet troops would evacuate Latvia at the end of hostilities if Latvia would agree to Anglo-Russian guarantees. The Latvian Government was still determined to "oppose by all means the entry of *any* foreign army whatsoever into our territory." [48]

The Estonian Minister to London had left his formal note at the Foreign Office on June 7. It cited press reports that Moscow had insisted on automatic assistance to Estonia in certain circumstances. The "Estonian Government would be compelled to consider such proposals as an unfriendly act directed against the neutrality of Estonia. The Estonian Government desire to believe that His Majesty's Government in Great Britain may see their way not to agree to such proposals in so far as they concern Estonia." [49] A month later, on July 10, Estonian Foreign Minister Selter expressed his concern in a conversation with the British Consul at Tallinn. Unlike Germany, Russia had exhibited an aggressive spirit toward the Baltic states and apparently intended to intervene in their affairs in the event, e.g., a pro-German government should come to power. Estonia could not even consider a Soviet guarantee since such an action would compromise its neutrality. If Russia subsequently reached an agreement with Germany rather than the West, "it would not be impossible that Germany would be prepared to give the Baltic States to Russia for a quid pro quo elsewhere." The Estonian Minister handed over a second note in London the same day: [50]

The Estonian Government . . . are compelled to consider any automatic assistance to Estonia given without her request and consent, as non-consistent with Estonia's neutrality, as well as with her sovereignty. . . . 'indirect aggression' . . . might involve quite unwarranted and inadmissible interference in the internal affairs of another country. The Estonian Government, fully cognizant of Estonia's sovereignty, could not admit the right of any foreign country to interfere in her internal affairs.

On June 18 Field Marshal Mannerheim had told the British Minister to Helsinki that only three possibilities existed: a Soviet agreement with Britain or Germany or neither. The second development would be the worst, but in case of war the third would be just as bad since Moscow would have a free hand once the belligerents were exhausted. He emphasized, however, that this was a "theoretical and international" view. "As a Finn, he must tell me that he would regard a compulsory guarantee by Russia as entirely unacceptable, and that the whole country was united on this point." [51]

The Finnish Minister to London called at the Foreign Office, ostensibly on his own, on June 27 and expressed concern about press reports that Britain had decided to accept the Soviet demands regarding guarantees. Finland had no objections to a British guarantee but was alarmed at the prospect of one by the U.S.S.R.; the Finns were convinced that Moscow planned a gradual infiltration of their country. The immediate danger from Germany was pointed out to the minister and especially the danger of a Soviet-German combination should the Moscow negotiations fail. He agreed that such a development would be disastrous but emphasized the harm that would result if Britain agreed to the Soviet demands: People in Finland would believe "that we were giving the Soviet a free hand there. The consequence would be to drive the Finnish Government into the arms of Germany."

The minister returned on July 5, this time on instructions, and questioned Halifax closely regarding the matter of guarantees. Nine days later the Finnish Minister called again and declared that German propaganda was increasing in Finland and was depicting Britain as prepared to trade Finnish neutrality, independence, and form of government for an agreement with the U.S.S.R. This time he left a formal note: [52]

> The Finnish Government cannot admit the right of any Power to come to their assistance for the purpose of resisting an alleged direct or 'indirect' aggression on Finland, in any other cases than when they themselves have asked for such assistance.
> The Finnish Government will consider as an aggressor any Power who, without their consent, attempts to render them armed assistance.
> The Finnish Government hope that His Majesty's Government will not into an international agreement introduce provisions which in some way or other might adversely affect their policy of strict neutrality.
> The Finnish Government consider that the acceptance of the notion of 'indirect aggression' might encourage other Powers to inadmissible interference in the internal affairs of Finland.

Even the Netherlands made an official protest in London on July 1 which it published two days later: "The Netherlands Government have in no way been consulted in these negotiations [in Moscow] and . . . take this opportunity to affirm once again the traditional Netherlands standpoint, to remain aloof from the rivalries which at present exist in Europe." [53]

In his telegram to Seeds of June 12 commenting on the latest interview with Molotov, the Foreign Secretary also opposed simultaneous signature of the political and military agreements. Such a demand revealed "a suspicion of our sincerity and *bona fides* which is most offensive and quite unjustifiable," especially since the British Government were prepared to start staff talks immediately after the political agreement was signed. One could only suspect that Moscow hoped "by this means to force us to accept military conditions which would be against our better judgement." Such a procedure was against the best interests of both sides; conclusion of a military agreement might require a great deal of time, and German propaganda could cite the delay as evidence that the political negotiations had broken down.

The same day, possibly after the telegram to Seeds was drafted, Halifax spoke to Maisky about the question of military talks. The Soviet Ambassador explained that his government's insistence on this point was probably due to its failure to secure a military agreement after the signature of the Franco-Soviet pact of 1935. He made a "personal" suggestion: his government might be satisfied if the political agreement required conclusion of the staff talks within a stated time. Three days later (July 15) the Foreign Secretary authorized Seeds, if he considered it desirable, to inform Molotov that the British Government were willing to start military talks immediately—even before the signature of the political agreement. In return, however, the Soviet Government would have to abandon the demand for simultaneous signature of the two agreements and accept the British position in regard to the wording of Article 1.[54]

Seeds and Naggiar presented Halifax' latest offer on July 17. But Molotov remained adamant: The British formula was unacceptable; "it was too vague and too restricted." He insisted on the terms "without threat of force" and "use of territory and forces." Molotov refused to be moved by the ambassadors' arguments and urged them to pass on to the next item. After some discussion of the Netherlands and Switzerland, Seeds brought up Halifax' objections to the simultaneous signature of the political and military agreements. Molotov immediately declared that his government insisted upon the two agreements being considered as one treaty. Unless Britain and France could agree, further conversations were useless: [55]

He begged us to put this point to our Governments and proposed that further discussion should be adjourned until an understanding on this point had been reached. . . . if this point of fundamental principle could be settled the question as to how agreement on the text of political articles was to be recorded was a technical matter of secondary importance. . . . He put definite question whether or not His Majesty's Government and French Government were really willing to open military conversations. We assured him that they were and the French Ambassador said he thought the French Government would be willing to begin military conversations at once without waiting for the signature of the political agreement. . . . I told him that we should be ready without further delay to start technical conversations, but only if agreement had been reached on the articles now under discussion. French Ambassador asked whether the idea of the Soviet Government was to open military conversations at once before conclusion of discussion on the political articles and parallel with those discussions. M. Molotov said that if the two

Governments made an official proposal in this sense he thought that the Soviet Government might agree.

After again asking the ambassadors to obtain a definite answer as to whether their governments would agree to consider the political and military agreements as an organic whole, Molotov started to rise, remarking that this question was crucial "and that nothing else mattered much." Seeds reminded him of the problem of indirect aggression, which London considered of supreme importance, and declared bluntly that the British Government felt they "were making fruitless concessions. Our stock of goodwill was not yet exhausted and His Majesty's Government would give full consideration to Soviet views regarding Article 6: in return we hoped for similar goodwill in regard to definition of indirect aggression. In reply he gave me no information beyond general assurance of goodwill."

In a letter to the Foreign Office on July 20, Strang commented on the course of the negotiations up to that time: [56]

Molotov does not become any easier to deal with as the weeks pass. . . . it is difficult to get to grips with him. He seems to be bored with detailed discussion . . . Indeed we have sometimes felt that the differences which have arisen between us might perhaps be based on some colossal misunderstanding. And yet we have usually come to the conclusion in the end that this is not so, and that Molotov has seen clearly the extent of the difference between the respective positions of the two sides.

On the whole the negotiations have been a humiliating experience. Time after time we have taken up a position and a week later we have abandoned it; and we have had the feeling that Molotov was convinced from the beginning that we should be forced to abandon it.

This was, I think, inevitable. . . . We are being urged by our press and by our public to conclude an agreement quickly; and the Russians have good reason to assume that we shall not dare to face a final breakdown of the negotiations.

10

Hitler Plays the Russian Card

July 19—August 25, 1939

On July 19 the French Embassy in London delivered to the Foreign Office a memo emphasizing the importance of a prompt agreement with the U.S.S.R. if war was to be avoided. The French Government considered the Soviet definition of indirect aggression preferable to a breakdown in the negotiations and urged that the two ambassadors in Moscow be instructed to accept Molotov's formula. The same day in Paris, Bonnet wrote a personal note to Halifax on the subject of Article 1: Although the two governments had already made very important concessions, a decisive moment was approaching and the failure of the conversations would be disastrous. "I myself fear that this could be the signal for German action against Danzig." Under these circumstances he and Daladier considered successful conclusion of the negotiations imperative.[1]

Two days later Halifax wired Seeds that, after careful consideration, the government had decided to accept the Soviet demand embodied in Article 6, i.e. the political agreement would be valid only when the military agreement had been signed. The cabinet had merely wished to avoid unnecessary delay in concluding the political agreement, but had never objected to the idea in principle. The question of indirect aggression, however, involved a matter of principle; "His Majesty's Government cannot be a party to an arrangement whereby they may be placed in position of becoming accessories to interference in the internal affairs of other States." They therefore insisted on the

196

substance if not the exact wording of the last British formula. At the same time, if this stand appeared to endanger the continuation of the conversations, the ambassador was to state that his government was prepared to start staff talks immediately and before final agreement on Article 1 and the protocol. Halifax hoped this offer "would avoid a definite break and would afford evidence in other quarters of practical co-operation between Russia, France and ourselves." [2]

The two ambassadors met with Molotov two days later on the afternoon of July 23. Seeds started the conversation by announcing that his government, after consulting with Paris, now agreed to the political and military pacts entering into force simultaneously. "M. Molotov expressed his keen satisfaction." The ambassador then proceeded to the problem of indirect aggression and the protocol and expressed hope that the Soviet Government was now willing to accept the last British drafts. After Naggiar declared this was also the position of his government, Molotov stated that he had already explained Soviet views; but he no longer considered the difficulties insurmountable and was convinced that a mutually satisfactory formula could be found. Was he correct in interpreting Seeds's statement as meaning that Britain and France were now ready to start the staff talks? The ambassador replied in the affirmative, but stated that London wished to reach agreement on the political points first. "M. Molotov repeated that he did not foresee any insuperable difficulty about Article 1 and the Protocol and for that reason it was necessary to start military conversations immediately. . . . it was essential that there should be no further delay about the opening of military conversations." Naggiar objected that it would hardly be possible to study the military problems before the main political base was established. While defining indirect aggression posed no insuperable difficulties, replied Molotov, it still required discussions which would delay the staff talks. In view of the international situation, the three governments should make concrete military arrangements as soon as possible. Naggiar again objected, stating that members of any French military mission would have to know the political basis for their conversations. The political basis was sufficiently clear, Molotov declared, and time should not be wasted while the few remaining details were settled. He also thought staff talks actually in progress would impress potential aggressors.

Seeds observed that his government intended to waste no time and he would report the conversation immediately. Pending a reply, however, he urged an effort to resolve the two remaining points. In return he was asked why time should be wasted on details and consideration of the essential problem, military conversations, delayed. The ambassador insisted that the definition of indirect aggression was a matter of principle, not detail, for the British Government. When Molotov repeated his assurances that the political problems could easily be settled with the staff talks underway, Seeds asked if the Soviet Government was prepared to accept the substance of the definition of indirect aggression proposed by London. "M. Molotov gave no reply to this question beyond repeating once again, this time in the name of the Soviet Government, that during military conversations outstanding political points could easily be settled." [3]

In a telegram to Halifax the same evening, Seeds pointed out that Molotov had been "obviously pleased" at Anglo-French agreement to simultaneous signature of the two pacts, and Soviet concessions on Article 1 might be hoped for with the military talks actually in progress. Although not optimistic as to their ultimate success and very doubtful of their early conclusion, the ambassador thought the initiation of such talks would give the Axis powers a "healthy shock." They would certainly have a greater effect upon public opinion than the declaration sought in the spring. In any event the dispatch of a military mission to Moscow was the only proof of British sincerity the Soviet Government was likely to accept.[4]

Halifax informed Soviet Ambassador Maisky on July 25 that the cabinet had decided to start military conversations as soon as possible. That evening he instructed Seeds to inform Molotov of the decision; at the same time the ambassador should make it clear that the British Government expected prompt resumption of discussion on the outstanding political points. Molotov received the two ambassadors again on the afternoon of July 27 and was informed officially that Britain and France intended to initiate staff talks in Moscow with the least possible delay. Some discussion of the definition of indirect aggression followed. Naggiar and Seeds restated their case, and Molotov answered in an inconclusive but friendly and reassuring manner. The conversation then turned to the public announcement of the dispatch of the military missions.[5]

In retrospect it is obvious that Stalin was seeking staff talks mainly for their effect upon Hitler. Although the arrival of Allied officers in Moscow should induce the Führer to accept a non-aggression pact with the U.S.S.R., it could conceivably produce an opposite reaction: Berlin might conclude that Anglo-French-Soviet agreement had been reached on all but a few details and that the Soviet Government had finally and definitely decided to join the Allies. Thus Molotov's reaction was unequivocally negative when Seeds suggested simultaneous, identical announcements in London, Paris, and Moscow and read a draft proposed by Halifax: The three governments "consider that such a measure of agreement has been reached on the provisions of the political Agreement which they propose to conclude that they can now proceed without delay to the consequential examination, which it was intended from the outset to undertake, of practical measures." For this purpose the British and French Governments "have decided to send to Moscow representatives of their General Staffs with a view to initiating technical conversations with the General Staff of the Soviet Union." The ambassadors had discussed the matter briefly during their previous interview, and Halifax had mentioned to Maisky a statement in Parliament. Molotov, therefore, apparently had precise instructions from Stalin on the subject. He immediately declared that any statement on the part of his government would be premature. Naggiar then pointed out that the British and French Governments would have to make statements to their respective parliaments, and Seeds explained that his government wished to be sure Moscow would issue nothing contradicting their announcement. "M. Molotov replied" that the British draft should be "more cautious in its terms. Present draft gave too optimistic an impression." He admitted that the Soviet Government planned no communiqué at all for the present and objected that the draft "we had proposed would create illusion that everything had been settled on the political side." Any joint communiqué "would have had to say that political conversations were not yet concluded; that discussions were still going on about the definition of indirect aggression, and that conversations were about to start on the most important part of the subject, namely, military questions." [6]

Chamberlain had apparently considered Molotov's objections when he announced the pending staff talks in Commons four days later (July 31) and added that it "is proposed that concurrently with the military conversations political discussions should continue with a view to reaching final conclusions on the terms of the political agreement." In concluding the debate on the subject, the Parliamentary Undersecretary of State for Foreign Affairs, R. A. Butler, explained that the main problem in the Moscow negotiations had been "whether we should encroach on the independence of the Baltic States." The government had no intention of doing so and the difficulty in finding a satisfactory formula was one of the main factors delaying an agreement. Moscow immediately seized on this statement, and in a communiqué in *Izvestia* on the morning of August 2 TASS declared that Butler was misrepresenting the attitude of the Soviet Government. The main problem was not the question of infringement of the independence of the Baltic states but rather of leaving no loophole for aggression. "One of the reasons for the delay in the negotiations lies in the fact that the British formula leaves such a loophole for an aggressor." [7]

Stalin's attempt, if such it was, to avoid the appearance of having definitely opted for the Anglo-French tie was unnecessary; by July 26 Hitler had decided to play the Russian card. According to Kleist (p. 46), news of the British intention to send a staff mission to Moscow reached Berlin on the 25th. Although no contemporary German account supports Kleist on this point, such early knowledge of British intentions was neither impossible nor improbable. Halifax had informed the Soviet Ambassador on the 25th, presumably not later than the afternoon, and "impressed upon M. Maisky that this information must be kept confidential for the present." But that same evening journalists in Paris and

London were aware that staff talks were imminent. The obvious conclusion is that Soviet diplomats deliberately "leaked" the news.[8]

During a long discussion with Ribbentrop in late July, Kleist warned against showing any eagerness in attempting to secure a pact with the U.S.S.R. and especially against offering any far-reaching concessions. A nonaggression pact was inherently desirable, particularly for the Soviet Union, and an excessively generous offer by one side would tend to reduce the value of the pact itself. Kleist expressed the opinion that mutually satisfactory relations and the elimination of tensions could be achieved within three to six months; Ribbentrop laughed and answered that he expected to arrive at this goal in fourteen days. "Politically, the problem of Russia is being dealt with here with *extreme urgency*," wrote Schnurre in Berlin to Schulenburg in Moscow on August 2, underlining the last two words. "During the last ten days," he continued, "I have daily had at least one direct or telephone conversation with the Foreign Minister and know that he is also constantly exchanging views with the Führer on this. The Foreign Minister is concerned to obtain some result in the Russian question as soon as possible, not only on the negative side (disturbing the British negotiations) but also on the positive side (an understanding with us)." [9]

The first German move was made on July 26; acting on orders from Ribbentrop who also prescribed the topics to be discussed, Schnurre invited Soviet chargé Astakhov and trade delegation chief Babarin to dinner at a Berlin restaurant. Schnurre started the discussion of political matters, which lasted until after midnight, by suggesting three stages in the improvement of Soviet-German relations: (1) fresh economic collaboration based on successful conclusion of the current economic negotiations; (2) the re-establishment of normal political relations, e.g., respectful treatment of each country in the other's press and attendance of diplomatic and other official representatives at various cultural and scientific affairs; and (3) a revival of the 1926 Berlin Treaty or a completely new agreement covering the vital interests of both states. Schnurre pointed out that the two countries had no conflicting interests either in Eastern Europe or the Far East and cited their common ideological opposition to Western "capitalist democracy."

Astakhov agreed with this exposition but brought up the Anti-Comintern Pact, close German-Japanese ties, and Munich, all of which had given the U.S.S.R. the feeling of being encircled and caused the Soviet Government to doubt the possibility of a rapid change in German policy. The chargé was possibly fishing for an indication of what Germany would demand in any delimitation when he declared that Berlin regarded Finland, the Baltic states, and Rumania as within its sphere of interest. Schnurre gave a reassuring answer and again mentioned a broad agreement which would take into account vital Soviet interests.

Evidently following Ribbentrop's instructions—which reflected Hitler's immediate concern—Schnurre then warned against a Soviet pact with Britain. "The time was opportune now" for an understanding with Germany "but would no longer be so after the conclusion of a pact with London." "What could Britain offer Russia?" asked Schnurre. "At best participation in a European war and the hostility of Germany, hardly a desirable end for Russia. What could we offer as against this? Neutrality and keeping out of a possible European conflict and, if Moscow wished, a German-Russian understanding on mutual interests." Astakhov apparently agreed and again sought to determine the extent of the "mutual interests." He inquired about German political aims in Rumania and the Baltic states and indicated Soviet approval of German annexation of Danzig and the Corridor; he also tried to get some indication of German intentions regarding Galicia and Eastern Poland. Schnurre answered that "no German-Russian clash of interests would result from all these questions." Astakhov promised to report the conversation to Moscow and in conclusion asked if a high German personality would express the same views in any conversation with a high Soviet personality. Schnurre replied in the affirmative.[10]

On July 29 Weizsäcker forwarded to Schulenburg a copy of Schnurre's memo on the conversation with the two Soviet officials and instructed the ambassador to determine Molotov's reaction if he saw "an opportunity of arranging a further conversation." Should Molotov display a less reserved attitude, Schulenburg was to express Schnurre's ideas more concretely. But Hitler and Ribbentrop were becoming impatient, and two days later Weizsäcker wired Schulenburg that Berlin desired an early interview and instructed him to report its date and time. The ambassador was unable to secure the audience immediately, and Ribbentrop himself spoke to Astakhov during the evening of August 2.[11]

The Foreign Minister posed two prerequisites for an improvement in relations with the U.S.S.R.: mutual noninterference in internal affairs and Soviet abandonment of a policy opposed to vital German interests. But renewed fear of a Soviet rebuff and exposure apparently accompanied Hitler's decision to make a serious approach. Ribbentrop merely repeated the statements Schnurre had already made, in somewhat stronger terms, and promised a more definite offer once Moscow had officially declared its "fundamental desire for remoulding our relations." In concluding the interview, he warned that the Germans desired no sensations. "If conversations such as ours were not handled with the discretion they deserved, they would have to be discontinued."[12]

Although Schulenburg had wired on August 2 that an interview with Molotov had been scheduled for the 3rd, Ribbentrop decided to continue the approaches in Berlin without waiting for the ambassador's report, and Schnurre received Astakhov at 12:30 on the afternoon of the 3rd. The chargé stated he had informed Molotov of the earlier dinner-conversation and that the latter had received the report with great interest. The Soviet Government also hoped for improved relations with Germany, and it too regarded the negotiation of an economic treaty as an appropriate first stage in achieving that goal. Molotov felt, however, that neither in Berlin or Moscow had the German Government made clear its attitude. Schnurre promised further talks in concrete terms if Moscow officially expressed such a desire; for its part the German Government would appreciate a clear statement of Russian interests. It also felt the talks should be continued in Berlin. If the Soviet Government agreed, appropriate instructions could be sent to Astakhov. The chargé was evidently aware of the reasons for German hesitancy and had taken Ribbentrop's warning to heart: "He assured me unasked [minuted Schnurre] that matters were being treated with absolute discretion on the Soviet side and particularly by himself in Berlin. Not even his colleagues at the Embassy were informed of these conversations." [13]

Stalin also appears to have hesitated at this stage, presumably fearing exposure of the talks in a German effort to prevent an Anglo-French-Soviet agreement. The first part of Schulenburg's interview with Molotov on August 3 was little more than a repetition of the Schnurre-Astakhov-Babarin conversation of the evening of July 26. Molotov cited the Anti-Comintern Pact, German support of Japan, and Soviet exclusion from the Munich meeting and declared that his government still had no proof of a change in Germany's attitude. When Schulenburg stated that Berlin maintained its demands on Poland but sought a peaceful solution, Molotov answered that the responsibility for a peaceful solution rested with Germany. The ambassador then denied that Germany alone was to blame for the deterioration in its relations with the U.S.S.R., mentioned the 1935 Soviet-French treaty, and warned against Soviet participation in a new anti-German combination. "Molotov replied that the present course taken by the Soviet Union was directed to purely defensive ends." Germany, on the other hand, had supported and encouraged Japanese aggression and, together with Italy, was pursuing an offensive policy. He promised, however, to inform his government which also desired improved relations.

Schulenburg received the impression that the Soviet Government was becoming more receptive to the idea of a *rapprochement*, "although the old mistrust of Germany persists." The ambassador felt that Moscow still intended to sign with Britain and France if they met all the Soviet demands. Molotov had seemed impressed, but "it will, nevertheless, require considerable effort on our part to cause a reversal in the Soviet Government's course." [14]

Although determined to treat with Hitler, Stalin seems to have taken what precautions he could against a German betrayal of the exchanges. The Soviet Ambassador to Ankara told Turkish Foreign Minister Saracoglu on August 4 that his government desired a bilateral secret agreement with Turkey and would welcome a visit to Moscow by the Foreign Minister for this purpose. Saracoglu received the impression that the Soviet Government desired to use him as an intermediary in the negotiations with the Western Allies. Stalin may have hoped this friendly approach to an ally of Britain and France would make any rumor or accusation of double dealing implausible. If such was the case, Turkey was selected because the attitude of Poland and Rumania precluded a similar approach to those countries. The Turkish Ambassador to Moscow called on Seeds on August 22, the day it became generally known that Germany and the U.S.S.R. were contemplating an agreement. He too "could not conceal his astonishment at the Soviet action," reported Seeds, "the Russian expressed readiness to conclude a pact with Turkey seemed a clear proof that they were not abandoning the anti-aggression nations." [15]

The next response to Berlin occurred on August 5 when Astakhov delivered Molotov's reply to the remarks Schnurre had made two days earlier: Moscow desired and was prepared to continue the conversations and considered the conclusion of the trade agreement as the first step in improving relations. The chargé admitted that his authority only extended to receiving the German views, but he considered the answer was a forward step; he also had the impression that even the last Schulenburg-Molotov interview had "ended on a positive note." Two days later (August 7) Potemkin remarked to Schulenburg that Astakhov was to receive wider instructions regarding the conversations.[16]

Schnurre reported to Ribbentrop at Fuschl (near Salzburg) on August 8 and received instructions for the next talk with Astakhov. The Anglo-French military mission was then at sea and arrived at Leningrad the following evening. The conversation on August 10 thus reflected the Foreign Minister's concern over the possibility of a Russian agreement with the West. Early in the discussion the Soviet chargé stated that he had again received explicit instructions to emphasize his government's desire for better relations with Germany. Schnurre in turn expressed regret at Molotov's failure to reveal any precise Soviet interests without a knowledge of which any concrete discussion would be impossible. It was especially important for Berlin to know the attitude and intentions of the U.S.S.R. with respect to Poland, since a conflict with that country might soon be forced on Germany. Soviet aims in the staff talks with the Western Allies also needed explanation. Schnurre assured the chargé that German objectives in Poland in the event of hostilities were limited and need not clash with Soviet interests, which must, however, be stated. If the Soviet Government was negotiating with Britain and France because of fear of Germany, Berlin was prepared to give any desired assurance. Astakhov then explained that the negotiations in Moscow had started at a time when Germany still displayed an intransigent attitude toward the Soviet Union. He felt that the outcome was now uncertain and that his government regarded the question as open. The chargé also considered it still too early to settle finally the problem of Poland.[17]

Astakhov called on Schnurre again on the 12th as a result of new instructions from Moscow. He stated that his government was interested in discussing several of the subjects already mentioned. According to the chargé, Molotov had emphasized that the discussions must develop "by degrees." It would also be much easier for the Soviet side if the talks were held in Moscow; Schulenburg could act for the Germans, or a special negotiator could be sent from Berlin.

At first Hitler and Ribbentrop thought to send Schnurre and, to give official weight, Dr. Hans Frank, Director of the National Socialist Legal Office and Minister without Portfolio in the German Government. Astakhov was informed of this on the evening of the 13th. Hitler, however, was thinking of going even further. On the 14th at Berchtesgaden he mentioned to Brauchitsch and Halder that he was considering sending a "prominent" person to Moscow with broad powers to negotiate. (Frank was evidently not a really "prominent" person.) [18]

Sometime during the 14th of August the Führer seems to have crossed, if not the Rubicon, at least the diplomatic Dvina. Late that evening in a "most urgent" telegram, Ribbentrop instructed Schulenburg to inform Molotov, among other things, that there "exist no real conflicts of interests between Germany and Russia," and that "German-Russian policy today has come to an historic turning-point." The ambassador was to point out that the alliance with the Western powers in 1914 had resulted in a Russian collapse: [19]

It is the compelling interest of both countries to avoid for all future time the destruction of Germany and of Russia in the interests of Western democracies.

The crisis which has been produced in German-Polish relations by English policy, as well as English agitation for war and the attempts at an alliance . . . make a speedy clarification of German-Russian relations necessary. Otherwise matters might, without Germany contributing thereto, take a turn which would deprive both Governments of the possibility of restoring German-Russian friendship and in due course clarifying jointly territorial questions in Eastern Europe. . . . Since, however, according to previous experience this clarification can be achieved only slowly through the usual diplomatic channels, I am prepared to make a short visit to Moscow in order, in the name of the Führer, to set forth the Führer's views to M. Stalin. In my view, only through such a direct discussion can a change be brought about, and it should not be impossible thereby to lay the foundations for a final settlement of German-Russian relations.

Ribbentrop directed his ambassador to read the instructions to Molotov verbatim but not to give him a copy. If necessary Schulenburg was to request an interview with Stalin himself to ensure that the communication suffered as little distortion as possible. The Foreign Minister also stated that he could make the visit only if assured of a long discussion with Stalin.

That afternoon, even before Ribbentrop's detailed instructions were wired from Berlin, Schulenburg had been directed to arrange an interview with Molotov for the following day. Thus at 8:00 on the evening of the 15th, after a few preliminary remarks, the ambassador read the slightly edited text of his instructions. Molotov listened closely as the communication was translated and ordered his secretary to make notes as detailed and accurate as possible. Although he could not give a definite answer immediately, Molotov declared that his government warmly welcomed Ribbentrop's offer. The visit would, however, require a great deal of preparation. In veiled terms (using a prediction of German intentions which he asserted Ciano had made at the end of June to the Soviet chargé in Rome) he then, for the first time, gave an indication of Soviet desires: (1) Germany to use its influence to improve Soviet-Japanese relations; (2) a joint "guarantee" of the

Baltic states; and (3) a nonaggression pact. As the conversation proceeded, Molotov abandoned some of his caution. The discussions of the last few weeks, he remarked, had given his government the impression that Berlin was really in earnest in its expressed desire to improve relations with the Soviet Union. "He regarded the statement which had been made today as decisive and as one in which this wish was especially pregnantly and clearly expressed." Molotov then bluntly asked how the German Government felt about the points mentioned. Toward the end of the conversation he indicated the primary question was that of a nonaggression agreement, and the main points should be considered promptly in order that Ribbentrop could come to Moscow prepared to make binding decisions.[20]

Schulenburg's telegraphic report on the interview was received in Berlin at 4:25 on the morning of August 16. At 2:30 that afternoon fresh instructions were sent from Berchtesgaden, and Weizsäcker was ordered to arrange for their immediate dispatch to Moscow. An hour later the State Secretary wired the ambassador to arrange another interview immediately. "Instructions for this are now being enciphered and will be sent to you in an hour at the latest." They left Berlin forty minutes later, but Weizsäcker's preliminary telegram was not deciphered in Moscow until 11:00 that evening, too late to contact the Narkomindel. An interview could not be requested until about 10:00 the next morning, the 17th. Ribbentrop could not contain his impatience, and shortly after noon Weizsäcker wired Schulenburg asking when he had requested the interview with Molotov and the time for which it had been scheduled. At about the same time, the German Embassy was informed that the ambassador would be received at 8:00 that evening.[21]

Schulenburg began the interview by reading the latest communication: Germany was prepared to sign a nonaggression pact, if desired one irrevocable for twenty-five years. Germany was also prepared to guarantee the Baltic states jointly with the U.S.S.R. and exert its influence toward better Russian-Japanese relations. In view of the danger of serious incidents involving Poland, Ribbentrop was ready to fly to Moscow any time after the 18th with full power from Hitler to negotiate and sign a treaty.

After the ambassador had finished, Molotov remarked that he would first read the official reply to the previous communication. Stalin was following the matter closely, he declared, was aware of all the details, and "in complete agreement with Molotov." In the official answer, after first laying the onus for German-Soviet enmity on Berlin, Stalin suggested as the first step in improved relations "the conclusion of a trade and credit agreement. . . . the second step, to be taken shortly thereafter, could be the conclusion of a non-aggression pact, or the reaffirmation of the Neutrality Pact of 1926, with the simultaneous conclusion of a special protocol defining the interests of the contracting parties in this or that question of foreign policy, and forming an integral part of the pact." Molotov then expressed his government's gratification with Ribbentrop's proposal to visit Moscow which emphasized the serious intentions of the German Government. "The journey by the Reich Foreign Minister, however, required thorough preparation. The Soviet Government did not like the publicity that such a journey would cause. They preferred to do practical work without much fuss." The official statement, continued Molotov, covered the basic Soviet views even though it had been prepared before the latest German communication was known. Both sides should immediately prepare drafts for a nonaggression pact (or reaffirmation of the neutrality treaty) and protocol.[22]

Although still cautious and unwilling to take more than one step at a time, Stalin apparently felt Hitler's agreement to his general conditions deserved some answer, even though indirect. The interview took place on the evening of the 17th; presumably that night or the next day Stalin ordered a communiqué which appeared in *Izvestia* on the 19th. The release cited reports in the Polish press that differences had arisen in the Anglo-French-Soviet staff talks over Soviet demands for support in the event of a conflict in the Far East. "Tass is authorized to state that this announcement is pure invention from the beginning to the end and that differences of opinion *which in fact exist* [italics supplied] are concerned with a completely different subject and have no connexion whatever with the question of the Far East." [23]

Schulenburg's report on the conversation was received in Berlin at 9:00 the following morning (August 18). At 6:53 that evening Weizsäcker wired the ambassador that fresh instructions were being drafted and directed him to "do everything in your power" to secure an interview with Molotov the next morning. At 7:45 the instructions were received from Berchtesgaden and by 10:48 they had been enciphered and were on their way to Moscow.

Ribbentrop instructed the ambassador to emphasize the imminence of a Polish-German war. Hitler considered clarified German-Soviet relations necessary before such a development, "if only to be able to take into account Russian interests in case of such a conflict, which would, of course, be difficult without such a clarification." Berlin had agreed to a nonaggression pact and a guarantee of the Baltic states and was willing to use its influence with Japan. In addition negotiations for the trade agreement had been completed. The nonaggression treaty presented no problems; Ribbentrop visualized a very simple formula: "Article 1. The German Reich and the U.S.S.R. will in no event resort to war, or to any other use of force with respect to each other. Article 2. This treaty shall enter into force immediately upon signature, and shall be valid and not liable to denunciation thereafter for a term of twenty-five years." The ambassador was to urge an immediate visit by his Foreign Minister who would come with full powers from Hitler to arrange details and sign the special protocol which, among other things, could settle spheres of interest in the Baltic area. In conclusion Ribbentrop directed the ambassador not to read the instructions, as previously, but rather press "emphatically, in the sense of the foregoing statements, for a rapid realization of my journey" and at the same time oppose with suitable arguments any new Soviet objections.[24]

Schulenburg met with Molotov again at 2:00 the next afternoon (the 19th). Although the latter admitted the importance of the proposed visit and emphasized that his government "understood and esteemed the underlying purpose," he still maintained that extensive preparations were necessary and not even an approximate date for the trip could be set. After all, the economic agreement had not yet been signed and published. "Molotov remained apparently unaffected by my protests, so that the first conversation closed with a declaration on the part of Molotov that he had imparted to me the views of the Soviet Government and had nothing to add to them." Schulenburg departed at 3:00 but scarcely half an hour later was informed that Molotov wished to see him again at 4:30. After apologizing, the latter stated that he had reported to his government which was willing to receive Ribbentrop about a week after the signing of the economic agreement had been announced. If the announcement were made the next day, the 20th, the German Foreign Minister could arrive in Moscow on August 26 or 27. "Molotov did not give reasons for his sudden change of mind. I assume [!] that Stalin intervened." At this meeting the ambassador was also given a Soviet draft of the nonaggression pact.[25]

The negotiations for the trade agreement had been concluded in Berlin on the evening of August 18 with both sides in complete agreement on the proposed text. Although the Soviet officials hinted they would require final approval from Moscow, it was decided that signature should take place at noon on Saturday the 19th. At 12:30 that day Schnurre was informed that definite word had not yet arrived from Moscow, and at 4:00 P.M. the Soviet delegation phoned that they would be unable to sign on the 19th. They requested further discussion on Monday, August 21. Later in the evening, however, Stalin wired his approval, and Schnurre and Babarin signed the treaty at 2:00 on the morning of the 20th. At the same time they agreed that the signature would be announced over the radio that evening and in the press the next morning, i.e. of August 21.[26]

Sometime before noon on the 20th (the telegram left Berlin at 12:35), Ribbentrop directed Schulenburg to report immediately by wire any further comment on the last two interviews or any other observations. Late that afternoon Weizsäcker instructed the ambassador to make an appointment at the Narkomindel for the same day in order to deliver an urgent personal message from Hitler to Stalin. The State Secretary's telegram was received at the embassy at 8:50 that evening and the Führer's communication shortly after midnight; Schulenburg replied that he could do nothing until the next day. At 1:43 P.M. on August 21 he reported he was to meet Molotov at 3:00 P.M. At that time he handed over a copy of Hitler's message together with a Russian translation, presumably on paper without any letterhead as ordered by Ribbentrop.

Hitler wrote that he welcomed the conclusion of the trade agreement as the first step in reshaping German-Soviet relations. With this act Germany was resuming a traditional attitude which had benefited both states in the past. The Führer also accepted the Soviet draft of the nonaggression pact but felt it imperative that certain questions connected with it be clarified as soon as possible.[27]

The substance of the supplementary protocol desired by the Government of the Soviet Union can, I am convinced, be clarified in the shortest possible time if a responsible German statesman can come to Moscow himself to negotiate. Otherwise the Government of the Reich are not clear as to how the supplementary protocol could be cleared up and settled in a short time.

The tension between Germany and Poland has become intolerable. Polish demeanour toward a great Power is such that a crisis may arise any day. Germany is at any rate determined, in the face of this presumption, from now on to look after the interests of the Reich with all the means at her disposal.

In my opinion, it is desirable, in view of the intentions of the two States to enter into a new relationship to each other, not to lose any time. I therefore again propose that you receive my Foreign Minister on Tuesday, August 22, but at the latest on Wednesday, August 23. The Reich Foreign Minister has the fullest powers to draw up and sign the nonaggression pact as well as the protocol. A longer stay by the Reich Foreign Minister in Moscow than one to two days at most is impossible in view of the international situation. I should be glad to receive your early answer.

ADOLF HITLER.

Molotov, having read the message, appeared deeply impressed and promised an immediate answer once Stalin had reached a decision. Two hours later Molotov handed over Stalin's reply: [28]

To the Chancellor of the German Reich, Herr A. Hitler. I thank you for the letter. I hope that the German-Soviet non-aggression pact will bring about a decided turn for the better in the political relations between our countries.

The peoples of our countries need peaceful relations with each other. The assent of the German Government to the conclusion of a non-aggression pact provides the foundation for eliminating the political tension and for the establishment of peace and collaboration between our countries.

The Soviet Government have instructed me to inform you that they agree to Herr von Ribbentrop's arriving in Moscow on August 23.

J. STALIN.

Stalin's reply arrived in Berlin at 9:45 P.M. on August 21 and was forwarded to Berchtesgaden an hour later. Hitler received the news with exultation; pounding the wall with both fists, he cried, "Now I have the whole world in my pocket!" [29]

Late in the afternoon of the 22nd, Ribbentrop arrived in Berlin from Berchtesgaden; the same evening he embarked for Moscow without any pronounced conviction that his mission would succeed but with an entourage of some thirty persons in two Condor transports—diplomatic experts, interpreters, press officials, and two photographers. Since it was impractical to fly directly to Moscow, the two aircraft landed at Königsberg later that night with an early departure planned for the next morning. Arriving at the Moscow airport shortly after noon on August 23, the party was greeted by Schulenburg and Deputy Foreign Commissar Potemkin; a swastika flag hastily prepared by the Soviet authorities was also in evidence.

Ribbentrop, Schulenburg, and Hilger were received in the Kremlin at 3:30 that afternoon; to their surprise Stalin as well as Molotov awaited them. Although his participation this early in the negotiations was unexpected, his presence allowed the discussion to proceed rapidly. The pact itself posed few problems since Hitler had already accepted the Soviet draft as a base. Stalin met the Germans half way in agreeing to a term of ten years (renewable for another ten years) and granted in full the Führer's desire for a treaty valid immediately upon signature. The settlement of these points seems to have required only three hours.

Ribbentrop then interrupted the talks to inform Hitler of a Soviet demand in connection with the special protocol. The Führer was willing to grant the U.S.S.R. Bessarabia, Finland, Estonia, Poland east of the rivers Narev,[30] Vistula, and San, and Latvia as far as the Düna. Stalin, however, demanded the Latvian ports of Libau and Windau. The message was telephoned from Moscow at 8:05 P.M. and Hitler's reply was received three hours later: "Yes, agreed." The German Foreign Minister returned to the Kremlin with most of his entourage, including the two photographers. The pact was quickly signed, and Ribbentrop then presented a draft for a joint communiqué announcing the signature. Stalin, however, objected to the rather extravagant terms Ribbentrop proposed to use in praising the new Soviet-German friendship. He reminded the Foreign Minister of the former bitterness of Soviet and German propaganda and suggested greater consideration for public opinion in the two countries.[31] Ribbentrop readily agreed to more moderate and restrained wording.

Once the official business had been concluded, a buffet was laid out in the conference room. Stalin himself poured the champagne for his guests. Toasts flowed as freely as the wine: "I know how much the German nation loves its Führer," said Stalin, "I should therefore like to drink to his health." He even managed a bit of German for the occasion: "Prost!" and "Zur Gesundheit!" It was almost 4:00 A.M. when the German delegation returned to its quarters and Ribbentrop reported the success of his mission directly to Hitler by telephone. He flew back to Berlin at 1:20 that afternoon.[32]

THE FRENCH GOVERNMENT had wished to send the staff missions to Russia by train through Germany. British Ambassador Henderson in Berlin, however, considered this route "unnecessarily provocative" and feared an incident might result. It was impossible to arrange air transport to Moscow, and the missions finally departed in a chartered steamer which docked at Leningrad during the night of August 9/10. The Allied officers arrived in Moscow on the morning of the 11th. Courtesy calls were made the same day and all members of the missions presented to Defense Commissar Voroshilov and Red Army Chief of Staff Shaposhnikov; Molotov himself received the heads of the missions, Admiral Drax of the Royal Navy and Général d'armée Doumenc of the French Army.[33]

The first official meeting of the three delegations took place the next morning, August 12. Voroshilov, Shaposhnikov, Kuznetsov (navy), Loktionov (air force), one other general officer, two interpreters, and a stenographer represented the U.S.S.R. General Doumenc, General Valin, five other officers, and three service attachés represented France. From the British forces were present Admiral Drax, Air Marshal Burnett, Major General Heywood, four other officers, and the three service attachés. After points of procedure and the time for future meetings had been agreed upon, Voroshilov produced an official document authorizing the members of the Soviet delegation to negotiate and sign a military agreement. What credentials and authority had the British and French missions, he asked. Displaying an order signed by Daladier, General Doumenc replied that he was authorized to sign a draft which would, however, have to be ratified by the French Government. Admiral Drax had no written credentials but stated he would take immediate steps to secure them. Although emphasizing the importance which his government attached to such credentials, Voroshilov declared that the talks need not be postponed until their receipt. He then invited the Allied missions to submit proposals for military cooperation; the Soviet delegation had prepared some plans but would first like to hear those of the British and French. Drax and Doumenc agreed, and after some general remarks the meeting ended.[34]

When the discussions resumed the next morning, General Doumenc gave a detailed exposition of the French Army's mobilization plans, number of divisions, timing, fortifications, communications, reserves of materiel, etc. He declared that offensives in certain areas were planned once any German offensive was repulsed. Even before such offensives developed, however, he felt that the Germans would hardly dare allocate less than forty divisions to the Western Front. Voroshilov then posed several questions and the meeting was adjourned until the afternoon. During the second session, in the process of answering Voroshilov's questions, General Heywood discussed the organization, expansion, and planned employment of the British Army, and General Valin made a few remarks on the French Air Force. In connection with the agenda for the next session, the Defense Commissar observed that before expounding on Soviet plans he should know what action the British and French staffs felt the Soviet Union should take in the event of a German attack in the west or against Poland, Rumania, or Turkey. To operate against Germany, Soviet forces would have to be based on the territory of other states.[35]

That night Stalin learned of Hitler's offer to send Schnurre and Frank to Moscow, and Voroshilov returned to the subject the following morning (August 14). In the event of a German attack on Britain and France, what were the Soviet forces expected to do? Could they cross Polish and Rumanian territory to contact the enemy? In reply Admiral Drax mentioned the moral effect upon Poland and Rumania of the knowledge that the Red Army was prepared to come to their aid. As operations developed, however, he felt the two countries would request Soviet aid. General Doumenc agreed and thought the Poles and Rumanians would beg for Soviet support. Voroshilov and Shaposhnikov expressed the fear that the request for aid might come too late. Admiral Drax then suggested adjournment, but the Defense Commissar objected. When Doumenc attempted to pass on to other matters and asked for an exposition of Soviet military plans, Voroshilov replied that without an unequivocal answer to his question regarding transit through Poland and Rumania further discussions would be useless. The British mission then withdrew for a private conference. Upon its return Admiral Drax made a statement for both Allied missions: Since Poland and Rumania were sovereign states, the simplest and most direct procedure would be for the Soviet Government to ask the two other governments. The Allied missions were willing, however, to ask their governments to pose the question in Warsaw and Bucharest. In the meantime, in view of the critical international situation, they urged that the discussions continue pending an answer. The Soviet delegation then retired to confer and prepare a written reply which their stenographer read upon their return to the conference room an hour later: [36]

Will the Soviet Military forces be allowed to pass through Polish territory, that is through the Wilno Gap and Galicia, and through Roumanian territory . . . France has already a treaty with Poland and Britain has guaranteed the integrity of Poland. . . . since the Soviet Union has no military agreement with Poland or Roumania, and since the danger of aggression in Europe is most likely to affect Poland, Roumania, France and England; to that extent the question of the rights of passage of Soviet Armed Forces across Poland and Roumania . . . should be decided by the Governments of France and Great Britain in consultation with the Polish and Roumanian Governments. . . . without a solution to this question . . . the Soviet Military Mission cannot recommend to its Government to take part in an enterprise so obviously doomed to failure.

The Soviet Military Mission asks that the replies to the questions by the British and French Governments should be expedited. Pending receipt of these replies the Soviet Military Mission considers that it is still possible to go into its plans for military collaboration against aggression in Europe.

The British and French missions agreed to ask their governments to determine the attitude of Poland and Rumania, and the Soviet delegation agreed that the next meeting would be devoted to Soviet military plans.

After a short preliminary exchange at the beginning of the next session (August 15), Shaposhnikov spoke of the planned employment of the Red Army. He first reviewed its strength in Europe, organization, mobilization plans, and railways and other communications. The Soviet Chief of Staff then gave a very interesting account of plans for three different contingencies. Since they reflect long-standing fallacies upon which Soviet foreign policy was then based and continued to be based, they must have actually embodied Stalin's views; i.e. had the pact with Hitler not been forthcoming and had he decided to combine with the West—on his own terms—these would have been the terms.

1) In case of a German attack on Britain and France, the U.S.S.R. proposed to put into the field a force equal to 70 per cent of the British and French forces engaged directly against Germany. If 90 divisions were deployed on the Western Front, the Soviet Union would deploy 63 infantry divisions, 6 cavalry divisions, and the necessary artillery, tanks and aircraft— altogether some 2,000,000 troops. Poland must put 40 to 45 divisions in action in line with her treaties with France and Britain, and the latter two countries must obtain Polish permission for the operation of Soviet forces on Polish territory.

2) Should Germany attack Poland and Rumania, the two countries must resist with all their forces and France and Britain must immediately declare war on Germany. Once Britain and France had secured Polish and Rumanian agreement, the U.S.S.R.

would deploy forces equal to those deployed by France and Britain directly against Germany. If the Allies used 90 divisions on the Western Front, the Red Army would engage 90 infantry divisions, 12 cavalry divisions, and the necessary artillery, tanks, and planes.

3) A third alternative envisioned Germany attacking the Soviet Union through Latvia, Estonia and Finland. In this case Britain and France must immediately declare war against Germany, and Poland must support them and also allow passage of the Red Army through northern and southern Poland. The U.S.S.R. proposed to deploy 120 infantry and 16 cavalry divisions, 5,000 pieces of heavy artillery, 9,000 to 10,000 tanks, and 5,500 planes. France and Britain must immediately attack Germany with the equivalent of 70 per cent of these forces, and Poland should contribute at least 45 infantry divisions.

In all three eventualities the British and French fleets would have the same task: to close the English Channel, blockade Germany's North Sea coast, control the Mediterranean and close the Suez Canal and the Dardanelles, and operate against enemy submarines and cruisers off Norway and Finland and around Murmansk and Archangel. Their most important task, however, would be to send a strong force into the Baltic. In this connection, Paris and London must secure the agreement of Finland, Estonia, and Latvia to British-French-Soviet occupation of certain ports and islands.[37]

At the next meeting on August 16, Air Marshal Burnett spoke of the policy, expansion, and training of the Royal Air Force and of aircraft production. General Valin then made a statement on the French Air Force, its materiel, personnel, ground organization, mobilization, supply services, and planned employment. Principles submitted earlier in a written statement by General Doumenc were then discussed briefly. Voroshilov rejected them as too general and abstract and demanded action on "the actual questions of the organisation for common action against aggression." The French general thereupon declared that he would like to draft some written terms based on the three plans presented by Shaposhnikov the day before, but the Defense Commissar in turn objected that it was too soon to draw up documents. The cardinal point was not yet decided: the "question of the rights of passage of Soviet troops over Polish and Roumanian territory to take part in common action against the aggressor." Doumenc again urged that an attempt be made to draft specific articles of a military agreement, but Voroshilov remained adamant. The discussion then turned to the agenda of the next meeting, and the Defense Commissar agreed to a statement on Soviet aviation. He also asked when a reply could be expected to the "cardinal" Soviet question regarding Poland and Rumania. If a lengthy delay were expected, he felt the talks should be adjourned indefinitely after the next session. Rejecting a suggestion by General Doumenc that the discussions might continue on the assumption of an affirmative answer, Voroshilov ended the meeting with the observation that the "Soviet Delegation will not be able to continue its conversations with the other delegations until they know the views of the British and French Governments on how they consider that the Soviet forces can intervene against aggression." [38] This session was held in the morning; the evening before Schulenburg had informed Molotov that Ribbentrop was prepared to visit Moscow.

The discussion of the following morning, August 17, opened with a statement by Army Commander Loktionov (the title of "general" had not yet been restored in the Red Army) on Soviet air strength: aircraft, aircraft production, training, and planned employment. Voroshilov then "answered" in general terms, evasively, or not at all a list of seven questions on logistic and political problems submitted earlier by the British and French (e.g., Soviet views on Germany's most likely course of action and tonnage that could be sent to Poland via Murmansk or the Black Sea). If an answer regarding Poland and Rumania were not received by the next morning, he then announced, the meetings would have to be suspended. When the Defense Commissar remained obdurate in the face of Allied protests and arguments, General Doumenc finally suggested that a date be set for the next meeting; if no reply had been received by then, the session could be postponed. Admiral Drax added that if the negotiations were adjourned indefinitely the French and British Governments would probably have to make a statement. The Soviet officers withdrew for a conference, and upon their return Voroshilov suggested 10:00 A.M. on August 20 or 21. Admiral Drax preferred the later date and the meeting ended.[39]

The last meeting opened on schedule. The credentials of the British mission had arrived in the interval and were duly read and translated. The Defense Commissar then officially suggested an indefinite suspension of the talks until the attitude of Poland and Rumania could be clarified. After the Allied missions had withdrawn for a short conference, Admiral Drax presented their formal reply:

We . . . find it difficult to understand your action in inviting our two missions to come to Moscow, when it was apparently your intention to put to them at once difficult political questions. The Soviet authorities must have been well aware that the answers to these questions would inevitably require reference to our Governments and by them to other Governments. It is obvious that this would entail delays which are surely undesirable from every point of view. The French and British Missions are therefore unable to accept any responsibility for the delays that have arisen. . . . in our opinion, useful work can be done by continuing these meetings and we are ready to do so at any time.

After hearing the Anglo-French statement the Soviet delegation withdrew to prepare its defense: "British and American troops, in the last World War," declared Voroshilov,

could not have taken part in the general action with the French Military forces, had they not had the opportunity of operating from French soil. . . . The Soviet Military Delegation cannot picture to itself how the Governments and General Staffs of Britain and France, in sending their missions to the U.S.S.R. for discussions to arrange a military convention, could not have given them some directives on such an elementary matter as the passage and action of Soviet armed forces against the troops of the aggressor, on the territory of Poland and Roumania, with which countries France and Britain have corresponding military and political agreements.

If, however, this axiomatic question is turned by the British and French into a great problem demanding long study, this can only show that there are reasons to doubt their desire to come to serious and effective cooperation with the U.S.S.R. In view of the above the responsibility for delay in drawing up a military convention, as for the interruption of the conversations, naturally falls on the British and French Delegations.

At the same time the Defense Commissar was careful not to slam the door too hard. He assured the Allied officers that his delegation was prepared to resume the discussions once an affirmative answer had been received regarding Poland and Rumania. They contemplated no statement to the press and reserved "the right, on the continuation of the talks, to put a series of questions which they may consider necessary." [40] But this was the end of the military staff talks, if indeed they may properly be termed that. That afternoon Schulenburg delivered Hitler's personal letter to Stalin and the latter agreed to Ribbentrop's flight to Moscow.

BEFORE THE DAY ENDED, Seeds, Naggiar, Drax, and Doumenc had met and discussed the formal warning of August 14, that the Soviet Government could not participate in "an enterprise so obviously doomed to failure" should Warsaw and Bucharest refuse to admit the Red Army. The two ambassadors feared Moscow would remain adamant on this point. "We are agreed," reported Seeds, "that as we from the outset have been petitioners in this matter of forming an anti-aggression front and have taken engagements with regard to Poland and Roumania, Soviet negotiators are justified in putting on Great Britain and France the onus of approaching those countries." [41]

Bonnet received the news early the next morning and immediately telephoned Polish Ambassador Lukasiewicz who was vacationing in Brittany. The ambassador arrived at the Quai d'Orsay that afternoon and was warned that anything could happen, including a German-Soviet combination at the expense of Poland, if his government refused to allow the entry of Soviet troops. Although the ambassador promised to report the conversation, he gave little hope of a positive reply. Would you, as a Frenchman, he asked Bonnet, allow the Germans to protect Alsace-Lorraine? General Musse, the French military attaché at Warsaw who was temporarily in Paris, was sent back to his post the same day with orders to use what arguments he could with the Polish General Staff. The next day Bonnet wired Ambassador Noël in Warsaw that he should insist on the necessity of Polish agreement and emphasize that France could not believe Poland would refuse to discuss the conditions of Soviet intervention and thereby "accept the responsibility for the failure of the military talks in Moscow and all the consequences thereof." On the 17th Halifax instructed British Ambassador Kennard to support his French colleague and suggested that he, too, might warn of the possibility of a German-Soviet agreement.[42]

The two ambassadors agreed that Noël should see Beck first, and the French Ambassador was received on the 18th. Although reserving a final reply until the next day, the Foreign Minister voiced several objections: (1) If Poland agreed to admit Soviet troops, Moscow would immediately disclose this information in Berlin and Hitler, with his anti-Communist orientation, would no longer hesitate to attack Poland.[43] (2) Ever since the beginning of the negotiations, Moscow had been seeking to throw the responsibility for their failure upon Warsaw. (3) Even should Poland agree, the U.S.S.R. could not be relied upon to keep any agreement and was, in fact, incapable of furnishing any real aid. General Musse spoke with the Polish Chief of Staff, General Stachiewicz, the same day; although the Chief of Staff promised to consider the French arguments carefully, his attitude was equally negative. Kennard's interview with Beck took place that evening and was even less successful than Noël's. Beck had learned in the meantime that Voroshilov wished to intervene through Galicia and the Vilna area; this was evidence, declared the Foreign Minister, that Soviet strategy was to separate Poland from Rumania and the Baltic states.[44]

Having consulted with Marshal Smigly-Rydz, Beck gave the considered reply of the Polish Government on the evening of the 19th. It was unequivocally negative, but in order not to complicate the situation in Moscow he agreed that the Anglo-French approach and its rejection should be treated as a purely unofficial exchange. The French and British military attachés had talked to the Chief of Staff that morning, before Beck had returned his negative answer. Although General Stachiewicz considered it useless to discuss transit of Soviet forces, he agreed to consult Smigly-Rydz before giving a final answer. The next morning (August 20) he informed the two attachés that, if it were made clear in Moscow that Red Army ground forces could never be admitted, the Polish General Staff was willing to consider a memorandum regarding Polish-Soviet military collaboration based on the Moscow staff talks.[45]

Even before learning of the flat Polish refusal, Bonnet had, on the evening of the 19th, instructed Noël to make a new effort. On the evening of the 20th he ordered the ambassador to see Beck and Smigly-Rydz together. All to no avail. "With the Germans," declared the Polish marshal, "we risk our liberty. With the Russians we lose our soul." [46]

On the 20th Naggiar had wired from Moscow urging an affirmative reply to the Soviet demand regarding transit. If Warsaw would not agree officially, the only solution was to refuse to take Polish objections seriously. Probably what Beck really wanted was to know nothing at all about the matter. Bonnet agreed and spoke to Daladier who also agreed and on the 21st instructed Doumenc directly to make any statement about Poland he considered necessary and sign the best agreement he could get, subject to subsequent approval by the French Government. At the same time Bonnet instructed Naggiar to inform Molotov that France agreed in principle to the passage of the Red Army through Poland once that country was at war with Germany. The Foreign Office was also requested to instruct Admiral Drax to support this move, but no decision was reached in London, and definite instructions were never sent.[47]

General Doumenc interpreted his instructions as a sign that the situation was growing very serious. The news on the morning of the 22nd of Ribbentrop's pending visit confirmed this view. The general decided to write Voroshilov that the French Government's answer to the cardinal Soviet point was in the affirmative and request a meeting that evening (the 22nd) at 6:00. After the general had explained his views at the British Embassy the same morning, his colleagues agreed that, since they had no instructions from London, they "should let Doumenc play his hand as best he could, and that if Voroshilov asked about the British reply we could only repeat that we had not received one yet."

Voroshilov gave no answer until 6:30 P.M. when a Soviet liaison officer arrived at Doumenc's quarters with word that the Defense Commissar wished to see him immediately, alone and without an interpreter. After informing Naggiar, who had similarly been summoned to an interview with Molotov, Doumenc went to Voroshilov's office expecting to find Admiral Drax there. After a few minutes' wait outside, he realized the admiral was not coming and, being informed that Voroshilov was waiting, he finally went in.

Without any excuse for his tardy reply to Doumenc's note, the Defense Commissar asked for proof that the French answer was in the affirmative; could the general produce the telegram from his government? He did not normally carry code messages in his pocket, Doumenc replied, and his statement must suffice: "I have no document, but my Government has informed me that the reply to the basic, essential question is in the affirmative. In other words, the Government has impowered me to sign a military convention under which authorisation will be given for the passage of Soviet troops at the points specified by you, that is to say, the Corridor of Vilno, and, if the actual circumstances demand it, Galicia and Roumania." Voroshilov immediately rejected this "affirmative" reply on the grounds that it was neither endorsed by the British nor made with the full knowledge and consent of Warsaw and Bucharest.[48]

BUT EVEN AT THIS LATE DATE, only hours before Ribbentrop's arrival, Stalin was reluctant to abandon completely the possibility of a treaty with France and Britain. He apparently still feared a German attempt to disrupt the military talks and plunge the U.S.S.R. back into the diplomatic isolation it had experienced immediately after Munich. "Please allow us to wait until the situation is clear," said Voroshilov to Doumenc, "that is to say, until we have the British Government's reply and until the position of Poland and Roumania seems clear to us." "But I fear one thing," warned the Defense Commissar, "the French and English sides have allowed the political and military discussions to drag on too long. That is why we must not exclude the possibility during this time, of certain political events. Let us wait." [49]

At the same time Molotov was assuring Naggiar that the fundamental policy of the U.S.S.R. had not changed; it was still determined to maintain peace and resist aggression. The Soviet Union had signed a number of nonaggression agreements, he reminded the ambassador, one with Poland in particular. In agreeing to negotiate another with Germany, he did not consider that his government was deviating from its general peaceful policy. He felt that it was necessary to mark time for a few days until the proper course was clear.[50]

Molotov received Seeds at 8:00, immediately after the interview with the latter's French colleague. The ambassador asked exactly what the Germans had proposed; nonaggression pacts could take various forms. Did the Soviet Government intend to stand idly by while Poland was overrun? Molotov "clearly did not like this questioning and could only say that we must wait and see how negotiations would work out." Seeds persisted: Was everything that had been achieved in building a system of general defense against aggression "to be rendered null. Would it not be possible to continue this good work?" Molotov finally replied "that it all depended on the German negotiations, but perhaps, after a bit, say a week, we might see."[51]

On the evening of the 22nd, the U.S. chargé in London reported that the Soviet Embassy there was busily disseminating the line that a pact with Germany in no way ruled out an Anglo-French-Russian defensive alliance. At almost the same time, the chargé in Germany telegraphed to Washington information received from a member of the Soviet Embassy in Berlin. The informant hinted that further Soviet negotiations with Britain and France were possible; even if a pact should be concluded with Berlin, flagrant German aggression against Poland might cause Russia to turn against Germany.

During the 22nd and even on the 23rd, the competent Soviet press officials in Moscow continued to assure foreign correspondents that a pact with Germany was not incompatible with a military agreement with Britain and France. It was in the best interests of all to relieve the tension between Germany and the Soviet Union, and there was no question of a pact which would encourage aggression. Naggiar mentioned these statements to Molotov on the 22nd, and the next afternoon Berlin brought the reports to Ribbentrop's attention in Moscow. On the margin of the telegram the Foreign Minister wrote: "Schulenburg: Molotov to take action against false reports. Departure of military missions." [52]

In the conversations with Seeds and Naggiar on the 22nd, Molotov attempted to blame the Allies for the stalemate in the staff talks and Ribbentrop's invitation to Moscow. The French Ambassador had only been directed to demand an explanation of the German Foreign Minister's visit. Halifax, however, had armed Seeds with instructions to accuse the Russians of negotiating in bad faith. Writing to the Foreign Secretary a week later, the stiff upper lip of His Majesty's Ambassador in Moscow curled momentarily: [53]

If I may be permitted a human touch at this serious moment I beg to be allowed to express my personal gratification at Your Lordship's instructions which enabled me, after months of patience and self-control, to accuse the Soviet Prime Minister to his face of 'bad faith,' a charge which an accuser cannot usually make and survive. That the accusation had to be made through a subservient and very frightened M. Potemkin as interpreter and witness was particularly galling to the recipient, who savagely asked whether those words figured textually in my instructions. But as the conversation continued on normal lines for some three-quarters of an hour after that incident, with M. Molotov in a reasonably amenable frame of mind, it is clear to me that even a Soviet statesman may sometimes feel that his particular ideology, or conception of conduct, is not quite unassailable.

By the morning of August 24, Admiral Drax and General Doumenc had decided to leave for home via Helsinki that evening if orders to the contrary were not received. Both the Foreign Office and the Quai d'Orsay felt, however, that the Soviet authorities should explicitly state that further negotiations were useless. Thus Drax and Doumenc, accompanied by the two military attachés, spoke with Voroshilov for the last time at 1:00 P.M. on the 25th. In "view of the changed political situation announced yesterday," they asked, is it "likely in your opinion that the Soviet Government will desire the Military Missions to continue their conversations." Unfortunately, the Defense Commissar replied, with the new political situation there was no point in continuing the talks. As the two Allied officers were leaving, he exclaimed that throughout the negotiations the Poles had declared they wanted no Soviet help; the Rumanians had said nothing at all. "Were we to have to conquer Poland in order to offer to her our help, or were we to go on our knees and offer our help to Poland? The position was impossible for us." Seeds and Naggiar had a similarly futile conversation with Molotov about five hours later. As the British Ambassador was leaving, "Molotov then adopted a manner of almost hearty simplicity and said what a pity it was we could not have helped negotiations to a successful issue by getting the consent of Polish and Roumanian Governments to the passage of troops." Naggiar, who remained behind, asked what the Soviet Government now proposed to do in the event of German action against Danzig, to which Molotov replied that his government could hardly assist Poland which was unwilling to accept Soviet assistance.[54]

IN A CONVERSATION WITH BULLITT on the afternoon of the 22nd, Daladier said he was unable to understand how the Russians had so completely deceived his government. He reminded the ambassador of at least six warnings he, Bullitt, had given since January, "that most serious negotiations were under way between the Germans and the Russians . . . he had told all the French Government services to attempt to verify my statements to him but had been reassured that there were no negotiations other than the commercial negotiations in progress between Germany and the Soviet Union."

Recent warnings had, however, been voiced—but not loudly or often enough to make any impression. Reporting on a conversation with Weizsäcker on August 15, British Ambassador Henderson mentioned that the State Secretary seemed much more detached and calm than at the time of the Munich crisis. He "professed to believe that Russian assistance to the Poles would not only be entirely negligible but that the U.S.S.R. would even in the end join in sharing the Polish spoils." At about the same time Theo Kordt of the German Embassy in London, who had just returned from Berlin, was warning Vansittart of the danger of a German-Soviet understanding, but Vansittart expressed great confidence over the situation in Moscow.

In a telegram of August 21, Seeds quoted a quite ominous passage in *Pravda*'s account that morning of the trade agreement: "It may prove to be an important step in the question of further improving not only economic but also political relations between the U.S.S.R. and Germany." On August 19 and 21 *Pravda* had printed stories from the London *Daily Worker* of August 7 and 8 charging fresh attempts at appeasement on the part of the British Government. In reporting the articles in another telegram of the 21st, Seeds merely pointed out that the Soviet Government had evidently withheld publication of the articles and was now printing them in connection with the trade agreement with Germany and at a delicate state in the Franco-British-Soviet negotiations. Naggiar seems to have been more alarmed. The same day he warned Paris that he would not be surprised if the Axis powers offered the U.S.S.R. parts of Poland, Rumania, and the Baltic states. No reliance could be placed in the ideological differences since Hitler and Mussolini were in such a tight spot they would hesitate at nothing. In view of recent nationalistic trends in the Soviet Union, Moscow might welcome such an offer.[55]

As on several earlier occasions, someone in the German Embassy evidently attempted to warn the Allies through the U.S. Embassy. On August 6 the chargé d'affaires telegraphed to Washington a detailed and accurate account of the Molotov-Schulenburg conversation of the 3rd. On the 16th Ambassador Steinhardt transmitted an account of the interview of the night before when Schulenburg had delivered Ribbentrop's offer to come to Moscow in person. (The only significant information which he lacked was that Ribbentrop himself proposed to make the trip.) "In view of the nature of the above information," wired the ambassador, "I venture to request the Department to use every means to protect the source and Moscow origin thereof." The next day in Washington, Undersecretary of State Sumner Welles informed the British Ambassador of the report and disclosed its source. "He made me promise not to disclose its identity to you by telegram," wired the ambassador on the evening of the 17th, "as he distrusted security of all cyphers. I am sending it by air mail due in England August 20." Unfortunately the letter was not received at the Foreign Office until the 22nd. The telegram itself reached the Central Department of the Foreign Office the same day! Steinhardt himself spoke to Seeds at 7:00 on the evening of the 23rd—after Stalin and Ribbentrop had already spent several hours together: [56]

The British Ambassador . . . was not only apparently in complete ignorance of the degree of agreement already reached between the German and Soviet Russian Governments but was also apparently oblivious to the gravity and portent of the impending Soviet-German agreement and the consequences to be anticipated therefrom. . . . The Ambassador apparently believed Molotov's assurances that a Soviet-German agreement would be limited to a nonaggression pact which would not be incompatible with an Anglo-French-Soviet alliance against aggression. I expressed incredulity at this point of view and informed the Ambassador in confidence that I had good reason to believe that agreement had been substantially reached between the German and Soviet Governments on far-reaching political matters prior to the decision to send Ribbentrop to Moscow and that Ribbentrop's presence here was largely theatrical to impress world opinion, particularly British and French. The Ambassador thanked me for expressing my "opinion" to him so frankly . . . the French and British Embassies here have apparently not only been in complete ignorance of the Soviet intentions vis-a-vis Germany but appear to have been entirely taken in by the reassurances conveyed to them by Molotov, and were still incredulous last night.

In the dispatch to London of August 29, Seeds admitted that the pact had come as something of a shock. He and Naggiar had half expected the Soviet Government to abandon the negotiations and had, "indeed, of late rather been working only with the hope that conversations could be carried on for a period long enough to tide over a critical period in European history." They were, in other words, prepared for eventual Soviet neutrality; "but I must frankly confess," added the ambassador, "that I did not contemplate that the Soviet Government, having reached the stage of military conversations which contemplated an attack by Soviet troops on Germany through Poland and Roumania, could have the duplicity to reach out the hand of friendship to the prime mover in the anti-Comintern and, what might be called, aggression front." [57]

Those British and French statesmen and diplomats who were surprised can hardly be blamed; until almost the very end, Hitler and Stalin also doubted the possibility of reaching an understanding. In seeking an agreement with the U.S.S.R., London and Paris followed the only course justified by the information available. Although they expected little of value in a purely military sense from a Russian alliance, the authorities of the Foreign Office and the Quai d'Orsay felt that such an alliance, insofar as it might deter Hitler, represented the last hope of saving the peace. This may have been the case. As we shall see in the next chapter, Hitler believed that Anglo-French determination to support Poland was based upon hope of Soviet assistance. Once they were deprived of that hope, he expected the British and French leaders to stand idly by, wringing their hands perhaps but not declaring war, while German forces overran Poland. An alliance between the U.S.S.R. and the Western powers might conceivably have delayed the outbreak of the war until the next spring. Given Hitler's mentality, however, the ultimate outcome could hardly have been peace. After Munich he had little difficulty in convincing himself of what he wanted to believe, and he wanted to believe that France and Britain would not fight over Poland.

In retrospect it is clear that, in 1939 as in 1941, only a direct German attack could have enlisted Stalin on the side of the Western Allies. Such a direct attack was of course impossible until Poland had been conquered and Rumania occupied. British and French leaders might have sacrificed Poland, Rumania, and the other small states of Eastern Europe had they been politically able to disregard their parliamentary oppositions and public opinion and morally capable of basing their policy on expediency and ruthlessness. Although this would have made a German attack on Russia possible (but hardly certain), surviving German and Soviet citizens would have agreed in 1945 that a policy based mainly on ruthless expediency is not necessarily sound.

11

Stalin Fans the Flames

August 22—September 17, 1939

As early as the end of July 1939, Ribbentrop remarked to Kleist that if Warsaw refused the "generous" German offers for a solution of the problems of Danzig and the corridor, a "complete" solution would be necessary. Since the Soviet Union would remain passive, Britain and France, in their present weakness, would be unable to fulfill their treaty obligations to Poland.[1]

Approximately two weeks later, on August 14, Hitler expressed to Brauchitsch and Halder his conviction that Britain would not fight. The worst that could be expected from the West in the event of an attack on Poland would be the recall of their ambassadors, an embargo on trade with Germany, and an appeal to the League of Nations. As an excuse Britain would cite the attitude of the U.S.S.R., the neutrals' opposition to the passage of troops, and the fact that the Anglo-Polish mutual defense treaty was not yet ratified. To ensure this result, however, the German armed forces must secure immediate successes; within one or two weeks it would have to be apparent that Poland was on the verge of collapse.[2]

On August 22 at Berchtesgaden, Hitler addressed the top officers of the three services and the staff chiefs of the Wehrmacht high command. His own existence was an essential factor in the current situation, declared the Führer. Never again would a German statesman enjoy the confidence and be able to exercise the authority that he did. The second favorable factor was Mussolini; his strong personality was the only guarantee of Italian loyalty. Among the Allies, conversely, there were no significant personalities. He was convinced that Chamberlain and Daladier would hardly bring themselves to decide on war; such a decision would be much more difficult for them than for him since they must risk much and could win little. Finally, it was important to test the new German Wehrmacht in a limited conflict before attempting a general settlement with the victors of 1918.

The situation was now advantageous for the isolation of Poland and thus for a complete solution of the Polish problem. Although an attack on Poland involved a gamble, he was fully convinced it would succeed. Britain and France had pledged assistance but were in no position to furnish any—nor had Polish-British negotiations yet resulted in the conclusion of a treaty. Although it appeared to him that no British statesman would risk war in view of the precarious world situation, England sought to avoid the mistake she had made in the fall of 1938, a premature capitulation, and would thus bluff to the last moment. France, because of her low birth rate, could not even consider the bloodshed of a long war. There were only two ways for the two countries to help Poland: through a blockade of Germany and through an attack in the west. The first would have no effect because of German expansion in the east; the second was hardly likely because of psychological factors (i.e. the bitter lessons of the futile attacks from 1915 to 1917).

Until now the Western powers had placed all their hope in Soviet Russia. But the nonaggression pact with Moscow would snatch this card from their hands and strongly influence their future decisions. Nevertheless, despite all the favorable factors, the behavior of France and Britain could not be predicted with absolute certainty. For this reason ruthless determination was necessary on the German side. The next morning Hitler set the time and date for the attack: 4:30 A.M. on August 26.[3]

Hitler expected the news of the Moscow agreement to paralyze the will of the French and British to resist; the Poles for their part feared that this might indeed be the case. Beck's first reaction was transmitted to Kennard immediately after the announcement of Ribbentrop's journey, at 1:30 on the morning of August 22. The ambassador reported that the Foreign Minister was "apprehensive of the possible effect on French and British public opinion as he fully realizes the value which they attached to Soviet coopera- tion." In a conversation with Sumner Welles in Washington later in the day, the Polish Ambassador was also concerned about the effect upon British and French public opinion and expressed fear that the British Government might again be forced into appease- ment.[4]

But Hitler's hopes were unwarranted and the Polish fears un- justified. Daladier admitted to Bullitt on August 22 that France was in "a most tragic and terrible situation." "Under the circum- stances," reported the ambassador,

he was faced with the alternative of sacrificing the lives of all able-bodied men in France in a war, the outcome of which would be to say the least doubtful; or the worse alternative of abandoning the commitments of France to support Poland which would be a horrible moral blow to the French people and would result in Germany swallowing one after another, Poland, Rumania, Hungary, Yugosla- via, Bulgaria, Greece and Turkey. In the end Germany would turn on France and England with all the economic resources of these countries at her disposal. . . .

I discussed the general situation at great length with Léger at the Foreign Office. . . .

Throughout our conversation politicians kept calling him on the telephone urging that it would be folly to go to war in support of Poland in view of the agreement between the Soviet Union and Germany. Léger replied to them as he did to me that France must fight since if Poland should be abandoned the whole of Eastern and Southeastern Europe would fall without a struggle into Hitler's hands and with the resources of this vast area behind him Hitler would be able to overwhelm France and England. . . .

In brief the opinion of Daladier, Gamelin, Darlan, Léger, Guy la Chambre [Minister for Air] and other Ministers with whom I have talked today is . . . that France must support Poland even though the successful issue of a war thus engaged may be most doubtful since the abandonment of Poland would mean that France and England would have to fight somewhat later in an even worse position and that they would lose their moral standing in the world.[5]

Similar bitter despair may have been felt in London, but only determination was expressed. At 1:15 P.M. on August 23 at Berchtesgaden, Ambassador Henderson gave Hitler a German translation of a personal message from Chamberlain:

Apparently the announcement of a German-Soviet Agreement is taken in some quarters in Berlin to indicate that intervention by Great Britain on behalf of Poland is no longer a contingency that need be reckoned with. No greater mistake could be made. Whatever may prove to be the nature of the German-Soviet Agreement, it cannot alter Great Britain's obligation to Poland . . .

It is alleged that if His Majesty's Government had made their position more clear in 1914, the great catastrophe would have been avoided. Whether or not there is any force in that allegation, His Majesty's Government are resolved that on this occasion there shall be no such tragic misunderstanding.

If the case should arise, they are resolved and prepared to employ without delay all the forces at their command, and it is impossible to foresee the end of hostilities once engaged. It would be a dangerous illusion to think that if war once starts it will come to an early end, even if a success on any one of the several fronts on which it will be engaged should have been secured.

During this first interview the Führer displayed almost hysterical agitation, but as soon as Henderson had left the room he slapped his thigh, laughed, and predicted, "Chamberlain won't survive that conversation: his Cabinet will fall this evening." Weizsäcker, who was present, objected that Britain would be unable to evade her promises and that Chamberlain would rally Parliament with a war-like declaration. "But my words were spoken into the air," wrote the State Secretary later.

Henderson received Hitler's formal reply that afternoon. By guaranteeing Poland, declared the Führer, Britain had ensured Polish intransigence and had, in effect, encouraged persecution of the German minority in Poland. Germany could no longer tolerate this situation, and the expressed British intention to aid Poland would have no effect on its determination to defend German interests. Should Britain start any mobilization, he, Hitler, would immediately mobilize the German forces.[6]

The next morning, of the 24th, Weizsäcker spoke to Hitler alone. The Führer seemed more receptive to advice and expressed his own doubts regarding Italy. The State Secretary agreed, cited Italian statements, and warned that Britain would aid Poland but Italy would not aid Germany. Hitler was not as indifferent to the prospect of a war with the Western powers as he had been the previous day and mentioned the possibility of a peaceful solution: Should the Poles waver a settlement by stages might be feasible, and the British might abandon the Poles as they had the Czechs. "He seemed to be uncertain," recalled Weizsäcker, "and at times I could imagine I had convinced him. But when, on August 24, after our return by plane to Berlin, it had become clear that the British Parliament had not done Hitler the favor he had hoped for, he was obviously disappointed." [7]

Shortly before noon on the 25th, Hitler called Paul Schmidt, the chief interpreter of the Auswärtiges Amt, to the Reichschancellery to translate especially significant passages from statements Chamberlain and Halifax had made in Parliament the day before. Admitting that the German-Soviet pact had been "a surprise of a very unpleasant character," Chamberlain stated that it was regarded in Berlin as a great diplomatic victory which rendered unlikely any French or British aid to Poland. "We felt it our first duty to remove any such dangerous illusion." Halifax had spoken in almost identical terms in the House of Lords. The Führer seemed to become thoughtful as he listened but said nothing. Presumably after Schmidt had finished, at about noon, Hitler sent a query to the Army high command: How long could he wait before giving the final order for the attack? The answer was 3:00 that afternoon.

At approximately 2:00 he received Ambassador Henderson. After reflecting upon the last conversation at Berchtesgaden and the speeches of Chamberlain and Halifax in Parliament, declared the Führer, he wished to make a move toward Britain that would be as decisive as the move with respect to Russia. After first claiming that Polish provocation had become "intolerable" and alleging that twenty-one new frontier incidents had occurred the previous night and declaring that Germany was "determined to abolish these Macedonian conditions on her eastern frontier," Hitler warned that conditions had changed since the last war—Germany would no longer have to fight on two fronts. The pact was "unconditional" declared the Führer. "Russia and Germany would never again take up arms against each other." In addition the political and economic agreements would "render Germany secure economically for the longest possible period of war." In conclusion Hitler promised to make a comprehensive offer to England once the Polish problem was solved: He would "not only guarantee existence of British Empire in all circumstances as far as Germany is concerned but also if necessary assure the British Empire of German assistance regardless of where such assistance should be necessary." [8]

At 3:00 P.M., after Henderson's departure, the Führer ordered that the attack on Poland should start at 4:30 the next morning. At about 5:00 he received the news that the formal Polish-British alliance, the terms of which had been arranged in April, was at that moment being signed in London. According to Paul Schmidt who was present, Hitler sat in deep thought until French Ambassador Coulondre was announced. During the ensuing half-hour conversation the Führer followed approximately the same line as with Henderson earlier, but Schmidt received the impression that his thoughts were elsewhere and he was quite evidently trying to cut short the interview. As Coulondre left, Italian Ambassador Attolico was waiting outside with a message from Mussolini: Italy was unprepared and could not support Germany in a general war. This was the last straw. Hitler immediately ordered General Keitel to summon the chiefs of the armed forces; the attack order must be recalled. Although Brauchitsch stated at 7:00 that the attack could still be halted, during the night senior staff officers feared that this might not be the case. In the end, however, the order reached all the advanced elements before zero hour.[9]

According to some accounts, Hitler had added that he needed time to negotiate when he informed Keitel that the attack must be stopped. As Kordt (pp. 239–40) later speculated, he may have hoped London and Paris would weaken once they had a few days to consider the significance of the German-Soviet pact and the impossibility of aiding Poland. In any case, between the 25th and 31st Ribbentrop did what he could to play up the significance of the new Soviet tie.

In an article of August 25, the *Neue Zürcher Zeitung* had stated that the Anglo-French negotiations in Moscow had sought mainly to insure Poland against an attack in the rear. Claiming that 250,000 Red Army troops had been withdrawn from the Polish border in the last few days, the paper saw no current threat to Poland from the east. On the 27th Weizsäcker instructed Schulenburg to determine, "in a cautious way," whether Soviet troops had actually been withdrawn and if so whether the withdrawal could not be cancelled: Any "appearance of Poland being threatened from the Russian side too would naturally contribute to easing the situation in the West and might even, in the end, bring about a remarkable reduction in the readiness to help Poland." Queried by the ambassador the next day, Molotov laughed and denied that there was any truth in the reports. One could not bother with all of the nonsense then appearing in the press, he declared.

Probably on the same day (28th), before Schulenburg's report on the conversation with Molotov had been received in Berlin, the Army General Staff ordered General Köstring, the military attaché in Moscow, to sound out his Soviet colleagues regarding any new measures on the Polish frontier. Berlin had still not received the ambassador's report at 10:00 that evening when Weizsäcker wired that the "highest quarters" were keenly interested in the matter and that Schulenburg should report by return telegram. Ribbentrop was unable to wait, however, and called his ambassador on the telephone. Informed that the report was false, the Foreign Minister asked him to try to secure a denial, as emphatic as possible. In a telegram fifty minutes later, Weizsäcker suggested an official statement in the Soviet press regarding troop concentrations on the Polish border.

The ambassador spoke to Molotov along these lines at 5:00 the next afternoon, August 29. Asked whether he or the authorities in Berlin believed the report, Schulenburg replied that they were well aware it was completely false. It was a propaganda trick and should be answered by counter propaganda; thus Berlin requested "a *dementi* in terms as emphatic and unequivocal as possible." Molotov promised to take up the matter at once with Voroshilov and others, i.e. Stalin. The next morning the Soviet press and radio featured a semiofficial release. Reports in the *Neue Zürcher Zeitung* and other foreign papers of troop withdrawals on the Soviet western border, declared TASS, were "not at all in accordance with the facts." To the contrary, "in view of the increasing gravity of the situation in the eastern territories of Europe and of the possibility of surprises, the Soviet Command has decided to increase the numerical strength of the garrisons on the western frontier of the U.S.S.R." [10]

Ribbentrop also did what he could to get a new Soviet Ambassador and military attaché assigned to Berlin as soon as possible.[11] On August 25 Weizsäcker wired Schulenburg that the Foreign Minister wanted him to speak to Molotov "at once" and request that a new ambassador and military representative be assigned to Berlin "without delay." Schulenburg mentioned the matter the same day, and Molotov promised that his government would do its best. The ambassador was convinced that a dearth of suitable candidates was causing the delay. Three days later Weizsäcker wired that because of the tense international situation the presence of a Soviet Ambassador and military representative was especially desirable. Schulenburg should again do what he could and report the results of his efforts by telegram. The ambassador spoke to Molotov the next day (August 29), and the latter replied that four officers (actually five) had been selected and were ready to leave. A new ambassador had not yet been selected, however. Although the Narkomindel informed Schulenburg on the 30th that the Soviet officers, military attaché, assistant military attaché, air attaché, and two secretaries, would leave by plane via Stockholm the next morning, they finally departed only on September 2.

An official of the Auswärtiges Amt telephoned Schulenburg on August 31 that Ribbentrop wished identical communiqués published in Berlin and Moscow: "In connection with the conclusion of the German-Russian Pact of Non-Aggression and Consultation, provision was made for the despatch of a Soviet Russian Military Delegation. This delegation, led by . . . has arrived in Berlin today." The next evening Molotov asked the ambassador to call and expressed his government's objections to the proposed communiqué: If released before the officers arrived it might make their journey dangerous. Even after their arrival, the Soviet Government preferred that nothing be said of a "Military Mission" and that the German press should merely refer to new military attachés. The Soviet press intended to adopt this line. Göring, however, used the pending assignments as best he could. On the afternoon of August 31 he informed British Ambassador Henderson that a "Soviet Military Mission" including two generals had arrived that day in Berlin.[12]

General von Brauchitsch had warned Hitler on the afternoon of August 28 that the troop concentration on the Polish border could not be maintained much longer. It would be necessary to either attack or withdraw the advanced formations. The Führer had thereupon tentatively ordered the attack for September 1 but had left open the possibility of again setting back the date or completely canceling the attack plans. He also mentioned to Brauchitsch that he was currently seeking to drive Poland into an unfavorable negotiating position and put her in the wrong. During the next day Hitler wavered between peace and war. Late that evening, however, he was inclining more and more toward war. "In two months Poland will be finished," he declared "and then we shall have a great peace conference with the Western Powers."

On the following afternoon, August 30, the armed services were ordered to make preparations for an attack at 4:30 on the morning of September 1. Any new delay would be of only a day's duration. Finally, at approximately 4:00 P.M. on August 31, Hitler gave the decisive order for the attack: It was to take place the next morning but zero hour was set at 4:45 on the advice of the Luftwaffe.

The Führer seems to have still believed that Britain and France, if they did declare war, would make no offensive moves unless forced to do so. On August 31 he refused to order the evacuation of civilians from the western frontier zones. "Instruction No. 1 for the Conduct of the War," issued to the services on August 31, clearly reflected this belief: [13]

In the west it is a matter of clearly leaving to England and France the responsibility for opening hostilities. Minor border violations are, for the time being, to be dealt with purely locally. The neutrality guaranteed by us of Holland, Belgium, Luxembourg and Switzerland is to be scrupulously respected. At no point will the German western border be crossed without my specific permission. At sea the same holds true for all warlike operations or all that may be so interpreted. The defensive measures of the Luftwaffe are, for the time being, to be limited to warding off enemy air attacks on the Reich border, whereby the borders of the neutral states are to be respected as long as possible.

German troops marched into Poland as scheduled on the morning of September 1, 1939. At noon Hitler briefly described to Ribbentrop the progress of the attack, observed that the campaign would be over before the Western powers could write their notes of protest, and asked for the latest news from Paris and London. Otto Abetz, Ribbentrop's specialist on French affairs who was also present, seized the opportunity to voice his conviction that France would fight this time even though the military situation was not in her favor. Throwing up his hands, the Führer jokingly begged Ribbentrop to spare him from the judgments of the experts. Our diplomats sit in every capital, said Hitler, and each is supposed to have his hand on the pulse of the nation to which he is accredited. But what happens when I ask these people for their opinion? The introduction of conscription means war, they warned. The occupation of the Rhineland means war, and also the *Anschluss* with Austria, the Sudeten crisis, and the occupation of Prague. The generals were no better. "You must understand," declared Hitler, "that I finally have no further use for the opinion of people who have misinformed or even lied to me a dozen times and prefer to rely on my own judgment which has advised me better on all these occasions than the responsible expert." [14]

In the afternoon of September 2, Fritz Hesse, the press attaché in London, telephoned Berlin that the British Cabinet would soon meet to decide on a short-term ultimatum; should Germany reject it, war would result. Two hours later Hewel, Ribbentrop's liaison officer with Hitler, called back to ask for more details and asked if there were any way of avoiding the conflict. Hesse replied that a prompt German evacuation of Poland and reparations for the damage done offered the only possibility. At 7:00 P.M. Hewel called again and then handed the phone to Ribbentrop who did not, however, identify himself. "You know who is speaking," he said, "please go to your confidant [Sir Horace Wilson] . . . and tell him this: the Führer is ready to move out of Poland and to offer reparation for the damage done on condition that we receive Danzig and the road through the Corridor,

if England will act as mediator in the German-Polish conflict."
The press attaché was authorized to submit the proposal to the
British Government and to commence negotiations immediately.
At Hesse's request Ribbentrop repeated the communication and
added: "So that there may be no misunderstanding, stress the
fact that you are acting on the express instructions of Hitler and
that this is no private step of mine."

Hesse was unable to meet with Sir Horace Wilson until 10:00
P.M. The latter appeared impressed by the proposal, but, after
walking up and down the room several times, he turned to the
press attaché and said there was no point in submitting it to the
cabinet. After the invasion of Poland no Englishman could consider Hitler's proposal; such consideration or any negotiations
were impossible as long as German troops remained on Polish
soil.[15]

Sometime after midnight on the night of September 2/3, the
British Embassy called the Reich Chancellery and requested an
audience for Henderson at 9:00 A.M. that he might hand over a
communication from the British Government. Aware that an
ultimatum was probably involved and having little desire to accept it personally, Ribbentrop ordered Paul Schmidt, who happened to be standing nearby, to receive the British Ambassador.
Henderson appeared at Ribbentrop's office in the Wilhelmstrasse
promptly at 9:00, shook hands with Schmidt, refused the offer of
a chair, and proceeded to read the ultimatum:

... unless not later than 11 A.M., British Summer Time, today
September 3, satisfactory assurances to the above effect ["that the
German Government had suspended all aggressive action against
Poland and were prepared promptly to withdraw their forces from
Polish territory"] have been given by the German Government and
have reached His Majesty's Government in London, a state of war
will exist between the two countries as from that hour.

With the document in his briefcase, Schmidt proceeded to
Hitler's office in the Reich Chancellery. The Führer was seated at
his desk and Ribbentrop stood near the window. Both loked up
anxiously as the interpreter entered. The latter remained some
distance in front of the desk and slowly translated the ultimatum.
As he finished perfect silence reigned. Hitler sat as though turned

to stone and stared straight ahead. Finally, turning to Ribbentrop who had remained as though paralyzed by the window, he asked, "What now?" [16]

ON SEPTEMBER 3 Ribbentrop informed Schulenburg that a decisive victory over the Polish forces was expected within a few weeks; for military reasons the German Army would have to continue its operations in that part of Poland allocated to the U.S.S.R. The Foreign Minister instructed his ambassador to point out to Molotov the desirability, at the proper time, of Red Army operations against Polish units in Eastern Poland and Soviet occupation of that territory. Schulenburg spoke with Molotov at 5:30 the next evening and the latter promised an early reply. But as Molotov admitted on the 10th, Stalin did not think any action would be necessary for several weeks; the early German successes came as a surprise in Moscow. On the 5th Stalin feared it was still too soon to commit himself irrevocably, and his reply, delivered by Molotov that day, reflected this caution: At a "suitable time it will be absolutely necessary for us to start concrete action. We are of the view, however, that this time has not yet come. . . . it seems to us that through excessive haste we might injure our cause and promote unity among our opponents." [17]

Nevertheless, by the 7th the Soviet Embassy staff in Paris had packed their documents and made the necessary preparations for an immediate departure; Léger told Bullitt that he expected an early Soviet attack on Poland. On the same day the Soviet military attaché in Berlin was recalled for consultations. The next evening Ribbentrop informed Schulenburg that the Polish Army had practically collapsed and requested him to again urge military action by the Red Army. On the 9th Molotov told the ambassador that the U.S.S.R. would take military action "within the next few days," and General Köstring received similar information from Red Army sources the same day. Also on the 9th, both the German and U.S. Embassies reported conclusive evidence of mobilization: the calling up of reservists, schools being prepared for use as hospitals, restrictions on the sale of gasoline, etc. Steinhardt, the U.S. Ambassador, later estimated that a million men had been mobilized, and Molotov told Schulenburg on the 10th that over three million men were under arms.

The mobilization created a minor panic; people withdrew money from savings banks, and their efforts to hoard food made the queues before food stores longer than ever. The calling up of workers also caused considerable confusion in transport and industry. The authorities, however, took steps against hoarding and maintained the stocks in the stores, and the panic soon subsided.

In announcing the mobilization on the 10th, TASS stated that it was connected "with the German-Polish war, which is taking on a broader and more threatening character." That afternoon Molotov told Schulenburg that the Red Army still needed two to three weeks to complete its preparations. His government had intended to justify its intervention on the grounds that Poland was disintegrating and the U.S.S.R. had to protect Ukrainians and White Russians "threatened" by Germany. But according to a statement by Brauchitsch reported by the DNB the previous day, an armistice was imminent. If Germany concluded such an armistice, it would preclude this justification. After checking with Berlin, the ambassador explained to Molotov that he had misinterpreted the announcement and no armistice was contemplated; the latter seemed satisfied and made no further mention of the matter.

Four days later he summoned the ambassador and announced that the Red Army had carried out its preparations sooner than expected. But in order to make the protection of Russian minorities a plausible justification, the Soviet Government did not intend to act until after the fall of Warsaw. The next evening (15th) Ribbentrop wired Schulenburg that he assumed Moscow had abandoned the idea of claiming to protect the Ukrainian and White Russian minorities. "The assignment of a motive of that sort would indeed be out of the question in practice." It would "make the two States appear as enemies before the whole world." Hitler evidently feared Western hopes might be aroused. In conclusion the Foreign Minister expressed the hope that Moscow would now set a definite date and hour for its intervention.

The ambassador spoke with Molotov along these lines on the afternoon of the 16th. The latter agreed that the proposed Soviet excuse would jar German sensibilities somewhat, "but asked us in view of the difficult situation of the Soviet Government not to stumble over this piece of straw. The Soviet Government unfortunately saw no possibility of any other motivation, since the Soviet Union had heretofore not bothered about the plight of its minorities in Poland and had to justify abroad, in some way or other, its present intervention." [18]

At 2:00 on the morning of September 17, Schulenburg, Köstring, and Hilger were summoned to the Kremlin. Stalin himself received them, and Molotov and Voroshilov were also present. "At 6:00 A.M., four hours from now," declared Stalin, "the Red Army will cross into Poland all along the border and the Red Air Force will begin bombarding the area east of Lvov." He requested that the German headquarters be notified immediately in order to avoid any incidents. General Köstring, surprised by the short notice, objected with some anxiety that advanced German units could not be notified in time to prevent clashes with Soviet troops. Voroshilov waved aside the objection and expressed his conviction that German organization would meet the test. Subsequent developments proved him right.

As the conversation continued, Stalin voiced doubts regarding German willingness to withdraw to the west of the agreed demarcation line. Some people in Germany, he remarked, might fear that the U.S.S.R. would make common cause with the defeated Poles. Schulenburg assured him Germany would fulfill its obligations and pointed out that a withdrawal would release troops for the Western Front. He trusted the German Government, Stalin replied, but soldiers were reluctant to abandon conquered territories. At this point Köstring declared that the German armed forces would obey the Führer's orders. Although Stalin then expressed himself as satisfied, the ambassador asked Berlin for authority "to make a further declaration of such a nature as to remove his last doubts." During the audience, Stalin also read the text of a note justifying the pending attack on Poland. Schulenburg objected to three points, and Stalin immediately revised the draft to the ambassador's satisfaction.[19]

At 2:15 A.M., while the conversation in the Kremlin was still in progress, one of Potemkin's assistants telephoned Polish Ambassador Grzybowski and requested his presence to receive an important communication from the Deputy Foreign Commissar. Forty-five minutes later Potemkin slowly read the text of a note signed by Molotov:

> The Polish-German War has revealed the internal bankruptcy of the Polish State. . . . The Polish Government has disintegrated, and no longer shows any signs of life. . . . Therefore the Agreements concluded between the U.S.S.R. and Poland have ceased to operate. Left to her own devices and bereft of leadership, Poland has become a suitable field for all manner of hazards and surprises, which may constitute a threat to the U.S.S.R. . . .
> The Soviet Government further cannot view with indifference the fact that the kindred Ukrainian and White Russian people, who live on Polish territory and who are at the mercy of fate, are left defenceless.
> In these circumstances, the Soviet Government has directed the High Command of the Red Army to order the troops to cross the frontier and to take under their protection the life and property of the population of Western Ukraine and Western White Russia.
> At the same time the Soviet Government proposes to take all measures to extricate the Polish people from the unfortunate war into which they were dragged by their unwise leaders, and to enable them to live a peaceful life.

When the Deputy Foreign Commissar had finished, Grzybowski flatly refused to communicate the note to his government. He protested the unilateral abrogation of the existing Soviet treaties with Poland and rejected Molotov's justifications for such a step. Poland's president and government were still on Polish soil, and Polish soldiers were still fighting. The minorities were as one with the Poles in their loyalty. "More than once in our conversations," said the ambassador, "you have appealed to Slavonic solidarity. At our side at this moment not only Ukrainians and White Russians, but also Czech and Slovak legions are fighting the Germans. Where is your Slavonic solidarity?" Serbia and Belgium were occupied during the first World War, he added, "but it entered no one's head to regard their obligations to these States as non-existent on that account. Napoleon was once in Moscow, but so long as Kutuzov's army existed it was considered that Russia existed."

Potemkin, taken aback, spoke of the ambassador's "historic responsibility" should he refuse to accept the document. Moscow no longer had a representative in Poland and could not inform the Polish Government in any other way. Grzybowski replied that he would do no more than inform his government of the aggression which had probably already taken place. "But I still hope that your Government will restrain the Red Army from invasion, and will not stab us in the back at the moment of our struggle against the Germans." Completely on the defensive, the Deputy Foreign Commissar then stated he would have to consult his government! Half an hour later, at 4:30 A.M., he returned and said that the Soviet Government could not alter its decisions. The ambassador answered that he could not change his and departed. He wired Beck shortly after 5:00 but the telegram was not received until 11:00 A.M. The Red Army had entered Poland on schedule at 6:00.

Later in the day Molotov spoke over the radio in terms similar to the note rejected by Grzybowski. Copies of the note were also sent to the embassies and legations of the European powers, the countries bordering on the Soviet Union, Japan, and the United States. In a covering note, however, Molotov stated, "the USSR will conduct a policy of neutrality in the relations between the USSR and your country"—and thus tacitly admitted that Soviet troops had in fact attacked Poland.[20]

At 3:00 on the afternoon of September 17, the draft of a joint German-Soviet communiqué was phoned from Berlin to the German Embassy in Moscow. Schulenburg submitted it to Molotov at 11:30 that evening. The latter immediately summoned Stalin who favored a joint announcement but felt that the German draft was too brutally frank. Stalin thereupon wrote a version of his own and requested that it be approved by Berlin:[21]

In order to avoid all kinds of unfounded rumors concerning the respective aims of the German and Soviet forces which are operating in Poland, the Government of the German Reich and the Government of the U.S.S.R. declare that the operations of these forces do not involve any aims which are contrary to the interests of Germany and of the Soviet Union, or to the spirit or the letter of the Nonaggression Pact concluded between Germany and the U.S.S.R. On the contrary, the aim of these forces is to restore peace and order in Poland, which had been destroyed by the disintegration of the Polish State, and to help the Polish population to re-establish new conditions of its political existence.

By noon the next day Ribbentrop had agreed, and the text of the communiqué was broadcast by both the German and Soviet radio late the same afternoon.

At this time Stalin had not yet developed the overconfidence that characterized his subsequent attitude toward Hitler. As we have seen, as late as September 17 he openly voiced his suspicions regarding German intentions. Apparently he did not consider the pact with Hitler a sure guarantee against a German attack; only an armed conflict between Germany and the Western powers would provide such insurance. Before dismissing Litvinov on May 3, 1939, Stalin had decided that Britain and France would fight over Poland and that the Poles themselves would resist German aggression. But in May Poland and the Western powers counted on benevolent Soviet neutrality at the very least. Hitler hoped and Stalin evidently feared that the German-Soviet pact might so discourage the Poles that they would be willing to come to terms with Berlin—or that Britain and France might now consider assistance to Poland hopeless. Thus between August 23 and September 3, when Britain and France declared war, Soviet spokesmen tried to depreciate the significance of the pact.[22]

On August 24 the Soviet Ambassador to Warsaw, Nikolay I. Sharonov, told Beck that the German-Soviet nonaggression agreement would not change relations between the U.S.S.R. and Poland. The Anglo-French negotiations in Moscow might even continue. The ambassador adopted a cordial tone and seemed willing to work for a speedy settlement of several minor problems. Three days later Voroshilov granted an "interview" to a "correspondent" of *Izvestia*. In addition to blaming the Western powers for the breakdown of the negotiations and the Soviet decision to sign an agreement with Germany, Voroshilov made one significant statement: [23]

The question of assistance in the form of raw materials and military supplies is a commercial one and there is no need to conclude a mutual assistance pact, still less a military convention, in order to supply Poland with these things. The United States of America and a number of other States have no mutual assistance pacts or military conventions with Japan and yet for the last two years they have been selling raw materials and military supplies to the Japanese, in spite of the fact that Japan is in a state of war with China.

While emphasizing the peaceful significance of the pact in an address to the Supreme Soviet on August 31, Molotov sought to give the impression that at most it would result only in strict Soviet neutrality. "In the present instance," he declared, "there is no question of a mutual assistance pact as in the case of the Anglo-Franco-Soviet conversations but only of a non-aggression pact." He also decried "those amateurs who read into the pact more than is written in it. For this purpose they set on foot all sorts of conjectures and insinuations in order to cast discredit upon the pact in various countries." Finally, toward the end of his speech, Molotov asked if it was "really difficult to understand that the U.S.S.R. is following, and will continue to follow, its own independent policy, the aim of which is to further the interests of the peoples of the U.S.S.R. and these interests only?" The same day a member of the Soviet Embassy in Berlin assured a member of the U.S. Embassy that the pact contained no secret clause for common military action against or partition of Poland. On the contrary, Moscow wished to maintain Poland and the Baltic states as buffers, and the agreement involved no support for German expansion.[24]

On September 1, after Hitler had attacked Poland but before Britain and France had declared war, Soviet Ambassador Sharonov cited Voroshilov's "interview" and asked Beck why the Polish Government was not negotiating with Moscow for supplies. Beck immediately sent a special courier with instructions for Grzybowski to approach Molotov on the subject. The courier did not arrive in Moscow until September 6, and the ambassador was unable to secure an interview until the 8th. The situation had changed radically since Voroshilov's statement, declared Molotov. Britain and France had entered the war and "Poland is now synonymous with England, so far as we are concerned." Soviet interests came first, and Moscow intended to remain outside the conflict. The U.S.S.R. could furnish no supplies not already promised according to the existing trade agreement. Nor could it allow the shipment of Western military supplies over Soviet territory. But even at this late date Molotov still hesitated to slam the door. "At the end of the conversation," wrote Grzybowski in Paris two months later, "M. Molotov stated that all he had said had been said in present conditions, but that circumstances might change. The phrase 'in present conditions' was several times repeated in his answers." [25]

As late as September 11, after the Polish Government had left Warsaw, Soviet Ambassador Sharonov was still making reassuring statements. In conversations with Beck and Szembek he emphasized that Soviet medical supplies would be available, perhaps even gasoline. France could also purchase Soviet supplies. "There are rumors here about mobilization in Russia," he said to Szembek. "I know nothing about it. At the most it would concern five annual levies, which is no great matter. Apparently the Germans are bombing certain points on the Soviet western frontier. The Soviets do not wish to have frontiers with totalitarian States. With France the Soviets have a non-aggression treaty and an agreement for mutual assistance." [26]

The antics of Stalin's trained poodles abroad, the leaders of the British and French Communist Parties, followed a similar pattern. With some minor differences they urged resistance to Germany before September 3; after that date Communist deputies and the one M.P. voted war credits and were among the most vociferous supporters of the Allied war effort. The September issue of the English-language edition of the *Communist International*, printed sometime after August 31, contained no less than four anti-Nazi articles and editorials. An abrupt about-face followed the Soviet attack on Poland, however. The British and French Communist Parties promptly adopted a completely defeatist attitude and did everything possible to sabotage the Allied war effort. According to the Comintern journal a year later, "some mistakes were made in the early days of the war, owing to an inadequate understanding of the imperialist nature of the policy of countries like Great Britain, France and America," but "these mistakes were very soon rectified."

These were no mistakes, however, but part of Stalin's deliberate policy. Until September 3 he wanted to encourage the British, French, and Poles; even after that date he still had doubts regarding Hitler. Thus there was no point in sacrificing prematurely his best agencies for influencing British and French public opinion. After the 17th he had committed himself irrevocably, and the position of British and French Communists was immaterial. The maintenance of their earlier patriotic attitude might even raise German doubts.

The French Communist Party, at least, seems to have received no direct instructions from Moscow until about September 20. For this reason it has been argued that Stalin deliberately left his foreign lackeys in the dark, hoping they would adopt a patriotic attitude; according to another view, indecision actually prevailed in Comintern headquarters in Moscow until after September 17. Since the successful members of the Communist apparatus, abroad as well as at home, owe much of their success to their ability to interpret and anticipate the devious twists of the Party line, direct orders were hardly necessary. The statements by Voroshilov and Molotov and the anti-German articles in the September issue of the *Communist International* were more than adequate and saved Stalin some embarrassment in international Party circles: It was not he who had to make the sudden about face but rather his followers abroad.[27]

Georgi Dimitrov, the leader of the Comintern, formally set forth the new line in November: [28] The "proletariat, the working people, have nothing to defend in this war," he wrote. "It is not their war, but the war of their exploiters. It brings them suffering, privation, ruin and death. Were they to support such a war they would merely defend the interests of their enslavers and oppressors . . ."

The Social-Democratic, "democratic" and "radical" flunkeys of the bourgeoisie are brazenly distorting the anti-fascist slogans of the people's front, and are using them to deceive the masses of the people and to cover up the imperialist character of the war. . . . In the present situation, working class unity can and must be achieved *from below* . . . in a resolute struggle against the treacherous leaders of the Social-Democratic parties. And this process will be facilitated to a great degree by the comradely relations that have been established in recent years between the Communists and a considerable section of the Social-Democratic workers . . . the Social-Democratic parties, under the weight of the criminal policy of their leaderships, will increasingly disintegrate, and the healthy proletarian section of these parties will join with the Communists . . .

In the preceding period the Communists strove to secure the establishment of a united popular front by agreements with the Social-Democratic and other petty bourgeois "democratic" and "radical" parties in the person of their leading bodies, on the basis of a common platform of struggle against facism and war. . . . Now the mustering of the working class . . . cannot be brought about without . . . the elimination of the influence of these agents of the bourgeoisie . . . their isolation from the masses of the working people.

Stalin apparently envisaged a repetition of World War I, a prolonged, indecisive, and bloody struggle accompanied by increasing war weariness. This would eventually result in mutinies such as that of the French Army in 1917 and in the German Navy at Keil in 1918. But this time well-disciplined and well-prepared Communist parties should be able to seize power according to the pattern in Petrograd in 1917. As Kerenski had sought to keep Russia in the war and thus paved the way for the October Revolution, so would the British and French Socialists, by supporting their national war efforts, pave the way for a revolution throughout Europe. The Communist Party of Great Britain was small and impotent and its propaganda had little influence. In France, however, the Communists achieved greater success—but not of the kind Stalin expected. Although not the decisive factor, Communist defeatist propaganda undoubtedly weakened the morale of the French Army and thus facilitated the German conquest of France in 1940.

DID STALIN START WORLD WAR II? Of course not, Hitler did—but Stalin's encouragement may have been a decisive factor in the decision to start it in 1939 rather than 1940 or even 1941. The pact with Russia would strike the last card from the hands of the Western powers, Hitler told his generals on August 22. As late as his speech to the Reichstag on October 6, 1939, when he offered a puppet Poland, Hitler still thought Paris and London would accept a peace pretty much on his terms. And even in the fall of 1940, when Britain still refused to make peace despite the fall of France, Hitler again thought to play the Russian card—this time in the form of a grand continental coalition which would finally compel the British to realize the hopelessness of their position.

Hitler's estimate of the political situation in August 1939 was far indeed from reality. Stalin, in contrast, played his hand with great caution and tactical skill. From 1934 until 1939, Moscow and the Communist parties in the West did everything possible to encourage British and French resistance to German and Italian aggression—resistance which could scarcely have involved the Soviet Union. And once the decision to stop Germany was made in Paris and London, in March 1939, Stalin then began to encourage Hitler, using the carrot of Astakhov's hints and finally the stick of the Anglo-French military mission to Moscow.

Hitler was mistaken in 1939, but Stalin's basic error was even greater: He helped upset the balance of power. With three or more approximately equal powers, a balance operates almost automatically. Should power A show signs of becoming too powerful and dangerous, powers B and C combine against it. Should power B become too powerful, A and C form an alliance against it. Once Hitler had conquered France, the Soviet Union was in mortal peril. But Stalin realized the danger only a month or so before the German attack. Stalin displayed great tactical skill indeed in 1939—and used it to lead Russia inevitably to the disaster of June 22, 1941.

APPENDICES
NOTES
BIBLIOGRAPHY

Appendices

APPENDIX A: Treaty Between Germany and the Union of Socialist Soviet Republics. Signed at Berlin, April 24, 1926 [League of Nations, *Treaty Series*, LIII, 388–96].

The German Government and the Government of the Union of Socialist Soviet Republics, being desirous of doing all in their power to promote the maintenance of general peace, and being convinced that the interests of the German people and of the peoples of the Union of Socialist Soviet Republics demand constant and trustful co-operation, have agreed to strengthen the friendly relations existing between them by means of a special Treaty and have for this purpose appointed as their Plenipotentiaries:

The German Government:

Dr. Gustav Stresemann, Minister for Foreign Affairs;

The Government of the Union of Socialist Soviet Republics:

M. Nikolai Nicolaiwitsch Krestinski, Ambassador Extraordinary and Plenipotentiary of the Union of Socialist Soviet Republics;

Who, having communicated their full powers found in good and due form, have agreed upon the following provisions:

Article 1. The relations between Germany and the Union of Socialist Soviet Republics shall continue to be based on the Treaty of Rapallo.

The German Government and the Government of the Union

of Socialist Soviet Republics shall remain in friendly touch in order to promote an understanding with regard to all political and economic questions jointly affecting their two countries.

Article 2. Should one of the Contracting Parties, despite its peaceful attitude, be attacked by one or more third Powers, the other Contracting Party shall observe neutrality for the whole duration of the conflict.

Article 3. If on the occasion of a conflict of the nature mentioned in Article 2, or at a time when neither of the Contracting Parties is engaged in warlike operations, a coalition is formed between third Powers with a view to the economic or financial boycott of either of the Contracting Parties, the other Contracting Party undertakes not to adhere to such coalition.

Article 4. The present Treaty shall be ratified and the instruments of ratification shall be exchanged at Berlin.

It shall enter into force on the date of the exchange of the instruments of ratification and shall remain in force for five years. The two Contracting Parties shall confer in good time before the expiration of this period with regard to the future development of their political relations.

In faith whereof the Plenipotentiaries have signed the present Treaty.

Done in duplicate at Berlin, April 24, 1926.

[signed] STRESEMANN.

[signed] KRESTINSKI.

Ministry of Foreign Affairs.

Berlin, April 24, 1926.

With reference to the negotiations upon the Treaty signed this day between the German Government and the Government of the Union of Socialist Soviet Republics, I have the honour, on behalf of the German Government, to make the following observations:

(1) In the negotiation and signature of the Treaty, both Governments have taken the view that the principle laid down by them in Article 1, paragraph 2, of the Treaty, of reaching an understanding on all political and economic questions affecting the two

countries, will contribute considerably to the maintenance of peace. In any case the two Governments will in their deliberations be guided by the need for the maintenance of the general peace.

(2) In this spirit also the two Governments have approached the fundamental questions which are bound up with the entry of Germany into the League of Nations. The German Government is convinced that Germany's membership of the League cannot constitute an obstacle to the friendly development of the relations between Germany and the Union of Socialist Soviet Republics. According to its basic idea, the League of Nations is designed for the peaceful and equitable settlement of international disputes. The German Government is determined to co-operate to the best of its ability in the realisation of this idea. If, however, though the German Government does not anticipate this, there should at any time take shape within the League, contrary to that fundamental idea of peace, any efforts directed exclusively against the Union of Socialist Soviet Republics, Germany would most energetically oppose such efforts.

(3) The German Government also proceeds upon the assumption that this fundamental attitude of German policy towards the Union of Socialist Soviet Republics cannot be adversely influenced by the loyal observance of the obligations, arising out of Articles 16 and 17 of the Covenant of the League and relating to the application of sanctions, which would devolve upon Germany as a consequence of her entry into the League of Nations. By the terms of these articles, the application of sanctions against the Union of Socialist Soviet Republics would come into consideration, in the absence of other causes, only if the Union of Socialist Soviet Republics entered upon a war of aggression against a third State. It is to be borne in mind that the question whether the Union of Socialist Soviet Republics is the aggressor in the event of a conflict with a third State could only be determined with binding force for Germany with her own consent; and that therefore, an accusation to this effect levelled by other Powers against the Union of Socialist Soviet Republics and regarded by Germany as unjustified, would not oblige Germany to take part in measures of any kind instituted on the authority of Article 16. With regard to the question whether, in a concrete case, Germany would be in a

position to take part in the application of sanctions at all, and to what extent, the German Government refers to the Note of December 1, 1925, on the interpretation of Article 16 addressed to the German Delegation on the occasion of the signing of the Treaties of Locarno.

(4) In order to create a secure basis for disposing without friction of all questions arising between them, the two Governments regard it as desirable that they should immediately embark upon negotiations for the conclusion of a general treaty for the peaceful solution of any conflicts that may arise between them, when special attention shall be given to the possibilities of the procedure of arbitration and conciliation.

I avail myself of this opportunity to renew to Your Excellency the assurance of my highest consideration.

[signed] STRESEMANN.

To M. Krestinski,
Ambassador of the Union of Socialist
Soviet Republics in Germany,
Berlin.

Embassy of the Union of Socialist Soviet
Republics in Germany.

Berlin, April 24, 1926.

Your Excellency,

In acknowledging receipt of the Note which you have addressed to me with regard to the negotiations on the Treaty signed to-day between the Government of the Union of Socialist Soviet Republics and the German Government, I have the honour, on behalf of the Union of Socialist Soviet Republics, to make the following reply:

(1) In the negotiation and signature of the Treaty, both Governments have taken the view that the principle laid down by them in Article 1, paragraph 2, of the Treaty, of reaching an understanding on all political and economic questions jointly affecting the two countries, will contribute considerably to the maintenance of peace. In any case the two Governments will in their deliberations be guided by the need for the maintenance of the general peace.

(2) The Government of the Union of Socialist Soviet Republics takes note of the explanation contained in Sections 2 and 3 of your Note concerning the fundamental questions connected with Germany's entry into the League of Nations.

(3) In order to create a secure basis for disposing without friction of all questions arising between them, the two Governments regard it as desirable that they should immediately embark upon negotiations for the conclusion of a general treaty for the peaceful solution of any conflicts that may arise between them, when special attention shall be given to the possibilities of the procedure of arbitration and conciliation.

I avail myself of this opportunity to renew to Your Excellency the assurance of my highest consideration.

[signed] KRESTINSKI.

To Dr. Stresemann,
Minister for Foreign Affairs,
Berlin.

APPENDIX B: Treaty of Mutual Assistance Between France and the Union of Soviet Socialist Republics. Signed at Paris, May 2, 1935 [League of Nations, *Treaty Series*, CLXVII, 396–406].

The Central Executive Committee of the Union of Soviet Socialist Republics and the President of the French Republic, being desirous of strengthening peace in Europe and of guaranteeing its benefits to their respective countries by securing a fuller and stricter application of those provisions of the Covenant of the League of Nations which are designed to maintain the national security, territorial integrity and political independence of States; determined to devote their efforts to the preparation and conclusion of a European agreement for that purpose, and in the meantime to promote, as far as lies in their power, the effective application of the provisions of the Covenant of the League of Nations;

have resolved to conclude a Treaty to this end and have appointed as their Plenipotentiaries:

The Central Executive Committee of the Union of Soviet Socialist Republics:

Monsieur Vladimir Potemkine, Member of the Central Executive Committee, Ambassador Extraordinary and Plenipotentiary of the Union of Soviet Socialist Republics accredited to the President of the French Republic;

The President of the French Republic:

Monsieur Pierre Laval, Senator, Minister for Foreign Affairs;

Who, having exchanged their full powers, found in good and due form, have agreed upon the following provisions:

Article 1. In the event of France or the Union of Soviet Socialist Republics being threatened with or in danger of aggression on the part of any European State, the Union of Soviet Socialist Republics and reciprocally France undertake mutually to proceed to an immediate consultation as regards the measures to be taken for the observance of the Provisions of Article 10 of the Covenant of the League of Nations.

Article 2. Should, in the circumstances specified in Article 15, paragraph 7, of the Covenant of the League of Nations, France or the Union of Soviet Socialist Republics be the object, notwithstanding the sincerely peaceful intentions of both countries, of an unprovoked aggression on the part of a European State, the Union of Soviet Socialist Republics and reciprocally France shall immediately come to each other's aid and assistance.

Article 3. In consideration of the fact that under Article 16 of the Covenant of the League of Nations any Member of the League which resorts to war in disregard of its covenants under Articles 12, 13 or 15 of the Covenant is *ipso facto* deemed to have committed an act of war against all other Members of the League, France and reciprocally the Union of Soviet Socialist Republics undertake, in the event of one of them being the object, in these conditions and notwithstanding the sincerely peaceful intentions of both countries, of an unprovoked aggression on the part of a European State, immediately to come to each other's aid and assistance in application of Article 16 of the Covenant.

The same obligation is assumed in the event of France or the Union of Soviet Socialist Republics being the object of an aggression on the part of a European State in the circumstances specified in Article 17, paragraphs 1 and 3, of the Covenant of the League of Nations.

Article 4. The undertakings stipulated above being consonant with the obligations of the High Contracting Parties as Members of the League of Nations, nothing in the present Treaty shall be interpreted as restricting the duty of the latter to take any action that may be deemed wise and effectual to safeguard the peace of the world or as restricting the obligations resulting for the High Contracting Parties from the Covenant of the League of Nations.

Article 5. The present Treaty, both the French and the Russian texts whereof shall be equally authentic, shall be ratified and the instruments of ratification shall be exchanged at Moscow as soon as possible. It shall be registered with the Secretariat of the League of Nations.

It shall take effect as soon as the ratifications have been exchanged and shall remain in force for five years. If it is not denounced by either of the High Contracting Parties giving notice thereof at least one year before the expiry of that period, it shall remain in force indefinitely, each of the High Contracting Parties being at liberty to terminate it at a year's notice by a declaration to that effect.

In faith whereof the Plenipotentiaries have signed the present Treaty and have thereto affixed their seals.

Done at Paris, in duplicate, this 2nd day of May, 1935.

[signed] V. POTEMKINE.

[signed] PIERRE LAVAL.

Protocol of Signature. Upon proceeding to the signature of the Franco-Soviet Treaty of Mutual Assistance of to-day's date, the Plenipotentiaries have signed the following Protocol, which shall be included in the exchange of ratifications of the Treaty.

I. It is agreed that the effect of Article 3 is to oblige each Contracting Party immediately to come to the assistance of the other by immediately complying with the recommendations of the Council of the League of Nations as soon as they have been issued in virtue of Article 16 of the Covenant. It is further agreed that the two Contracting Parties will act in concert to ensure that the Council shall issue the said recommendations with all the speed required by the circumstances and that, should the Council nevertheless, for whatever reason, issue no recommendation or fail to reach a unanimous decision, effect shall none the less be given to the obligation to render assistance. It is also agreed that the undertakings to render assistance mentioned in the present Treaty refer only to the case of an aggression committed against either Contracting Party's own territory.

II. It being the common intention of the two Governments in no way to contradict, by the present Treaty, undertakings previously assumed towards third States by France and by the Union of Soviet Socialist Republics in virtue of published treaties, it is agreed that effect shall not be given to the provisions of the said Treaty in a manner which, being incompatible with treaty obligations assumed by one of the Contracting Parties, would expose that Party to sanctions of an international character.

III. The two Governments, deeming it desirable that a regional agreement should be concluded aiming at organising security between Contracting States, and which might moreover embody or be accompanied by pledges of mutual assistance, recognise their right to become parties by mutual consent, should occasion arise, to similar agreements in any form, direct or indirect, that may seem appropriate, the obligations under these various agreements to take the place of those assumed under the present Treaty.

IV. The two Governments place on record the fact that the negotiations which have resulted in the signature of the present Treaty were originally undertaken with a view to supplementing a Security Agreement embracing the countries of North-Eastern Europe, namely, the Union of Soviet Socialist Republics, Germany, Czechoslovakia, Poland and the Baltic States which are neighbours of the Union of Soviet Socialist Republics; in addition to that Agreement, there was to have been concluded a Treaty of Assistance between the Union of Soviet Socialist Republics, France and Germany, by which each of those three States was to have undertaken to come to the assistance of any one of them which might be the object of aggression on the part of any other of those three States. Although circumstances have not hitherto permitted of the conclusion of those Agreements, which both Parties continue to regard as desirable, it is none the less the case that the undertakings stipulated in the Franco-Soviet Treaty of Assistance are to be understood as intended to apply only within the limits contemplated in the three-party Agreement previously planned. Independently of the obligations assumed under the present Treaty, it is further recalled that, in accordance with the Franco-Soviet Pact of Non-Aggression signed on November 29th, 1932, and moreover, without affecting the universal character of the undertakings assumed in that Pact, in the event of either Party becoming the object of aggression by one or more third European Powers not referred to in the above-mentioned three-party Agreement, the other Contracting Party is bound to abstain, during the period of the conflict, from giving any aid or assistance, either direct or indirect, to the aggressor or aggressors, each Party declaring further that it is not bound by any Assistance Agreement which would be contrary to this undertaking.

Done at Paris, this 2nd day of May, 1935.

[signed] V. POTEMKINE.

[signed] PIERRE LAVAL.

APPENDIX C: Treaty of Mutual Assistance Between the Czechoslovak Republic and the Union of Soviet Socialist Republics. Signed at Prague, May 16, 1935 [League of Nations, *Treaty Series*, CLIX, 348–61].

The President of the Czechoslovak Republic and the Central Executive Committee of the Union of Soviet Socialist Republics, being desirous of strengthening peace in Europe and of guaranteeing its benefits to their respective countries by securing a fuller and stricter application of those provisions of the Covenant of the League of Nations which are designed to maintain the national security, territorial integrity and political independence of States, determined to devote their efforts to the preparation and conclusion of a European agreement for that purpose, and in the meantime to promote, as far as lies in their power, the effective application of the provisions of the Covenant of the League of Nations, have resolved to conclude a Treaty to this end and have appointed as their Plenipotentiaries:

The President of the Czechoslovak Republic:
Monsieur Edouard Beneš, Minister for Foreign Affairs;
The Central Executive Committee of the Union of Soviet Socialist Republics:
Monsieur Serge Alexandrovsky, Envoy Extraordinary and Minister Plenipotentiary of the Union of Soviet Socialist Republics;
Who, having exchanged their full powers, found in good and due form, have agreed upon the following provisions:

Article 1. In the event of the Czechoslovak Republic or the Union of Soviet Socialist Republics being threatened with or in danger of aggression on the part of any European State, the Union of Soviet Socialist Republics and reciprocally the Czechoslovak Republic undertake mutually to proceed to an immediate consultation as regards the measures to be taken for the observance of the provisions of Article 10 of the Covenant of the League of Nations.

Article 2. Should, in the circumstances specified in Article 15, paragraph 7, of the Covenant of the League of Nations, the Czechoslovak Republic or the Union of Soviet Socialist Republics be the object, notwithstanding the sincerely peaceful intentions of both countries, of an unprovoked aggression on the part of a European State, the Union of Soviet Socialist Republics and reciprocally the Czechoslovak Republic shall immediately come to each other's aid and assistance.

Article 3. In consideration of the fact that under Article 16 of the Covenant of the League of Nations any Member of the League which resorts to war in disregard of its covenants under Articles 12, 13 or 15 of the Covenant is *ipso facto* deemed to have committed an act of war against all other Members of the League, the Czechoslovak Republic and reciprocally the Union of Soviet

Socialist Republics undertake, in the event of one of them being the object, in these conditions and notwithstanding the sincerely peaceful intentions of both countries, of an unprovoked aggression on the part of a European State, immediately to come to each other's aid and assistance in application of Article 16 of the Covenant.

The same obligation is assumed in the event of the Czechoslovak Republic or the Union of Soviet Socialist Republics being the object of an aggression on the part of a European State in the circumstances specified in Article 17, paragraphs 1 and 3, of the Covenant of the League of Nations.

Article 4. Without prejudice to the preceding provisions of the present Treaty, it is stipulated that should either of the High Contracting Parties become the object of an aggression on the part of one or more third Powers in conditions not giving ground for aid or assistance within the meaning of the present Treaty, the other High Contracting Party undertakes not to lend, for the duration of the conflict, aid or assistance, either directly or indirectly, to the aggressor or aggressors. Each High Contracting Party further declares that it is not bound by any other agreement for assistance which is incompatible with the present undertaking.

Article 5. The undertakings stipulated above being consonant with the obligations of the High Contracting Parties as Members of the League of Nations, nothing in the present Treaty shall be interpreted as restricting the duty of the latter to take any action that may be deemed wise and effectual to safeguard the peace of the world or as restricting the obligations resulting for the High Contracting Parties from the Covenant of the League of Nations.

Article 6. The present Treaty, both the Czechoslovak and the Russian texts whereof shall be equally authentic, shall be ratified and the instruments of ratification shall be exchanged at Moscow as soon as possible. It shall be registered with the Secretariat of the League of Nations.

It shall take effect as soon as the ratifications have been exchanged and shall remain in force for five years. If it is not denounced by either of the High Contracting Parties giving notice thereof at least one year before the expiry of that period, it shall remain in force indefinitely, each of the High Contracting Parties being at liberty to terminate it at a year's notice by a declaration to that effect.

In faith whereof the Plenipotentiaries have signed the present Treaty and have thereto affixed their seals.

Done at Prague, in duplicate, this 16th day of May, one thousand nine hundred and thirty-five.

[signed] DR. EDOUARD BENES.
[signed] S. ALEXANDROVSKY.

Protocol of Signature. Upon proceeding to the signature of the Treaty of Mutual Assistance between the Czechoslovak Republic and the Union of Soviet Socialist Republics of to-day's date, the Plenipotentiaries have signed the following Protocol, which shall be included in the exchange of ratifications of the Treaty.

I. It is agreed that the effect of Article 3 is to oblige each Contracting Party immediately to come to the assistance of the other by immediately complying with the recommendations of the Council of the League of Nations as soon as they have been issued in virtue of Article 16 of the Covenant. It is further agreed that the two Contracting Parties will act in concert to ensure that the Council shall issue the said recommendations with all the speed required by the circumstances and that, should the Council nevertheless, for whatever reason, issue no recommendation or fail to reach a unanimous decision, effect shall none the less be given to the obligation to render assistance. It is also agreed that the undertakings to render assistance mentioned in the present Treaty refer only to the case of an aggression committed against either Contracting Party's own territory.

II. The two Governments declare that the undertakings laid down in Articles 1, 2 and 3 of the present Treaty, concluded with a view to promoting the establishment in Eastern Europe of a regional system of security, inaugurated by the Franco-Soviet Treaty of May 2nd, 1935, will be restricted within the same limits as were laid down in paragraph 4 of the Protocol of Signature of the said Treaty. At the same time, the two Governments recognise that the undertakings to render mutual assistance will operate between them only in so far as the conditions laid down in the present Treaty may be fulfilled and in so far as assistance may be rendered by France to the Party victim of the aggression.

III. The two Governments, deeming it desirable that a regional agreement should be concluded aiming at organising security between Contracting States, and which might moreover embody or be accompanied by pledges of mutual assistance, recognise their right to become parties by mutual consent, should occasion arise, to similar agreements in any form, direct or indirect, that may seem appropriate, the obligations under these various agreements to take the place of those resulting from the present Treaty.

Done at Prague, this 16th day of May, 1935.

[signed] Dr. Edouard Benes.

[signed] S. Alexandrovsky.

APPENDIX D: Treaty of Nonaggression Between Germany and the Union of Soviet Socialist Republics. Signed at Moscow, August 23, 1939 [*D German FP*, ser. d., vii, 245–47].

The Government of the German Reich and the Government of the Union of Soviet Socialist Republics, desirous of strengthening the cause of peace between Germany and the U.S.S.R., and proceeding from the fundamental provisions of the Treaty of Neutrality, which was concluded between Germany and the U.S.S.R. in April 1926, have reached the following agreement:

Article I. The two Contracting Parties undertake to refrain from any act of violence, any aggressive action and any attack on each other either severally or jointly with other Powers.

Article II. Should one of the Contracting Parties become the object of belligerent action by a third Power, the other Contracting Party shall in no manner lend its support to this third Power.

Article III. The Governments of the two Contracting Parties will in future maintain continual contact with one another for the purpose of consultation in order to exchange information on problems affecting their common interests.

Article IV. Neither of the two Contracting Parties will join any grouping of Powers whatsoever which is aimed directly or indirectly at the other Party.

Article V. Should disputes or conflicts arise between the Contracting Parties over questions of one kind or another, both Parties will settle these disputes or conflicts exclusively by means of a friendly exchange of views or if necessary by the appointment of arbitration commissions.

Article VI. The present Treaty shall be concluded for a period of ten years with the proviso that, in so far as one of the Contracting Parties does not denounce it one year before the expiry of this period, the validity of this Treaty shall be deemed to be automatically prolonged for another five years.

Article VII. The present treaty shall be ratified within the shortest possible time. [Instruments of ratification were exchanged on September 24.] The instruments of ratification will be exchanged in Berlin. The treaty shall enter into force immediately upon signature.

Done in duplicate in the German and Russian languages. Moscow, August 23, 1939.
For the Government
of the German Reich:
v. RIBBENTROP

With full power of the
Government of the U.S.S.R.:
V. MOLOTOV

Secret Additional Protocol. On the occasion of the signature of the Non-Aggression Treaty between the German Reich and the Union of Soviet Socialist Republics, the undersigned plenipotentiaries of the two Parties discussed in strictly confidential conversations the question of the delimitation of their respective spheres of interest in Eastern Europe. These conversations led to the following result:

1. In the event of a territorial and political transformation in the territories belonging to the Baltic States (Finland, Estonia,

Latvia, Lithuania), the northern frontier of Lithuania shall represent the frontier of the spheres of interest both of Germany and the U.S.S.R. In this connection the interest of Lithuania in the Vilna territory is recognized by both Parties.

2. In the event of a territorial and political transformation of the territories belonging to the Polish State, the spheres of interest of both Germany and the U.S.S.R. shall be bounded approximately by the line of the rivers Narev, Vistula, and San.

The question whether the interests of both Parties make the maintenance of an independent Polish State appear desirable and how the frontiers of this State should be drawn can be definitely determined only in the course of further political developments.

In any case both Governments will resolve this question by means of a friendly understanding.

3. With regard to South-Eastern Europe, the Soviet side emphasizes its interest in Bessarabia. The German side declares complete political *désintéressement* in these territories.

4. This Protocol will be treated by both parties as strictly secret.

Moscow, August 23, 1939.
For the Government of
the German Reich:
v. RIBBENTROP

With full power of the
Government of the U.S.S.R.:
V. MOLOTOV

Notes

PREFACE

1. Ivan M. Maisky, Soviet Ambassador to Britain from 1932 until 1943, demonstrated this quite inadvertently in the second volume of his *Vospominaniya Sovetskogo Posla* (Moscow: Izdatel'stvo "Nauka," 1964) covering the period from 1932 until the Nazi-Soviet agreement of 1939. In a 538-page volume ostensibly explaining the events leading to World War II and published twenty-five years after it started, this high ranking Soviet diplomat could cite the following:

	Titles	*Times Cited*
Non-Soviet sources	26	165
Published since 1945	12	64
From non-Soviet archives	4 (10 vols.)	45
Soviet sources	16	68
Published since 1945	7	22
From Soviet archives	1	13

The one title from Soviet archives fills thirty-five pages of the journal *Mezhdunarodnaya Zhizn'* (Feb. 1959, pp. 144–58; Mar. 1959, pp. 139–58), "Peregovory Voennykh Missiy SSSR, Anglii i Frantsii v Moskve v Avguste 1939 g.," the minutes of the staff talks between the Anglo-French and Soviet military delegations in Moscow in August 1939. But this same material had been published five years earlier by the British Foreign Office in *Documents on British Foreign Policy*.

Nor is it possible to argue that Maisky was merely attempting to convict the Western "imperialists" with their own words. He quotes a minute by Karl Schnurre, a German Foreign Office official, of a conversation with Georgi Astakhov, the Soviet chargé in Berlin, on May 5, 1939. According to Schnurre, Astakhov had cautiously tried to determine the German reaction to the dismissal of Soviet Foreign

271

Commissar Litvinov two days earlier. Maisky doubts that "Schnurre accurately conveys what Astakhov said in this connection (of this, naturally, it is impossible to be in any way certain) . . . But in all probability Schnurre himself actually raised the question," concludes Maisky, "and only in his record of the conversation represented the affair as if the question came from Astakhov" (II, 513–14).

The point is that Maisky could only quote a captured German document published sixteen years earlier by the U.S. Department of State. He was unable to quote Astakhov's own report on the conversation which should be in the Soviet Foreign Ministry (or K.G.B.?) files in Moscow.

CHAPTER I

1. U.S. Department of State, *Foreign Relations of the United States* (Washington: G.P.O., continuing series, hereafter cited as *FRUS*), 1932, III, 560; see also 1931, III, 27, 67.

2. *FRUS*, 1932, IV, 7–8. Jane Degras (ed.), *Soviet Documents on Foreign Policy* (London: Oxford University Press, 1951–53), II, 532.

3. *FRUS*, 1932, IV, 315.

4. *FRUS*, 1933, III, 68–70.

5. *Ibid.*, 195–96.

6. League of Nations, *Official Journal*, Supplement 112, pp. 98–99.

7. *FRUS*, 1933, III, 228–30.

8. E. L. Woodward and Rohan Butler (eds.), *Documents on British Foreign Policy 1919–1939* (London: H.M. Stationery Office, 1949——, hereafter cited as *D British FP*), 2nd s., VII, 581–83.

9. Degras, III, 23.

10. *FRUS*, 1933, III, 412–16.

11. *FRUS, The Soviet Union*, 54; 1934, III, 109–11.

12. *D British FP*, 2nd s., VI, 773–74.

13. *Ibid.*, 845–48.

14. *FRUS*, 1934, III, 230–31.

15. *Ibid.*, 231–32, 291–92; 1935, III, 103. In his memoirs Eden wrote of his astonishment at the depths of Soviet suspicion of British policy, "not so much in Stalin's mind, or Litvinov's, but often revealed in casual comment and conversation. An almost Machiavellian subtlety was attributed to us in encouraging Hitler to satisfy his appetites in the east at Russia's expense." (*Facing the Dictators*— Boston: Houghton Mifflin, 1962—pp. 139, 170, 181.)

16. *FRUS*, 1936, IV, 64–65. Degras, III, 164–70.

17. *FRUS*, 1936, IV, 100, 101–2.
18. *Ibid.*, 162, 165.
19. Degras, III, 219–20. U.S. Department of State, *Documents on German Foreign Policy* (Washington: G.P.O., 1949——, hereafter cited as *D German FP*), ser. d, I, 734. *FRUS*, 1936, IV, 426–29, 451–52. The Anti-Comintern Pact had in itself little real significance. When he concluded the agreement with Stalin in 1939, Hitler ignored its most important provision, Article II of the secret annex: "For the duration of the present Agreement, the High Contracting States will conclude no political treaties with the Union of Soviet Socialist Republics contrary to the spirit of this Agreement without mutual consent."
20. *N.Y. Times*, May 16, 1937. *The Times* (London), May 17. Degras, III, 242–44. *FRUS*, 1937, III, 920–28.
21. *FRUS*, 1937, III, 827–28.
22. *Ibid.*, 635–36.
23. *FRUS*, 1938, III, 455–85. *The Times* (London), Jul. 4, 1938. *N.Y. Times*, Jul. 4, 14, 16–31; Aug. 1–16, 1938. Clark W. Tinch, "Quasi-war Between Japan and the U.S.S.R., 1937–1939," *World Politics*, III (Jan. 1951), 178–82. Martin Blumenson, "The Soviet Power Play at Changkufeng," *World Politics*, XII (Jan. 1960), 249–63. The only thorough account of the Changkufeng fighting, however, and the one upon which much of this is based, is a manuscript, as yet unpublished, by Alvin D. Coox. During ten years in Japan he examined practically all the published and many unpublished records and interviewed survivors who had participated in the fighting or held important positions at the time—from the General Staff in Tokyo to the Japanese Embassy in Moscow and the headquarters of the brigades and regiments involved. The statement of General Suetaka is quoted by Coox from Kunihiko Akaishizawa, *Chokoho* (*Changkufeng*—Tokyo, 1941), pp. 318–24.
24. There is some evidence that Heydrich, the Nazi S.S. official, using handwriting specimens dating from the pre-1933 cooperation of Reichswehr and Red Army, forged documents implicating the Soviet marshal in an anti-Stalin plot and secret dealings with the German General Staff—and then transmitted the forgeries to the Soviet N.K.G.B. But the testimony of Walter Schellenberg, the only survivor who might have been in a position to say what happened, is confused to say the least. Even according to his account this incident can hardly have started the purge of the Red Army; Schellenberg states that the N.K.G.B. received the documents in mid-May, but Tukhachevsky had already been demoted to the command of a military district by May 11. (Peter Kleist, *Zwischen Hitler und*

Stalin, 1939–1945—Bonn: Athenäum Verlag, 1950—fn., p. 212. Walter Schellenberg, *The Labyrinth*—New York: Harper and Bros., 1956—pp. 25–28.)

25. *FRUS, The Soviet Union*, 320–22, 374–76, 389–94, 506–7. Count Jan Szembek, *Journal 1933–1939* (Paris: Librairie Plon, 1952), 263–65. *D German FP*, ser. d, i, 904–9, 910–12, 915–16. Degras, iii, 218–19, 265–66, 269–72, 314–15. See also National Archives roll 312—522/237310 and 1542—3168/D674840.

26. *The Times* (London), Jul. 4, 1938. *N.Y. Times*, Jul. 22, Aug. 4, 1938.

CHAPTER 2

1. Gustav Hilger and Alfred G. Meyer, *The Incompatible Allies* (New York: Macmillan, 1953), 253. Degras, iii, 1.

2. *D German FP*, ser. c, i, 14, 21–22. Norman H. Baynes, *The Speeches of Adolf Hitler* (London: Oxford University Press, 1942), ii, 1019. See also Rudolf Nadolny, *Mein Beitrag* (Wiesbaden: Limes Verlag, 1955), 133–34.

3. *D German FP*, ser. c, i, 241–42, 252, 418–19.

4. *Ibid.*, 450. N. Rudolph, "The Intensification of the Versailles Antagonisms and the Menace of a New Imperialist War," *Communist International*, x, no. 9 (May 15, 1933), 292. Unless otherwise indicated, references to the Comintern journal are to the English-language edition. Ten to fifteen per cent of the articles dealing with international relations did *not* appear in the Russian edition.

5. *D German FP*, ser. c, i, 567, 581–82, 590–92. Degras, iii, 21–23.

6. Hilger & Meyer, 256–57. *D German FP*, ser. c, i, 273, 363, 422, 467–68 (fn. 12), 523, 741–43, 822.

7. *D German FP*, ser. c, i, 798, 845–47, 850–55, 862–64, 872–73, 883; ii, 35, 47–48, 53–54. Degras, iii, 31–32.

8. N. Rudolph, "The Foreign Policy of German Fascism and War Preparations Against the U.S.S.R.," *Communist International*, x, no. 12 (Jun. 22, 1933), 438–39. *FRUS, The Soviet Union*, 53; 1934, iii, 111. *D German FP*, ser. c, ii, 297.

9. The Anti-Comintern Pact lay more than two years in the future (Nov. 1936), and in 1933 and 1934 Moscow can hardly have had any reason to suspect a German-Japanese understanding. As late as October 1934, State Secretary Bülow instructed the German Ambassador in Tokyo to avoid "any close relations . . . which might lay us open to being suspected of wishing to render assistance against Russia." Otherwise, should a war break out in the Far East, "moves would probably be made against us in order to make certain that we did not

attack Russia in the rear or even merely cause disquiet." The ambassador replied on December 14 that he was restricting relations with the Japanese Foreign Minister to a minimum; the service attachés were doing the same with respect to the Japanese Army and Navy. (*D German FP*, ser. c, III, 480.)

10. *D German FP*, ser. c, I, 64, 71, 87.

11. *Ibid.*, 357.

12. *Ibid.*, ser. c, I, 884–85; II, 40, 53 (fn. 3). *D British FP*, 2nd s., VII, 602–3.

13. *D German FP*, ser. c, II, 128–29, 421–22, 458. *D British FP*, 2nd s., VII, 630–31, 632, 637, 646–47. Karl Radek, editor of *Izvestia*, had urged the idea unofficially during a visit to Warsaw in the summer of 1933 (Col. Jozef Beck, *Final Report*—New York: Robert Speller & Sons, 1957—pp. 31–33).

14. *D German FP*, ser. c, II, 338, 377.

15. Beck, 51–53. Degras, III, 73–75.

16. *D German FP*, ser. c, II, 683–85, 686, 731–34, 746–47, 763–64. Degras, III, 79–83.

CHAPTER 3

1. *D British FP*, 2nd s., VI, 753–56. For an account of French-Soviet relations from the evacuation of the Rhineland in 1930 to the signing of the alliance in 1935, see William Evans Scott, *Alliance Against Hitler: The Origins of the Franco-Soviet Pact* (Durham, N.C.: Duke University Press, 1962).

2. *FRUS, The Soviet Union*, 53–54. Degras, III, 45, 48, 51.

3. *D British FP*, 2nd s., VI, 704, 707–8, 803–22. *D German FP*, ser. c, II, 880–81, 902–4.

4. *D German FP*, ser. c, I, 717, 833; II, 83.

5. *Ibid.*, ser. c, II, 276.

6. Degras, III, 46, 54–57. *D German FP*, ser. c, II, 302.

7. *D German FP*, ser. c, II, 333–34, 352.

8. Degras, III, 70.

9. Nadolny, 167–68. *D German FP*, ser. c, III, 20, 111–12.

10. *D German FP*, ser. c, III, 396–402, 446–49. Degras, III, 96–98. Scott, 186–89, 207–13. See also Laval's remarks to a German diplomat in Paris in March 1937, National Archive roll 296—653/253169–73.

11. Hilger & Meyer, 269–71. *D German FP*, ser. c, IV, 138, 453–54, 778–79, 897–99, 932–33. Degras, III, 153–55.

12. *D British FP*, 2nd s., VI, 770, 805, 876.

13. Georgi Dimitroff [Dimitrov], "A Congress of the Mobilization of Forces on a Broad Scale Against Fascism and War" (lead

article) and "The Fascist Offensive and the Tasks of the Communist International in the Fight for the Unity of the Working Class Against Fascism," *Communist International*, XII, no. 17–18 (Sept. 20, 1935), 1159–67, 1188–1247.

14. Louis Fischer, *Men and Politics* (New York: Duell, Sloan and Pearce, 1941), 377, 382. D *German FP*, ser. d, III, 89.

15. David T. Cattell, *Soviet Diplomacy and the Spanish Civil War* (Berkeley & Los Angeles: U. of Calif. Press, 1957), 35.

16. *FRUS*, 1936, II, 461. Louis Fischer, *The Soviets in World Affairs* (Princeton: Princeton U. Press, 1951), I, 237, 264–65.

17. Degras, III, 273–75.

18. Fischer, *Men and Politics*, 413, 530.

19. Alexander Orlov, *The Secret History of Stalin's Crimes* (New York: Random House, 1953), 238. David T. Cattell, *Communism and the Spanish Civil War* (Berkeley & Los Angeles: U. of Calif. Press, 1956), 76–79.

20. League of Nations, *Official Journal*, 1935, pp. 1141–42.

21. *Ibid.*, Supplement 138, p. 73.

22. Degras, III, 150.

23. League of Nations, *Official Journal*, 1936, pp. 319–20.

24. *Ibid.*, Supplement 169, pp. 82–83.

25. *FRUS, The Soviet Union*, 285–86; 1936, I, 200–201.

26. Degras, III, 216.

27. D *German FP*, ser. c, v, 298–99, 488–94, 512, 571–73, 964–66, 1066–70, 1115–18. Documents on the Kandelaki-Schacht conversations are filmed on National Archives roll 282—393/212210–15, also on 1057—1907/429293–300, and will presumably appear in D *German FP*, ser. c, VI: "It would be somewhat different," Neurath concluded, "if the situation in Russia should develop toward an absolute despotism based on the military. In such a case, of course, we dare not miss the moment for again making connections with Russia."

28. *The Times* (London), Jan. 15, 25, 1937. *FRUS*, 1937, I, 40. *N.Y. Times*, Feb. 10, 1937.

29. *N.Y. Times*, Apr. 7, May 19, 1937. *The Times* (London), Apr. 14, May 19, 1937. See also National Archives roll 282—393/212222 and 1057—1907/429302–11.

30. *FRUS, The Soviet Union*, 387–88.

31. *FRUS*, 1937, I, 158, 186–88. See also D *German FP*, ser. d, I, 55–67, 81, 122–23, 1144.

32. Degras, III, 266–68. "Dimitroff [Dimitrov] Speaks to His Electors," *Communist International*, XV, no. 1 (Jan. 1938), 10. National Archives roll 312—523/237663–70. *N.Y. Times*, Dec. 2, 1949. *FRUS*, 1938, I, 6.

33. This reference was to Chamberlain's rebuff of a peace move Roosevelt had wished to make; at the time, however, it might have been interpreted as applying to Germany (Eden, 622–45, 682).

34. Part vii, "Strategy and Tactics," of "The Foundations of Leninism" in *Works* (Moscow: Foreign Languages Publishing House, 1953), vol. 6, p. 161.

35. A serial account of the Hottelet interview appeared in the *Washington Post*, January 21–25, 1952, a few days after Litvinov's death. General Smith's account was published as a Prefatory Note (pp. 7–8) to *Notes for a Journal*, falsely attributed to Litvinov (New York: William Morrow & Co., 1955).

CHAPTER 4

1. *FRUS, The Soviet Union*, 533–34. *D British FP*, 3rd s., i, 54; unless otherwise indicated, subsequent references are to the 3rd Series.

2. *D British FP*, i, 65.

3. *Ibid.*, 62–64. Degras, iii, 276–77. Soviet Ambassador Maisky presented an official version of Litvinov's remarks to the British Foreign Office on March 17, together with a covering note stating that they represented the official views of the Soviet Government. Assuming that Moscow was in effect proposing an international conference, Halifax, the new Foreign Secretary, politely rejected the proposal in a note of March 24: "A conference only attended by some of the European Powers, and designed less to secure the settlement of outstanding problems than to organise concerted action against aggression, would not necessarily, in the view of His Majesty's Government, have such a favourable effect upon the prospects of European peace." (*D British FP*, i, 101.) The white flag of appeasement was already nailed to the mast.

4. *FRUS*, 1938, i, 41–42.

5. Quoted in *International Press Correspondence*, v. 18, no. 22 (Apr. 30, 1938), 486.

6. The British Government "is now ready to sacrifice the interests of peace by betraying Austria and Czechoslovakia to Hitler as it has already betrayed Spain and China." "Hatred of Communism, hatred of the People's Front, hatred of democracy are a mainspring of Chamberlain's policy." "The new foreign Secretary, Lord Halifax, was chosen precisely because of his extremely subservient attitude to fascist Germany, precisely because he was the candidate of the Cliveden clique of the pro-fascist millionaires." "To resist this there is only one effective means—the unity of the working class, the unity

of all progressive and peace-loving forces." (R. Page Arnot, "Chamberlain Kowtows to Fascist Aggressors," *Communist International*, xv, no. 4—Apr. 1938—pp. 400–404.)

For the Chamberlain government, a peace front with the Soviet Union "constitutes a greater evil than the risk of war: for with fascism curbed and peace preserved the way would be open for an extension of the People's Front, for the struggle of the oppressed classes . . . with those very interests which Chamberlain represents, the interests of a handful of millionaires, monopolists and big landlords." "Chamberlain's calculation is to divert German aggression away from the colonies and against Czechoslovakia, the Balkans and the USSR." "If the significance of the present situation . . . is driven home effectively throughout the working class and the mass of the people of Britain, then it will be possible to look forward to the early building up of a wide democratic front of peace in Britain, united in struggle against fascism and war and against the pro-fascist Chamberlain government." (R. Page Arnot, "The Struggle to Establish a Democratic Peace Front in England," *Communist International*, xv, no. 6—June 1938—pp. 536–41.)

"Whose is the responsibility for this brazen insolence and murderous activity of fascism . . . The responsibility lies with the reactionary clique of British Conservatism." "To German fascism they lent their aid, giving it the possibility of rearming. For them it is a bloodthirsty ruffian, a 'strong-arm-man' to be used against the international working class and the democratic movement of the people.

"They gave their blessing to its invasion of Austria. Stealthily, covertly, they direct it toward the east, against the land of the Soviets.

"Responsibility also lies with the French reactionary bourgeoisie. By capitulating to German fascism they helped to give it strength."

"Put no faith, comrades, in those who assert that you have not at your disposal the means whereby to make governments conduct a policy of struggle against the aggressors." "Without the working class no train is moved, no steamer sails, no ship is laden, no one can hush the voice of thousands of demonstrators.

"But, brother proletarians, for your strength to be brought into action requires working class unity."

"In the name of millions of workers . . . the Communist International again proposes to the Socialist and Trade Union Internationals to establish a united international working class front." ("May First Manifesto of the Executive Committee of the Communist International," *Communist International*, xv, no. 5—May 1938—pp. 411–14.)

7. *FRUS, The Soviet Union*, 572.

8. "Provocative Fascist Broadcast Exposed by Soviet Union," *International Press Correspondence*, v. 18, no. 25 (May 14, 1938), 606. G. Friedrich, "Cuckoo's Eggs in the Communist Press," *Communist International*, xv, no. 6 (June 1938), 574–78. Friedrich cited a "new false dispatch in the same *Rote Fahne*." Under the headline "Voroshilov to the Worker Delegates: The Red Army is Ready," *Rote Fahne* reported that Voroshilov had addressed a delegation of foreign workers in the Kremlin. Friedrich commented that "the only thing that is true in this report is that a reception actually took place in the Kremlin, but . . . for a delegation of the participants in the parade on Red Square." Friedrich's article also appeared in *International Press Correspondence*, v. 18, no. 28 (June 11, 1938), 703–5.

9. D *German FP*, ser. d, 11, 267–69; unless otherwise indicated, subsequent references are to Series D.

10. *FRUS*, 1938, 1, 492.

11. D *British FP*, 1, 184–85, 317, 332, 340, 341. D *German FP*, 11, 198, 304, 315–16, 318–19, 320, 327.

12. "Czechoslovakia and World Peace," lead editorial, *Communist International*, xv, no. 7 (Jul. 1938), 603–7.

13. Degras, 111, 292–94. *FRUS, The Soviet Union*, 587.

14. Quoted in "The Chief Danger to Peace," *World News and Views*, v. 18, no. 36 (Jul. 23, 1938), 853.

15. D *British FP*, 11, 107, 266. *FRUS*, 1938, 1, 547–48.

16. Degras, 111, 286–87, 294.

17. *FRUS*, 1938, 1, 65–68, 548.

18. *Ibid.*, 546, 548.

19. D *British FP*, 11, 277–78, 280, 283–84, 285, 680–82.

20. D *German FP*, 11, 715, 751–52.

21. D *British FP*, 11, 309, 312, 313–14.

22. D *German FP*, 11, 786–98. D *British FP*, 11, 338–51, 373–99, 405.

23. Czechoslovakia, Ministerium für auswärtige Angelegenheiten, and U.S.S.R., Ministerium für auswärtige Angelegenheiten, *Neue Dokumente zur Geschichte des münchener Abkommens* (Prague: Orbis, 1959), 91–93, 96–97. Beneš later wrote that he had objected to the loss of time involved in an appeal to the League. The Soviet Minister again wired Moscow and received an answer the same day: The U.S.S.R. would come to the aid of Czechoslovakia immediately following an appeal to Geneva without waiting for a resolution. On the 22nd, however, Deputy Foreign Commissar Potemkin asked Fierlinger, the Czech Minister in Moscow, why Prague had never posed

the question of unconditional Soviet support (*Neue Dokumente,* 120); and on the 23rd Litvinov declared that Prague "had not raised the question of Soviet assistance independently of assistance by France." For a detailed examination of the evidence see Boris Celovsky, *Das münchener Abkommen von 1938* (Stuttgart: Deutsche Verlags-Anstalt, 1958), 375–78.

24. D *British FP*, ii, 431–36, 437–39, 440, 441–45, 449–50.

25. D *German FP*, ii, 870–79. D *British FP*, ii, 463–73.

26. D *British FP*, ii, 499–508. D *German FP*, ii, 898–908.

27. League of Nations, *Official Journal,* Supplement 183, pp. 77–78; italics supplied.

28. *FRUS,* 1938, i, 634. The Soviet chargé also remarked that although it might linger on for some time, the Franco-Soviet pact was dead for all practical purposes.

29. D *British FP*, ii, 457–58, 459, 460, 479, 481, 483, 488.

30. Fierlinger, the Czechoslovak Minister in Moscow, told Deputy Foreign Commissar Potemkin on the 22nd that Prague regarded the pact with the U.S.S.R. as still valid, and the latter made no objection. (C.S.R. & U.S.S.R., *Neue Dokumente,* 120.)

31. League of Nations *Official Journal,* Supplement 189, pp. 34–35.

32. D *British FP*, ii, 480.

33. *Ibid.,* 497–98.

34. *Ibid.,* 518–19, 520–35, 537–40, 550.

35. *Ibid.,* 541–42, 554–57.

36. *Ibid.,* 559, 564–67, 576–78.

37. *Ibid.,* 586, 587, 589, 590, 592, 593–94.

38. *FRUS,* 1938, i, 695–97.

39. D *German FP*, ii, 998. In 1933 Ramsay MacDonald and Sir John Simon had discussed a four-power pact (France-Britain-Italy-Germany) with Mussolini.

40. D *British FP*, ii, 623–25.

CHAPTER 5

1. General Maurice Gustave Gamelin, *Servir* (Paris: Librairie Plon, 1946–47), ii, 230.

2. *FRUS,* 1938, i, 500–504, 507–8. On May 22 Foreign Minister Comnen told the French Ambassador to Bucharest that seven Czech planes had recently flown over Rumania, en route from Russia, in perfectly innocent circumstances, but the Polish Minister in Rumania had demanded an explanation. (Georges Bonnet, *La Défense de la*

Paix 1936–1940—Geneva: Éditions du Cheval Ailé, 1946–48—I, 131.)

3. Colonel Firebrace, the British military attaché, had written a similar evaluation in Moscow on April 18: "Both my [French and Czech] colleagues consider that the Red Army would have to advance through Poland as this offers the only theatre of war in which it could develop its numerical and mechanical superiority. Passage through Roumania would be very difficult as the country is unfavourable for operations of large forces. In the same way attack through Latvia and Lithuania must be restrained to small forces unless Polish territory is violated. . . .

"I myself agree that the only way in which Soviet Russia could directly advance in strength to the support of Czechoslovakia would be through Poland. Advance through Roumania, even with moderate forces, would leave Poland, obviously a possible opponent, on the flank, and would in any case be unlikely to present a serious threat [to Germany] . . . I cannot see that in any circumstances she [Poland] would allow of the passage of Soviet troops through her country." (*D British FP*, I, 172–73.)

4. D British FP, I, 482.

5. *FRUS*, 1938, I, 564. D British FP, II, 287–89, 318.

6. D British FP, II, 441. Gamelin, II, 352, 357.

7. Bonnet, I, 132. D British FP, I, 480–81; II, 82–83, 190.

8. Robert Coulondre, *De Stalin à Hitler* (Paris: Librairie Hachette, 1950), 152–53. C.S.R. & U.S.S.R., *Neue Dokumente*, 51. The Soviet Government may have returned to the theme later. Bullitt told Bonnet on August 26 that according to his information Moscow had asked the French Government if they would be obliged to support Poland "in case Germany should invade Czechoslovakia and France should then attack Germany and Polish troops should occupy the Teschen District." The French Foreign Minister confirmed that an inquiry had been made in exactly this form. He had replied that France would not be under any obligation to support Poland. "Bonnet went further and said that recent conversations between the French and Russian Governments led him to believe that if Germany should enter Czechoslovakia the first additional war to start would be war between the Soviet Union and Poland." (*FRUS*, 1938, I, 555–56.)

9. L. B. Namier, *Europe in Decay* (London: Macmillan, 1950), 286–87. C.S.R. & U.S.S.R., *Neue Dokumente*, 123. Degras, III, 305.

10. D German FP, II, 897–98, 948–50.

11. Beck, 168.

12. *FRUS*, 1938, I, 84.

13. Gamelin, II, 279. Celovsky, 203 (fn. 4), 205. Bonnet, I, 126. N. P. Comnène [Comnen], *Preludi del Grande Dramma* (Rome: Edizioni Leonardo, 1947), 39. See also *D German FP*, ser. c, v, 174, 648–49, 670–71, 736–37, 950.

14. Bonnet, I, 125. C.S.R. & U.S.S.R., *Neue Dokumente*, 42–45. *D British FP*, IV, 426.

15. Bonnet, II, 408. *D British FP*, II, 235, 255.

16. Bonnet, I, 199; II, 408. C.S.R. & U.S.S.R., *Neue Dokumente*, 64–71. Winston S. Churchill, *The Gathering Storm* (London: Cassell & Co., 1948), 229–32. *D British FP*, II, 229–30, 489. On September 8 Maisky told Halifax that Litvinov had suggested to Paris a joint Anglo-French-Soviet note to Berlin. The Soviet Ambassador observed that such a move would probably attract U.S. support. But Halifax remained noncommittal. According to Bonnet, Litvinov mentioned the proposal again at Geneva on September 11 and seemed disappointed at the lack of a positive reaction. (*D British FP*, II, 272, 294.)

17. Bonnet, I, 200–203; II, 409. Celovsky, 322–24. Comnène, *Preludi*, 83–86, 90; also in *La Suisse*, Aug. 8, 1946, cited by Bonnet, II, 410. See also *D German FP*, II, 981, and *D British FP*, III, 46.

18. *D British FP*, II, 355.

19. *D German FP*, II, 250. The Czechoslovak Government had obtained the rights to build a new-type Soviet medium bomber and had purchased a number as models for Czech factories. During a meeting of the council of the Little Entente at Sinaia on May 4 and 5, Czechoslovak Foreign Minister Krofta told Fabricius, the German Minister to Bucharest, that his government had purchased twenty of the bombers and that seven or nine had already been ferried across Rumania. On July 19 the Rumanian air and military attaché in Warsaw informed the German air attaché that about thirty-five of the aircraft had crossed Rumania since the end of May. The Rumanian Government had insisted that the planes be unarmed, have Czech markings, and be flown by Czech pilots. The ferry crews evidently travelled through Poland and Rumania to Russia by rail. Some forty or fifty of the aircraft were delivered altogether. (*D German FP*, II, 256, 500–501, 587–88, 855. Celovsky, 379. C.S.R. & U.S.S.R., *Neue Dokumente*, 32. Szembek, 326.)

20. *D German FP*, II, 434, also 573–76.

21. *Ibid.*, 500–501, 701.

22. Szembek, 325–26, 336–37. *D German FP*, II, 726.

23. *D German FP*, II, 746.

24. *Ibid.*, 981.

25. *FRUS*, 1938, I, 37–38. U.S.S.R., Ministry of Foreign Affairs,

Documents and Materials Relating to the Eve of the Second World War (Moscow: Foreign Languages Publishing House, 1948), I, 103.

26. *D British FP*, I, 162–65.

27. *Ibid.*, 161–62.

28. *Ibid.*, 213, 218. At the meeting in London on September 25 Daladier again stressed the quantitative strength of the U.S.S.R. in the air: "Colonel Lindberg . . . had said that the Russian air force had not the same prototypes as the German air force, but war was not conducted with planes capable of travelling at 500 miles per hour. What really mattered was the total number, and in this respect Russia could hold her own with Germany." (*D British FP*, II, 533.)

29. *D British FP*, I, 346, 420–24.

30. *D German FP*, II, 434.

31. *D British FP*, I, 303–7. In his report of April 18, Colonel Firebrace had referred to the French military attaché as a person "whose judgment does not inspire confidence." Reporting on the conversation, Vereker observed that Coulondre may have had "insufficient confidence in his own Military Attache, who was not present" but that "his main object was simply to clear his mind and to be able to go to Paris fortified by an independent and unbiased third party opinion." General Gamelin (I, 116, 137–38) admits that after 1937 the consensus of the intelligence received in Paris was that the Red Army was in the midst of a crisis.

32. U.S.S.R., *Documents and Materials*, I, 113, 118. *FRUS*, 1938, I, 58.

33. *D British FP*, II, 509. General Vuillemin, the French air chief, had mentioned this at a meeting of the Comité permanent de la Défense nationale on March 15, 1938 (Gamelin, II, 324).

34. *D German FP*, II, 602, 631, 667.

35. *D British FP*, II, 219–20.

36. Bonnet, II, 410.

37. *D German FP*, II, 177, 180, 231–32.

38. *Ibid.*, 348.

39. League of Nations, *Official Journal*, 1938, pp. 340–41. *D German FP*, I, 917–18; see also 1134–35.

40. *D German FP*, II, 358–62; I, 864.

41. *Ibid.*, II, 363–64, 423–26. Tippleskirch made a very similar evaluation in a memo of July 5 (*ibid.*, 467–69).

42. *Ibid.*, I, 920–21. *FRUS, The Soviet Union*, 584.

43. Degras, III, 286–87. *D German FP*, I, 924.

44. *D German FP*, II, 630.

45. *D British FP*, II, 140–42. The basic reason for the conversation,

evidently undertaken with Schulenburg's approval, was to impress the British with the necessity of adopting an unequivocal line in dealing with Hitler. The German Ambassador's secretary declared that "Ribbentrop shared, or affected to share the Fuhrer's optimism and the certainty that Great Britain would in no circumstances move and that Germany would be able to invade Czechoslovakia with impunity was reflected with alarming clearness in the despatches and instructions which went out from the Wilhelmstrasse. This, our informant said, was very disturbing to professional diplomats like his Ambassador, who saw their country about to involve herself in a war in which the odds would in their opinion be heavily against her. . . . The blame, they felt, would lie to a certain extent with His Majesty's Government who, as in 1914, had failed to make their position sufficiently clear. The only hope in their opinion would be for a representative of His Majesty's Government to inform the Fuhrer himself quite categorically that in certain circumstances Great Britain would quite certainly go to war in defence of Czechoslovakia. This might well have the necessary deterrent effect." Members of the German Embassy expressed themselves in similar terms to the U.S. chargé (*FRUS*, 1938, I, 557).

Schulenburg worded a dispatch of August 26 (supplementing an earlier telegram on the interview with Litvinov) in a way which he evidently hoped would make an impression in Berlin: The "overwhelming conviction of the Diplomatic Corps here is that, in the event of a German-Czech armed conflict, France would attack Germany, and Great Britain would be at France's side. The members of the British and French Embassies here have repeatedly told us this. As far as the Soviet Union is concerned, my colleagues here believe that she will do as little as possible, so that at the end of the war she will have an intact army at her disposal. In consequence, the Soviet Union would in the end be the only one to gain." (*D German FP*, II, 631.)

46. *D German FP*, I, 921; II, 632, 654.

47. *Ibid.*, II, 601. G. Ciano, *Ciano's Hidden Diary 1937–1938* (New York: E. P. Dutton, 1953), 148.

48. *D German FP*, II, 476, 686–87, 727–30.

49. *Ibid.*, IV, 606.

50. Ministerstvo Inostrannykh Del S.S.S.R. i Ministerstvo Inostrannykh Del Ch.S.R., *Novye Dokumenty iz Istorii Myunkhena* (Moscow: Gosudarstvennoe Izdatel'stvo Politicheskoy Literatury, 1958). The German-language edition, *Neue Dokumente . . .*, published in Prague in 1959 with some slight additional material in the notes, has been used for this study.

51. C.S.R. & U.S.S.R., *Neue Dokumente,* 112, 144, 145-46.
52. Gamelin, II, 285.
53. *D British FP,* II, 276-77.

CHAPTER 6

1. Degras, III, 306-7.
2. "The Pravda on Chamberlain's Triumph," *World News and Views,* v. 18 (Oct. 8, 1938), 1115.
3. Degras, III, 308-11.
4. *D British FP,* III, 67.
5. "The Conspiracy of Munich," *Communist International,* xv (Oct. 1938), 875.
6. Quoted in "The Balance of Munich," *World News and Views,* v. 18 (Oct. 29, 1938), 1186.
7. Quoted in "British Determined to Establish Domination over France," *World News and Views,* v. 18 (Nov. 26, 1938), 1278.
8. "Against Munich—Working Class Unity!" and J. R. Campbell, "Who are the Friends of Chamberlain in the British Labor Movement?" *Communist International,* xvi (Feb. and Mar. 1939), 99-104, 249.
9. Degras, III, 307-8. *D British FP,* III, 153-54.
10. Quoted in "The Consequences of Munich," *World News and Views,* v. 18 (Oct. 29, 1938), 1186.
11. *D British FP,* III, 280, 541-42. *FRUS, The Soviet Union,* 731-32.
12. *Communist International,* xvi (Jan. 1939), 27, 46, 58, 87-88.
13. *FRUS,* 1938, I, 651. *D British FP,* IV, 373.
14. *D German FP,* v, 87-88. *FRUS,* 1938, I, 664-65; 1939, I, 118-19.
15. Polish Ministry for Foreign Affairs, *Polish White Book* (New York: Roy Publishers, 1940), 16-17, 23-24, 29, 31, 43-44. *D British FP,* I, 274.
16. *Polish White Book,* 25-26. Szembek, 28, 32-34, 38-39.
17. *Polish White Book,* 36-38, 39. Szembek, 199, 222-23, 247.
18. Szembek, 275-77. *Polish White Book,* 44-45. The two translations of Szembek's memo on the conversation conflict on the point indicated.
19. U.S.S.R., *Documents and Materials,* I, 149. Szembek, 329.
20. D. Gard, "The Foreign Policy of German Imperialism," *Communist International,* xi (Jul. 20, 1934), 462.
21. "Germany as the Chief Instigator of War in Europe" and O. Piatnitsky, "Some Problems of the Present International Situation,"

Communist International, XII (Apr. 20 and June 5, 1935), 383–91, 611–21.

22. Degras, III, 156, 164–65.

23. J. Lenski, "Build up a Mighty Front of Freedom and Peace" and "Urgent Questions of the People's Front in Poland," *Communist International,* XIII (June and Oct. 1936), 764–73, 1280–91.

24. *FRUS, The Soviet Union,* 293.

25. David J. Dallin, *Soviet Espionage* (New Haven: Yale University Press, 1955), 124–25. Dallin cites an unpublished Gestapo report of Dec. 21, 1942. Schellenberg (p. 282) mentions von Scheliha's arrest in 1942.

26. Hilger & Meyer, 288–89.

27. Szembek, 358–59. Degras, III, 312.

28. *D British FP,* III, 419. *D German FP,* V, 136. Degras, III, 314 (TASS release of Dec. 21, 1938).

29. Report to Berlin of Dec. 3, 1938, *D German FP,* V, 138–40.

30. "Poland appears to be awakening . . . The Polish official news agency, *Pat,* stresses the fact that in Warsaw this declaration is interpreted as a gesture aimed, in the first place at Germany . . . the Polish people realise that their country is the next victim marked down by Hitler . . ." ("Foreign Political Review of the Week," *World News and Views,* v. 18—Dec. 3, 1938—p. 1300.)

31. Coulondre, 165, 168–69. Angelo Rossi, *Les Communistes Français Pendant la Drole de Guerre* (Paris: Les Iles d'Or, 1951), 12, 14.

32. Coulondre, 171.

33. *D British FP,* III, 193. *FRUS, The Soviet Union,* 592; 1938, I, 106. France, Ministère des Affaires Étrangères, *French Yellow Book* (London: Hutchinson & Co., 1940), 43. Chvalkovsky's fears may or may not have been genuine. Beneš and Jan Masaryk had mentioned this danger several times before Munich—probably in order to muster British and French support for Czechoslovakia. (*D German FP,* II, 64; *FRUS,* 1938, I, 31, 410–12, 500, 739.)

34. *D German FP,* V, 105–7, 127–29.

35. *Ibid.,* 152–61. *Polish White Book,* 53.

36. *D British FP,* VI, 248. Beck, 171–73. *FRUS,* 1939, I, 1. Szembek, 407, 408.

37. *D German FP,* V, 160–61, 167–68. Joachim von Ribbentrop, *The Ribbentrop Memoirs* (London: Weidenfeld & Nicolson, 1954), p. 101, fn. Beck, 173. Szembek, 413–15.

38. *D German FP,* I, 902–3, 912–15, 926–28; VII, 623–26. Hilger & Meyer, 283–84.

39. *D German FP,* IV, 607–9.

40. *Ibid.,* 616, 618–20.

41. *Ibid.*, 620–21. Merekalov had been Deputy Commissar for Foreign Trade before his appointment to Berlin.

42. *Ibid.*, 621–22.

43. *D British FP*, IV, 24–25, 35.

44. *FRUS*, 1939, I, 313.

45. Kleist, 20–21. Hilger & Meyer, 285–86. Shortly after Ribbentrop's return from Warsaw, he may have considered a break in diplomatic relations with the U.S.S.R., possibly to convince the Poles of his good faith. On February 6 Wiehl advised against such a move because of the need of German industry for even the small amounts of Soviet raw materials it was then receiving (memo, Wiehl to Ribbentrop, *D German FP*, IV, 624–25). Some inconclusive economic discussions were held in Moscow during February, but on March 11 German economic authorities, because of new domestic demands, decided that they would be unable to make the necessary deliveries to Russia. They decided to continue the negotiations "in a dilatory fashion." Should the situation improve in the near future it might still be possible to conclude an agreement. Nothing important was said on the subject, however, until May 20. (*D German FP*, IV, 630–31; VI, 729–31.)

46. *FRUS*, 1939, I, 314.

47. *D British FP*, IV, 106–7, 115, 123–24. *FRUS, The Soviet Union*, 737. Litvinov evidently attempted to use the threat of a German-Soviet rapprochement as late as March 1939 during Soviet-Japanese negotiations for a fisheries convention (*D German FP*, VI, 55–56).

48. *D British FP*, IV, 34, 70–71. *FRUS*, 1939, I, 17, 30.

49. J. V. Stalin, *Report on the Work of the Central Committee to the Eighteenth Congress of the C.P.S.U. /B./* (Moscow: Foreign Languages Publishing House, 1939). See also the May Day Manifesto of the Executive Committee of the Comintern and the "Eighteenth Congress . . . ," which were written shortly after Stalin's speech (*Communist International*, XVI—Apr. 1939—pp. 292, 296–97).

50. *D German FP*, V, 524–32. *D British FP*, IV, 397–98, 421, 430–31, 454–55, 456, 474–76.

51. *D British FP*, IV, 584–85.

52. *Ibid.*, 509–10.

53. *Ibid.*, 511–12, 523–24.

54. *Ibid.*, 570–71; V, 235. Degras, III, 324–25.

55. Alfred Bilmanis, *Latvian-Russian Relations, Documents* (Washington: Latvian Legation, 1944), 188–89. August Rei, *Nazi-Soviet Conspiracy and the Baltic States* (London: Boreas, 1948), 35. *D British FP*, V, 350–51.

56. Degras, III, 315.

57. *D British FP*, IV, 448–50.

58. Wipert von Blücher, *Gesandter zwischen Diktatur und Demokratie* (Wiesbaden: Limes Verlag, 1951), 140–42. R. Magnus, "Neutrality of the Scandinavian Powers is Aid to the Aggressor," *Communist International*, XV (Sept. 1938), 836. K. G. Mannerheim, *The Memoirs of Marshal Mannerheim* (New York: E. P. Dutton, 1954), 292–301. John E. Wuorinen (ed.), *Finland and World War II* (New York: Ronald Press Co., 1948), 44–48.

59. Szembek, 436–37, 443, 470. As early as April 4 TASS denied reports in the French press that Russia had promised war materials to Poland in the event of a war with Germany (Degras, III, 328).

60. *D British FP*, V, 349–50.

61. *Ibid.*, 215, 349. *D German FP*, VI, 246, 316. FRUS, *The Soviet Union*, 934, 935.

62. *D British FP*, IV, 568–70.

63. The only German reaction recorded in the published diplomatic correspondence took place on March 21, before Hudson's visit, when Berlin queried the Moscow and London Embassies regarding a Helsinki report that Hudson was authorized to invite Litvinov to London. (*D German FP*, VI, 98 fn.)

64. FRUS, *The Soviet Union*, 61.

CHAPTER 7

1. Erich Kordt, *Nicht aus den Akten* (Stuttgart: Union deutsche Verlagsgesellschaft, 1950), 298.

2. Ernst von Weizsäcker, *Memoirs* (Chicago: Henry Regnery Co., 1951), 176. *D German FP*, IV, 190–202, 203–6, 221–24. FRUS, 1939, I, 14. *D British FP*, VI, 736–38.

3. *D British FP*, IV, 360–61, 366–67. FRUS, 1939, I, 72. On the following day Rumanian Foreign Minister Gafencu told the British Minister that Tilea, acting without authority or cause, had greatly exaggerated the situation and that Rumanian-German commercial negotiations were proceeding normally (*D British FP*, IV, 369–70; FRUS, 1939, I, 74–75). It is possible that Tilea was in fact acting on King Carol's instructions and sought to draw the British Government's attention to the potential if not actual German threat to Rumania; see Andreas Hillgruber, *Hitler, König Carol und Marschall Antonescu* (Wiesbaden: Franz Steiner Verlag, 1954), 35.

4. Private letter or diary entry quoted by Keith Feiling, *The Life of Neville Chamberlain* (London: Macmillan, 1946), 403.

5. *D British FP*, IV, 505–6.

6. *Ibid.*, 372.

7. Bonnet had approached the Soviet Ambassador to Paris on the 18th and had received a similar reply (*D British FP*, IV, 422–23; *FRUS*, 1939, I, 79). Bonnet's first thought was that this was merely Litvinov's way of evading the issue, as the Rumanians would certainly never agree to such a conference in Bucharest.

8. *D British FP*, IV, 385, 392–93.

9. Degras, III, 322–23. *D British FP*, IV, 446–47.

10. *D German FP*, VI, 47.

11. Private letter or diary entry quoted by Feiling, 402–3. *D British FP*, IV, 400.

12. Degras, III, 324. *D British FP*, IV, 429–30, 466.

13. *D British FP*, IV, 428, 453–54.

14. *Polish White Book*, 70–71. Beck desired a bilateral agreement which would exclude France as well as the U.S.S.R. in order to avoid any appearance of an effort to "encircle" Germany (Szembek, 433–34).

15. Alarming but unfounded reports of an imminent German attack on Poland had been received and the question of what the British Government would do in such a case had been raised in Parliament. The question was to be answered on the 31st, and Chamberlain, aided by Halifax and Cadogan, drafted the declaration on the afternoon of the 30th. "Normally, when any grave new step in foreign policy is in contemplation, its implications, political and military, are thoroughly canvassed by Ministers with their civilian and military advisers. In the case of the Polish declaration, the idea seems to have sprung fully grown from the Ministerial mind." (William Strang, *Home and Abroad*—London: Andre Deutsch, 1956—p. 161.)

16. *D British FP*, V, 6–7, 12.

17. *Polish White Book*, 72–73. *D German FP*, VI, 203–4, 205–7. Memos of Mar. 10 and Apr. 17, 1939 by Fabricius, the German Minister in Rumania, filmed on National Archives roll 1029— 1776/406277 and 406281. Grigore Gafencu, *Last Days of Europe: A Diplomatic Journey in 1939* (New Haven: Yale University Press, 1948), 47–49, 51; Gafencu had planned a stopover in Warsaw but had abandoned the idea upon the advice of Fabricius who had warned that, with the existing Polish-German tension, such a move would spoil the atmosphere for Gafencu's talks in Berlin (Hillgruber, 49–50). Helmuth Greiner, *Die oberste Wehrmachtführung* (Wiesbaden: Limes Verlag, 1951), 30.

18. *D. British FP*, V, 75–76.

19. Gafencu, *Last Days of Europe*, 85–86. *D German FP*, VI, 278–83, 290–93. *FRUS*, 1939, I, 175–76.

20. Feiling, 407–8.
21. D British FP, v, 104.
22. Ibid., 206.
23. Kordt, 306. Kleist, 26–27.
24. Kleist, 27–30.
25. FRUS, 1939, I, 139–40.
26. D German FP, vi, 266–67.
27. D British FP, iv, 574–75.
28. Ibid., v, 201–2.
29. Ibid., 215. D German FP, vi, 267.
30. D British FP, v, 221–22.
31. Ibid., 223–24.
32. Ibid., 368.
33. Ibid., 400, 542.
34. Tinch, 182–86. D German FP, vi, 942–43; vii, 27–28. FRUS, 1939, iii, 46, 50, 63.

CHAPTER 8

1. D German FP, vi, 259–60.
2. D British FP, v, 433. Coulondre, 270–71. French Yellow Book, 134–36.
3. French Yellow Book, 132–34. D British FP, v, 463. Szembek, 455.
4. D British FP, v, 622, 634. On May 8 Potemkin had told Gafencu in Bucharest that the Axis powers were "spreading the false rumour that the U.S.S.R. is ready to come to an understanding with Germany and Italy. That is the sort of tactics they use, particularly in Berlin, to prevent an agreement between London, Paris and Moscow." (Grigore Gafencu, Prelude to the Russian Campaign— London: Frederick Muller Ltd., 1945—p. 240, fn.)
5. D British FP, vi, 14.
6. D German FP, vi, 429, 460, 535–36.
7. Hilger & Meyer, 293–97. Kleist, 37–38.
8. FRUS, 1939, I, 318–21. This information was given to the U.S. Embassy in Moscow by a member of the German Embassy. Subsequent accounts of German-Soviet negotiations from the same source agreed almost exactly with the reports sent to Berlin. Schulenburg or some other senior member of the embassy may have desired to keep the British and French informed but hesitated to do so directly. The ambassador apparently went beyond the extremely narrow instructions he later received from Ribbentrop (Kordt, 309–10; Kleist.

43–44) but could not report such deviations to Berlin. No such inhibitions applied in the case of the U.S. Embassy, and the State Department may well have had more precise information than the Wilhelmstrasse.

9. *D German FP*, VI, 559–60. *FRUS*, 1939, I, 321–22.

10. In order to disarm any rumors which the limited German-Soviet feelers might have launched, Molotov, in a speech to the Supreme Soviet on May 31, briefly surveyed economic negotiations with Germany in 1938 and early 1939. "Judging by certain signs," he declared, "it is not impossible that the negotiations will be resumed" (Degras, III, 337). A month later (June 28) Daladier told Bullitt "that the Soviet Government had repeatedly assured the French and British Governments that it was not negotiating in any way with the German Government" (*FRUS*, 1939, I, 278).

11. *D German FP*, VI, 547, 558.

12. Kordt, 309. *D German FP*, VI, 586–87.

13. *D German FP*, VI, 589–93, 598. Italy, Ministero degli Affari Esteri, *I Documenti Diplomatici Italiani* (Rome: La Libreria dello Stato, 1952——, hereafter cited as *DDI*), 8th s., XII, 32–34.

14. *DDI*, 8th s., XII, 44–45. *D German FP*, VI, 598, 601–7.

15. *D German FP*, VI, 610, 627–28. *FRUS*, 1939, I, 323–24.

16. *D German FP*, VI, 686–87, 728–29, 747.

17. *Ibid.*, 741–42. *FRUS*, 1939, I, 326.

18. Kordt, 310, Kleist, 45.

19. *FRUS*, 1939, I, 326–27. *DDI*, 8th s., XII, 297–98.

20. Drafted on or before June 12; *D German FP*, VI, 687, 711, 746–48.

21. *D German FP*, VI, 788.

22. Hungary had annexed Ruthenia, the Ukrainian-inhabited extreme eastern section of Czechoslovakia, following German occupation of the Czech lands on March 15, 1939. Germany had concluded nonaggression treaties with Latvia and Estonia on June 7, 1939, and in Article 4 of the German-Lithuanian treaty of March 22, 1939—returning Memel to the Reich—both parties agreed to refrain from using force against each other. (*D German FP*, V, 531, fn.; VI, 664.)

23. *D German FP*, VI, 805–7, 834–36. *FRUS*, 1939, I, 327–29.

24. Telegram of June 27; *D German FP*, VI, 790–91.

25. *Ibid.*, 800–802, 810, 813.

26. *Ibid.*, 894–95.

27. *Ibid.*, 808, 839, 975–76. Hilger & Meyer, 298.

28. *D German FP*, VI, 820–21, 870–71, 910–11.

29. *Ibid.*, 889, 928–29.

30. *Ibid.*, 936–38.

31. *D British FP*, VI, 447, 449.
32. *D German FP*, VI, 955–56.

CHAPTER 9

1. *D British FP*, V, 215, 228–29.
2. *Ibid.*, 266–69, 294–95, 357–59, 448–50.
3. *Ibid.*, 357–59.
4. *Ibid.*, 483–87.
5. *Ibid.*, 479–80.
6. Degras, III, 330. *D British FP*, V, 491–92, 520–21, 528–29.
7. *D British FP*, V, 558–59.
8. *Ibid.*, 572.
9. *Ibid.*, 404, 564–65.
10. *Ibid.*, 573, 589–90, 604, 631. *FRUS*, 1939, I, 256–57, 261.
11. Paris proposed the following formula: "If France and Great Britain found themselves at war with Germany as result of executing engagements taken by them to prevent all changes by force of *status quo* in Central or Eastern Europe, Russia would immediately assist them. If as result of the help given by Russia to France and Great Britain in above conditions Russia found herself at war with Germany, they would immediately assist her. The three Governments will concert without delay nature, in both cases, of this assistance and will take all steps to assure its full efficacy."

During a conversation with the Soviet Ambassador to Paris a few days later, Bonnet disclosed this draft and modified the second sentence to meet the ambassador's objections: "If the U.S.S.R. found itself in a state of war with Germany as a result of the action which it had taken with a view to preventing all changes by force of the existing *status quo* in Central or Eastern Europe, France and Great Britain would immediately lend it aid and assistance."

Molotov questioned Seeds about the French modification during the interview of May 8 and the British Ambassador, who knew nothing about the French draft, was forced to perform some strenuous verbal gymnastics. Bonnet evidently realized, or was informed of, his blunder and in mid-May ordered the French chargé in Moscow to allow Seeds to take the lead in conducting the negotiations. (*D British FP*, V, 294–95, 377–78, 405, 406, 486, 565–66, 572.)

12. *D British FP*, V, 623–25, 634.
13. *FRUS*, 1939, I, 252, 255. *D British FP*, V, 594–95, 645–47. *French Yellow Book*, 149.
14. *D British FP*, V, 678–81, 688–89.
15. *Ibid.*, 710–12.

16. *Ibid.*, 719–20, 725–27. On May 10 the Finnish Foreign Minister had told the British Minister in Helsinki that Finland would reject any German offer of a nonaggression pact provided the country were not guaranteed by Russia in any way. Public opinion, however, would consider a Soviet guarantee a menace, even one operative only "if desired," and would force acceptance of any subsequent German offer. The Finnish Minister to London made a similar statement to Halifax at about the same time. (*Ibid*, 495–96, 522.)

In a conversation with the British representative at Tallinn on May 15, the Estonian Foreign Minister expressed the hope that in the event of a general war the British Government might induce Moscow to refrain from aggression against Estonia. The next day the Estonian chargé in London asked if a Soviet guarantee of his country was contemplated. (*Ibid.*, 560, 572–73.)

Latvian Foreign Minister Munters spoke with Halifax at Geneva on May 22 and "threw out idea that any arrangements reached between Great Britain, France and Russia might if they covered Baltic states at all take the form of some kind of guarantee of . . . [their] neutrality." (*Ibid.*, 648–49.)

Even the Bulgarian Minister to London had something to say on the subject. He told the Foreign Secretary on May 11 that his government had received no offer of a Soviet guarantee. Passing through Sofia, however, Potemkin had emphasized Moscow's intention of maintaining the traditional Russian interest in Balkan affairs. The Bulgarian Government preferred that any Soviet assistance be in the form of munitions rather than troops which the U.S.S.R. might be reluctant to withdraw. (*Ibid.*, 530–31.)

17. Degras, III, 336–37. *D British FP*, V, 737.

18. *D British FP*, V, 753–54.

19. *FRUS*, 1939, I, 266–70.

20. *D British FP*, V, 787–88. Although he can hardly have been averse to arousing anxiety in Berlin, Stalin apparently did not wish to discourage Hitler. Thus at a diplomatic reception on June 10, when Italian Ambassador Rosso asked Potemkin if Strang's journey meant that the negotiations were entering a decisive stage, the Deputy Foreign Commissar expressed strong doubts and said that "some important points" still remained to be settled. (*DDI*, 8th s., XII, 166–67.)

21. *D British FP*, VI, 50–51, 54–56. *D German FP*, VI, 717–18.

22. *D British FP*, VI, 65, 115–16. Strang, 175.

23. *D British FP*, VI, 34–39, 116–19.

24. *Ibid.*, 84–87, 89–91. Degras, III, 349.

25. *D British FP*, VI, 119.

26. *Ibid.*, 103–5.
27. *Ibid.*, 91–93, 140–42.
28. *Ibid.*, 142, 143.
29. *Ibid.*, v, 736.
30. *FRUS*, 1939, I, 272. *D British FP*, VI, 152–53.
31. *French Yellow Book*, 154–55. *D British FP*, VI, 2, 5.
32. *French Yellow Book*, 158–59.
33. *D British FP*, VI, 705.
34. Kordt, 313–16.
35. *D British FP*, VI, 138–40, 160–61.
36. *FRUS*, 1939, I, 276. *D British FP*, VI, 173–74, 193.
37. Before this offer could be presented to Molotov, an article by Politburo member A. Zhdanov appeared in *Pravda* on June 29. According to Schulenburg, the consensus of opinion among the foreign diplomats in Moscow was that the Soviet Government was seeking (1) to influence British and French public opinion and thus force British agreement to the Soviet terms, and (2) to blame Britain and France for the slowness of the negotiations and possibly for their breakdown. "The Anglo-Franco-Soviet negotiations," wrote Zhdanov, "have reached an impasse. In spite of the extreme clarity of the attitude of the Soviet Government and in spite of all their efforts . . . no real progress can be observed . . . My opinion is . . . that the English and French Governments do not want an agreement on terms of equality with the U.S.S.R. . . . The Anglo-Soviet negotiations, . . . reckoning from the 15th April, . . . have now lasted for seventy-five days. Of this period, the Soviet Government only required sixteen days for the preparation of their replies to the various English drafts and proposals: the remaining fifty-nine days were wasted in procrastination and delay on the part of the English and French. . . . The well known example of this sort of artificially-created stumbling blocks in the negotiations is provided by the question of a tripartite guarantee of immediate assistance to Latvia, Estonia and Finland . . . It seems to me that the English and French do not want a real agreement or one acceptable to the U.S.S.R.: the only thing they really want is to talk about an agreement and, by making play with the obstinacy of the Soviet Union, to prepare their own public opinion for an eventual deal with the aggressors." (*D German FP*, VI, 808–9. *D British FP*, VI, 217–19. Degras, III, 352–54.)
38. *D British FP*, VI, 229–32.
39. *Ibid.*, 251–52, 272–73.
40. *Ibid.*, 249–50.
41. *French Yellow Book*, 180. *FRUS*, 1939, I, 279–80, 281–82.
42. *FRUS*, 1939, I, 281. *D British FP*, VI, 276–78, 279–81.

43. *D British FP*, VI, 308–10.
44. *Ibid.*, 310–13.
45. *Ibid.*, 333–36.
46. *Ibid.*, 24–25; V, 658–59, 746.
47. *Ibid.*, VI, 48–49. See also *FRUS, The Soviet Union*, 937–38.
48. Bilmanis, 191.
49. *D British FP*, VI, 95–96.
50. *Ibid.*, 325–27, 382–83.
51. *Ibid.*, 120–21.
52. *Ibid.*, 307–8, 264–66, 413–15.
53. *Ibid.*, 226–27, 254.
54. *Ibid.*, 335, 339, 360.
55. *Ibid.*, 375–77.
56. *Ibid.*, 422. Although the negotiations had arrived at an impasse, Potemkin carefully avoided giving that impression in a conversation with the Italian Ambassador on the 21st. The parties had already achieved appreciable results, said the Deputy Foreign Commissar, but a lively discussion was still going on regarding certain points. The talks would probably continue for a long time and no member of the Soviet Government expected a vacation that summer. (*DDI*, 8th s., XII, 480, 502.)

CHAPTER 10

1. *D British FP*, VI, 396–98.
2. *Ibid.*, 427–29.
3. *Ibid.*, 456–60.
4. *Ibid.*, 460–61.
5. *Ibid.*, 478, 484–85, 521–22. This was the last exchange of political views except for an inconclusive discussion on August 2. On August 3 Seeds wired home that Molotov apparently intended to make no new proposal in the near future. If the British Government intended to maintain their stand, he recommended that they also "make no new proposal for the time being. Such a pause in the conversations at the present stage would do no harm . . . In that event it might be useful for Mr. Strang to return and report and return again." Halifax agreed and Strang left for London four days later. (*D British FP*, VI, 575, 592.)
6. *D British FP*, VI, 492, 522–25.
7. *Ibid.*, 559. Degras, III, 356. Molotov also adopted an aggrieved attitude in discussing Butler's statement with Seeds that same afternoon (*D British FP*, VI, 570–74.)

8. *D British FP*, VI, 485. *N.Y. Times* and *The Times* (London), July 26, 1939. On the evening of the 25th the *N.Y. Times* correspondent in London cabled that the British Government were considering "opening staff talks immediately." The same day the correspondent of *The Times* in Paris reported "the belief, if not the conviction, that the British Government are about to send a military mission to Moscow" and that the French would also send a mission. Under the head "Plan for Immediate Staff Talks," *The Times* of the 26th reported that "it has been suggested that military talks should soon be begun" and went on to speculate regarding the head of a mission. In Telegram 268 from London, received at the Auswärtiges Amt at 11:10 P.M. on the 26th, German Ambassador Dirksen said the Foreign Office was probably preparing a communiqué on the impending staff talks (National Archives roll 104—103/111493).

9. Kleist, 47. *D German FP*, VI, 1047–48.

10. *D German FP*, VI, 1006–9, 1015.

11. *Ibid.*, 1015–16, 1022–23.

12. *Ibid.*, 1049–50.

13. *Ibid.*, 1048–49, 1051–52.

14. *Ibid.*, 1059–62.

15. *D British FP*, VI, 623; VII, 384. When the Turkish Government expressed willingness to consider a Soviet draft of the proposed treaty, Moscow had replied in mid-August with a questionnaire on Turkish intentions which hardly reflected any Soviet urgency or, indeed, any real desire for a pact (*ibid.*, VI, 661; VII, 10).

16. *D German FP*, VI, 1067–68, 1072.

17. *Ibid.*, VII, 17–20, 20–21.

18. *Ibid.*, 58–59, 68–69. Greiner, 36–37. Franz Halder, *Kriegstagebuch* (Stuttgart: W. Kohlhammer Verlag, 1962–64), I, 11.

19. *D German FP*, VII, 62–64.

20. *Ibid.*, 59, 87–90, 99–100. See also *DDI*, 8th s., XIII, 47–48, and *FRUS*, 1939, I, 334–35.

21. *D German FP*, VII, 76–77, 81, 84–85, 100, 102. From this time until Ribbentrop's departure for Moscow on August 22, the code department of the Auswärtiges Amt was barely able to handle the load imposed on it. During such momentous days the Führer considered inspiring scenery more important than the ready availability of expert advice in Berlin. His instructions from Berchtesgaden were enciphered in Berlin and then dispatched to Moscow. Similarly, Schulenburg's telegrams from Moscow had to be deciphered in Berlin and then forwarded to Berchtesgaden. (Kordt, 323–24.) Even Ribbentrop was absent from Berlin; following his usual practice, he stayed at Fuschl near Salzburg in order to be near the Führer.

22. *D German FP*, VII, 84–85, 114–16.

23. *Ibid.*, 130. *D British FP*, VII, 74.

24. *D German FP*, VII, 120, 121–23.

25. *Ibid.*, 134, 149–51. Stalin's draft consisted of five articles and a "postscript":

Article 1: The signatories promised to refrain from any "violence and any aggressive action whatsoever against each other, or from an attack on each other either severally or jointly with other Powers."

Article 2: If one party were attacked by a third power, the other party would lend no support to that power.

Article 3: Any disputes and conflicts between the signatories were to be settled peacefully "through mutual consultation or, if necessary, through the creation of suitable arbitration commissions."

Article 4: In contrast to Ribbentrop, Stalin contemplated only a five-year treaty which could be extended for another five years.

Article 5: Stalin also differed with the German Foreign Minister on another point; he felt that the agreement should be valid upon ratification, which, however, should take place as soon as possible.

Postscript: The agreement must contain, as one of its integral parts, a protocol "covering the points in which the Contracting Parties are interested in the field of foreign policy."

26. *D German FP*, VII, 132–33, 152. The agreement provided for German credits of 200 million Reichsmarks at four and one half per cent interest for an average term of seven years. The Soviet Government was to use the credits for specialized German industrial products including machine tools and certain items of armament. Although Moscow promised to deliver 180 million Reichsmarks' worth of raw materials within the next two years, these deliveries were to be considered "current business" and were to be paid for by additional German industrial products. For the text of the treaty, a supplementary exchange of letters between Schnurre and Babarin, and the text of a protocol of August 26 covering changes in the value of the Reichsmark, see *D German FP*, VII, 142–48, 345–46.

27. *D German FP*, VII, 155, 156–58, 161–62, 164, 167.

28. *Ibid.*, 167–68.

29. Hilger & Meyer, 300.

30. Because of haste and the inadequate map used (!) all the participants mistakenly thought that the upper Narev extended to the border of East Prussia. At Molotov's request the matter was adjusted by an exchange of letters between himself and Schulenburg on August 28. The amended protocol provided for the division of

Poland along the "line of the Rivers Pisa, Narev, Vistula and San."
(*D German FP*, VII, 295–96, 356.)

31. According to Hilger (pp. 309–11) the average Soviet citizen reacted with satisfaction and relief to the announcement of the pact in the Soviet press on the morning of August 24. The earlier propaganda against Nazi Germany had evidently had little effect on the masses. Many Party members, however, were dismayed and some expressed fear that Germany might turn on the U.S.S.R. after overcoming Poland. To counteract these sentiments special meetings were held for members of the Party apparatus at which it was explained that the pact was merely a convenient political move and not necessarily permanent. Schulenburg reported in similar terms on September 6 (*D German FP*, VIII, 12–13).

32. Hilger & Meyer, 300–304. Kordt, 324. Kleist, 54–62. Ribbentrop, 109–15. *D German FP*, VII, 179–80, 200, 220, 221, 223, 250. Ribbentrop's account conflicts slightly in some of its factual details (e.g., time of arrival in Moscow) with that of Hilger. Since he wrote his "memoirs" hastily in the shadow of the gallows in 1946, his account has been disregarded in these cases.

33. *D British FP*, VI, 533, 535, 543, 545–46, 561–62; VII, 45–47.

34. *Ibid.*, VI, 674, 683; VII, 563–65. In a letter to the Director of Military Operations and Intelligence of the War Office on August 17, General Heywood remarked "that whilst sitting at meetings, at which every word is taken down by the Soviet shorthand-writer, Voroshilov is extremely careful in his statements, but directly that you get outside the conference room, at meals and in conversation, he cracks jokes and is out to be friendly. . . . although he claims to have plenipotentiary powers, apparently he is only a paper plenipotentiary, because on the two occasions that we put definite questions which required a decision, he had to ask for an adjournment, in one case for a quarter of an hour, which lasted over an hour, obviously, to consult 'Uncle Joseph.' " (*D British FP*, VII, 602.)

35. *D British FP*, VII, 565–70.

36. *Ibid.*, 570–75. Bonnet, II, 276.

37. *D British FP*, VII, 575–81. "I am inclined to believe," wrote General Heywood to the War Office on August 17, "that what the Soviet really want is the cover of our flags and our consent to the utilization of these ports. Token Naval Anglo-French forces would probably meet their requirements, even if it was only an Allied Port Commission in each place!" (*Ibid.*, 601.)

38. *Ibid.*, 581–84.

39. *Ibid.*, 584–89.

40. *Ibid.*, 589–93.

41. *Ibid.*, 1–2.

42. Bonnet, II, 275–80. *D British FP*, VII, 39–41.

43. Beck may have sought to reassure Hitler on this point, indirectly, two weeks earlier. Polish Ambassador Grzybowski, who had returned to Moscow from leave early in August, spoke to Italian Ambassador Rosso on the 5th. When the latter remarked that the military negotiations would be fruitless unless Poland agreed to accept Soviet aid, Grzybowski replied that Warsaw would never allow Soviet troops to set foot on Polish soil or Soviet aircraft to be based on Polish airfields. Rosso passed the information on to Schulenburg who reported it to Berlin on August 10. (*DDI*, 8th s., XII, 603. *D German FP*, VII, 13.)

44. Bonnet, II, 280–81. *D British FP*, VII, 53–54, 61, 69–70.

45. Bonnet, II, 282. *D British FP*, VII, 84–86, 91–92.

46. Bonnet, II, 282–84. *D British FP*, VII, 77–78. In a conversation with U.S. Ambassador Biddle at the end of July or the beginning of August, Beck had discounted the likelihood of a German-Soviet agreement: "he pointed out that, while it might be possible for the two capitals to see eye to eye in terms of commerce and other economic aspects, the broad gap between the two doctrines of Naziism and Communism was a fundamental hindrance to complete agreement. . . . Beck felt that it would be less difficult for the Western European democracies to adjust their line of thought in event they sought an understanding with the Axis powers than it would be for either Naziism or Communism to adjust their respective lines of thought were either or both in search of a common understanding." (*FRUS*, 1939, I, 331.)

On August 18 a presumably important Polish figure (identified only as "X") expressed to Szembek the opinion that Moscow was actually fishing for Soviet-Polish staff talks! He was not alarmed by rumors of a German-Soviet agreement; economic negotiations were in progress—but in Berlin which proved that Mikoyan was not greatly interested. (Szembek, 489.)

Polish obduracy softened moderately, however, with the announcement of Ribbentrop's pending journey to Moscow, broadcast by the German radio late in the night of August 21/22 and published in the German and Soviet press the next morning. Late in the evening of August 22, Bonnet wired Noël to make a final effort and emphasize that Poland could neither morally nor politically refuse "this last chance to save the peace." Beck received the two ambassadors on the 23rd (Kennard had been instructed to support his French colleague), and after much discussion a formula was agreed upon. General Doumenc was authorized to state that "we have learnt for certain that in the event of common action against German aggression collaboration, under technical conditions to be settled subsequently between Poland and U.S.S.R. is not excluded," and that the French and British General Staffs felt that all possibilities of such collaboration should be examined immediately. But the pact with Germany was concluded before this "offer" could be made known in Moscow. (Bonnet, II, 289–90. *D British FP*, VII, 117, 130, 149–50, 161.)

47. Bonnet, II, 284. *D British FP*, VII, 106–8, 119, 120–21, 604.

48. *D British FP*, VII, 604–6, 608, 609–10. Bonnet, II, 285. Although Voroshilov may well have suspected the true nature of the answer from Doumenc's initial statement, he was suspiciously prompt in asking the most embarrassing questions. At the same time Molotov was making exactly the same objections in his conversation with Naggiar, that Britain had not associated itself with the reply and that it was made without Polish approval (Bonnet, II, 296). Molotov was hardly the person to pose such perspicacious objections without having been primed beforehand. Although Soviet cryptographers may have broken the French or British codes, the most likely explanation, if one is required, was that members of both Allied missions, few of whom were "old Moscow hands," had spoken too freely of the matter since that morning. Many of them were quartered outside embassy premises in rooms that were certainly well furnished with hidden microphones.

49. *D British FP*, VII, 611–12. This is apparently the official Soviet version of the conversation as taken down by two Russian stenographers; General Doumenc requested and was promised a copy at the end of the interview.

50. Bonnet, II, 296.

51. *D British FP*, VII, 142–43.

52. *FRUS*, 1939, I, 305, 338. *DDI*, 8th s., XIII, 107. *D British FP*, VII, 384–85. Bonnet, II, 296. *D German FP*, VII, 208–9.

53. *D British FP*, VII, 385.

54. *Ibid.*, 184, 187–88, 205–6, 224, 237, 247, 268, 278, 613–14.

55. *FRUS*, 1939, I, 302. Kordt, 336–37. *D British FP*, VII, 31, 98–99. Bonnet, II, 286.

56. *FRUS*, 1939, I, 332–33, 334–35, 343–44. *D British FP*, VII, 41–42, 154–55, 156.

57. *D British FP*, VII, 384.

CHAPTER 11

1. Kleist, 47.

2. Greiner, 36. *D German FP*, VII, 553. Halder, I, 8–12.

3. *D German FP*, VII, 200–205, 557–59. Greiner, 38–43. Greiner bases his summary of the Führer's speech upon the account given him by Colonel Warlimont immediately after the latter's return to Berlin from Berchtesgaden on August 22. The next day he filled out the account by consulting the shorthand notes Admiral Canaris had made. See also Halder, I, 23–26.

4. *D British FP*, VII, 116. *FRUS*, 1939, I, 301.

5. *FRUS*, 1939, I, 301–4. Léger had expressed similar views to the British chargé that morning (*D British FP*, VII, 131).

6. *D British FP*, VII, 161–63, 170–72, 177–79. Weizsäcker, 203–4.

7. Weizsäcker, 204. According to Kleist (p. 66) Hitler summoned the German press chief and demanded the latest news of the cabinet crises in Paris and London. Asked of which cabinet crises he spoke, the Führer answered, "Naturally the British and French cabinets. No democratic government can survive that has received such a defeat and at the same time been made so ridiculous as Chamberlain and Daladier have through our Moscow treaty."

8. Paul Schmidt, *Statist auf diplomatischer Bühne 1923–45* (Bonn: Athenäum Verlag, 1954), 449. Greiner, 46. *D British FP*, VII, 227–29.

9. Schmidt, 450–53. Greiner, 46–47. Kordt, 327–28. Coulondre, 288. *D German FP*, VII, 560. Fritz Hesse, *Hitler and the English* (London: Allan Wingate, 1954), 78. Walther Hofer, *War Premeditated 1939* (London: Thames & Hudson, 1955), 95–96, 192–93. All of the existing accounts of the events of the afternoon and early evening of August 25 in Berlin were written after the end of the war. It is thus difficult to determine whether Hitler learned of the Anglo-Polish pact before or after the conversation with Coulondre. The two persons who could be expected to know give conflicting testimony: According to Schmidt, Hitler received the information before 5:30, while Fritz Hesse, the press attaché in London, claims he phoned the news to Berlin at around 6:00. The treaty was actually signed at approximately 5:30, and the problem seems to be whether Hesse stated that it was *being* signed or *had* been signed. In a chronology of the events of August 25, entered in his diary three days later, General Halder wrote (I, 39): "16.30 [4:30 P.M.] Anglo-Polish Pact announced."

10. *D German FP*, VII, 362–63, 380, 386–87, 408, 409, 419, 438–39.

11. After reporting to Moscow for consultations in the spring, Ambassador Merekalov had never returned from his "vacation." Stalin may have felt that there was less chance of rumors of German-Soviet feelers being taken seriously in the West if the U.S.S.R. were represented in Berlin only by a chargé d'affaires.

12. *D German FP*, VII, 296, 379–80, 419–20, 446, 460, 466, 494, 509. *D British FP*, VII, 454. In a report of September 15, Italian Ambassador

Attolico referred to the "so-called 'Soviet military mission' to Berlin which has already caused so much talk and given occasion for so many inferences and deductions" (*DDI*, 9th s., I, 138).

13. Weizsäcker, 208. Greiner, 50–51. *D German FP*, VII, 478, 565, 568, 569.

14. Kleist (pp. 94–96) is—alas!—the only authority for this statement.

15. Hesse, 83–86. *D German FP*, VII, 527–28.

16. Schmidt, 462–64. *D British FP*, VII, 535. Schmidt had no choice, but Weizsäcker evaded the French ultimatum and arranged for Coulondre to present it to Ribbentrop personally at 12:30 P.M. (*D German FP*, VII, 532–34).

17. *D German FP*, VII, 540–41; VIII, 2–4, 44.

18. *Ibid.*, VIII, 33–34, 35, 36, 44–45, 56, 60–61, 68–70, 76–77. *FRUS*, 1939, I, 419; *The Soviet Union*, 779–80, 791. Degras, III, 372.

19. Hilger & Meyer, 312–13. *D German FP*, VIII, 79–80, 92.

20. *Polish White Book*, 189–90, 211–12. Degras, III, 374–76. The Convention on Definition of Aggression, signed on July 3, 1933 by the U.S.S.R., Poland, and most of the other states bordering on the Soviet Union, stated that "no act of aggression . . . can be justified on either of the following grounds, among others: (a) The internal condition of a State: E.g., its political, economic, or social structure; alleged defects in its administration; disturbances due to strikes, revolutions, counter revolutions, or civil war."

21. *D German FP*, VIII, 95–97. The German draft had read: "In view of the internal incapacity of the Polish State and of the splitting apart of the nationalities living in its former territory, the Reich Government and the Government of the U.S.S.R. consider it necessary to bring to an end the intolerable political and economic conditions existing in these territories. They regard it as their joint task to restore peace and order in these, their natural spheres of interest, and to bring about a new order by the creation of natural frontiers and viable economic organizations."

22. On August 18, the Soviet chargé in Rome had assured the British Ambassador that Mussolini would not carry his support of Hitler to the point of armed conflict with Britain and France (*D British FP*, VII, 71–72), but this was part of the earlier general policy of encouraging resistance to Germany. Similarly, Stalin saw no reason to discourage Hitler. At Moscow on the night of August 23/24, Ribbentrop had remarked that Britain was weak and wanted others to fight "for her presumptuous claim to world domination. M. Stalin eagerly concurred and observed as follows: The English Army was weak; nor was the British Navy as important as it had formerly

been. England's air arm was being increased, to be sure, but there was a lack of pilots. If England dominated the world in spite of this, that was due to the stupidity of the other countries that always let themselves be bluffed. It was ridiculous, for example, that a few hundred Englishmen should dominate India." At the same time, however, Stalin "expressed the opinion that France still had an army worthy of consideration." (*D German FP*, VII, 227.)

23. *FRUS*, 1939, I, 366–67. *D British FP*, VII, 217, 346–48. Degras, III, 361–62.

24. *D British FP*, VII, 615–22. Degras, III, 363–71. *FRUS*, 1939, I, 345–46.

25. *FRUS*, 1939, I, 348–49. *D British FP*, VII, 499. *Polish White Book*, 187, 188, 209–10.

26. Beck, 220. *Polish White Book*, 188–89.

27. Franz Borkenau, *European Communism* (New York: Harper & Brothers, 1953), 236–41, 243, 298–302. A. Rossi, *The Russo-German Alliance, August 1939—June 1941* (Boston: Beacon Press, 1951), 103–7; *Drole de Guerre*, 45–47 and *passim. Communist International*, XVI, no. 9 (Sept. 1939): editorial, "The Guarantee of a New Germany," 969–72; editorial, "Thaelmann, the Great Symbol," 973–74; F. Lang, "The Nature of German Fascism," 993–1001; Kurt Funk, "Germany and Europe," 1021–25; XVII (Sept. 1940): editorial, "A Year of Imperialist War," 582. The July 1939 Russian-language issue of the Comintern journal (no. 7) seems to have appeared on schedule. The next issue, however, of "August–September" (double no. 8–9), contained Molotov's report of October 31 to the Supreme Soviet and must have been printed in November. It did *not* carry any anti-German articles.

28. "The War and the Working Class of the Capitalist Countries" (lead article), *Communist International*, XVI, no. 11 (Nov. 1939), 1102–10. A similar appeal was made to the Austrians in the same issue: "The Viennese worker, the Tyrolean or Carinthian peasant have no interests to defend in Poland or in France. This is not their war. On the contrary, it is directed against them also." (F. Furnberg, "The Austrian People's Struggle for Freedom," 1149–50.) This was not printed in the Russian edition (double no. 8–9), however, and was practically the last article with an anti-German flavor to appear in the Comintern journal until after the German attack on Russia in 1941.

Selected Bibliography

Beck, Col. Jozef. *Final Report.* New York: Robert Speller & Sons, 1957.

Beloff, Max. *The Foreign Policy of Soviet Russia 1929–1941.* 2 vols. London: Oxford University Press, 1947–49.

Bennett, Thomas Hanley. *The Soviets and Europe 1938–1941.* Geneva: Imprimeries Populaires, 1951.

Bilmanis, Alfred. *Latvian–Russian Relations, Documents.* Washington D.C.: The Latvian Legation, 1944.

Blumenson, Martin. "The Soviet Power Play at Changkufeng," *World Politics,* XII, no. 2 (Jan. 1960), 249–63.

Bonnet, Georges. *La Défense de la Paix 1936–1940.* 2 vols. Geneva: Éditions du Cheval Ailé, 1946–48.

Borkenau, Franz. *European Communism.* New York: Harper & Brothers, 1953.

Cattell, David T. *Communism and the Spanish Civil War.* Berkeley & Los Angeles: University of California Press, 1956.

———. *Soviet Diplomacy and the Spanish Civil War.* Berkeley & Los Angeles: University of California Press, 1957.

Celovsky, Boris. *Das münchener Abkommen von 1938.* Stuttgart: Deutsche Verlags-Anstalt, 1958.

Churchill, Winston S. *The Gathering Storm.* London: Cassell & Co., 1948.

Communist International. "Organ of the Executive Committee of the Communist International, published twice a month in English, Russian, German, French, Chinese and Spanish" (masthead statement). Changed to monthly with issue of January 1936, XIII, no. 1.

Comnène [Comnen], N. P. *Preludi del Grande Dramma.* Rome: Edizioni Leonardo, 1947.

Coox, Alvin D. "Changkufeng, 1938," unpublished manuscript. Fuchu City, Japan, 1964.

Coulondre, Robert. *De Stalin à Hitler*. Paris: Librairie Hachette, 1950.

C.S.R., Ministerium für auswärtige Angelegenheiten, and U.S.S.R., Ministerium für auswärtige Angelegenheiten. *Neue Dokumente zur Geschichte des münchener Abkommens*. Prague: Orbis, 1959. German-language edition of U.S.S.R. & C.S.R., *Novye Dokumenty* . . .

Dallin, David J. *Soviet Russia's Foreign Policy 1939–1942*. Translated by Leon Dennen. New Haven: Yale University Press, 1942.

D British FP—Documents on British Foreign Policy 1919–1939, eds. E. L. Woodward and Rohan Butler. London: H.M. Stationery Office, 1949———. Third Series unless otherwise indicated.

DDI—I Documenti Diplomatici Italiani. Rome: La Libreria dello Stato, 1952———.

Degras, Jane (ed.). *Soviet Documents on Foreign Policy*. 3 vols. London: Oxford University Press, 1951–53.

D German FP—Documents on German Foreign Policy 1918–1945. Washington D.C.: Government Printing Office, 1949———. Series d unless otherwise indicated.

Doumenc, Gen. Joseph Édouard. "Non, la France et l'Angleterre ne sont pas responsables du pacte germano-soviétique," *Carrefour*, Jun. 3, 1947 (Canadian ed.).

Eden, Anthony, 1st Earl of Avon. *Facing the Dictators*. Boston: Houghton Mifflin Co., 1962.

Fabry, Philipp W. *Der Hitler-Stalin Pakt*. Darmstadt: Fundus Verlag, 1962.

Feiling, Keith. *The Life of Neville Chamberlain*. London: Macmillan & Co., 1946.

Fischer, Louis. *Men and Politics*. New York: Duell, Sloan, and Pearce, 1941.

———. *The Soviets in World Affairs*. 2 vols. Princeton: Princeton University Press, 1951.

France, Ministère des Affaires Étrangères. *The French Yellow Book*. London: Hutchinson & Co., 1940.

FRUS—Foreign Relations of the United States. Washington D.C.: Government Printing Office, continuing series.

Gafencu, Grigore. *Last Days of Europe: A Diplomatic Journey in 1939.* Translated by E. Fletcher-Allen. New Haven: Yale University Press, 1948.

———. *Prelude to the Russian Campaign.* Translated by E. Fletcher-Allen. London: Frederick Muller Ltd., 1945.

Gamelin, Gen. Maurice Gustave. *Servir.* 3 vols. Paris: Librairie Plon, 1946–47.

Germany, Auswärtiges Amt. See *D German FP.*

Great Britain. *Parliamentary Debates, Fifth Series.* London: H.M. Stationery Office, continuing series.

Great Britain, Foreign Office. See *D British FP* and *D German FP.*

Greiner, Helmuth. *Die oberste Wehrmachtführung 1939–1943.* Wiesbaden: Limes Verlag, 1951.

Halder, Gen. Franz. *Kriegstagebuch.* 3 vols. Stuttgart: W. Kohlhammer Verlag, 1962–64.

Hesse, Fritz. *Hitler and the English.* Edited and translated by F. A. Voigt. London: Allan Wingate, 1954.

Hilger, Gustav, and Meyer, Alfred G. *The Incompatible Allies: A Memoir-History of German-Soviet Relations 1918–1941.* New York: The Macmillan Co., 1953.

Hillgruber, Andreas. *Hitler, König Carol und Marschall Antonescu: die deutsch-rumänischen Beziehungen 1938–1944.* Wiesbaden: Franz Steiner Verlag, 1954.

International Press Correspondence. Communist weekly published in London; title changed to *World News and Views* with vol. 18, no. 33, Jul. 2, 1938.

Italy, Ministero degli Affari Esteri. See *DDI.*

Kleist, Peter. *Zwischen Hitler und Stalin 1939–1945.* Bonn: Athenäum Verlag, 1950.

Kordt, Erich. *Nicht aus den Akten.* Stuttgart: Union deutsche Verlagsgesellschaft, 1950.

Nadolny, Rudolf. *Mein Beitrag.* Wiesbaden: Limes Verlag, 1955.

Poland, Ministry for Foreign Affairs. *The Polish White Book.* New York: Roy Publishers, 1940.

Rei, August. *Nazi-Soviet Conspiracy and the Baltic States: Diplomatic Documents and Other Evidence.* London: Boreas, 1948.

Ribbentrop, Joachim von. *The Ribbentrop Memoirs.* Translated by Oliver Watson. London: Weidenfeld and Nicolson, 1954.

Rossi, Angelo. *Les Communistes Français Pendant la Drole de Guerre.* Paris: Les Iles d'Or, 1951.

———. *The Russo-German Alliance, August 1939—June 1941.* Boston: The Beacon Press, 1951.

Schellenberg, Walter. *The Labyrinth.* New York: Harper & Brothers, 1956.

Schmidt, Paul. *Statist auf diplomatischer Bühne 1923-45.* Bonn: Athenäum Verlag, 1954.

Scott, William Evans. *Alliance Against Hitler: The Origins of the Franco-Soviet Pact.* Durham, N.C.: Duke University Press, 1962.

Stalin, J. V. *Report on the Work of the Central Committee to the Eighteenth Congress of the C.P.S.U. /B./* [delivered March 10, 1939]. Moscow: Foreign Languages Publishing House, 1939.

Strang, William, 1st Baron Stonesfield. *Home and Abroad.* London: Andre Deutsch, 1956.

Szembek, Count Jan. *Journal 1933-1939.* Paris: Librairie Plon, 1952.

Tinch, Clark W. "Quasi-War Between Japan and the U.S.S.R., 1937-1939," *World Politics,* III, no. 2 (Jan. 1951), 174-99.

U.S., Department of State. See *D German FP* and *FRUS.*

U.S., National Archives, Microfilm Collection T-120 (Auswärtiges Amt documents).

U.S.S.R., Ministerstvo Inostrannykh Del, and C.S.R., Ministerstvo Inostrannykh Del. *Novye Dokumenty iz Istorii Myunkhena.* Moscow: Gosudarstvennoe Izdatel'stvo Politicheskoy Literatury, 1958.

U.S.S.R., Ministry of Foreign Affairs. *Documents and Materials Relating to the Eve of the Second World War.* 2 vols. Moscow: Foreign Languages Publishing House, 1948.

Weizsäcker, Ernst von. *Memoirs of Ernst von Weizsäcker.* Translated by John Andrews. Chicago: Henry Regnery Co., 1951.

Woodward, E. L., and Butler, Rohan. See *D British FP.*

World News and Views. See *International Press Correspondence.*

Date Due

DEC 8 '77			
JAN 23 78			
FEB 23 78			